Education in a new South

Crisis and Change

Robert J. Balfour

CAMBRIDGE
UNIVERSITY PRESS

University Printing House, Cambridge CB2 8BS, United Kingdom

Cambridge University Press is part of the University of Cambridge.

It furthers the University's mission by disseminating knowledge in the pursuit of education, learning and research at the highest international levels of excellence.

Information on this title: education.cambridge.org/

© Cambridge University Press 2015

First published 2015

Printed in the United Kingdom by Printondemand-worldwide, Peterborough

A catalogue record for this publication is available from the British Library

Includes bibliographical references and index
ISBN 13-9781107447295 Paperback

CONTENTS

LIST OF TABLES AND FIGURES

Chapter 1

Tables:

Chapter 2

Tables:

Chapter 3

Tables:

LIST OF ACRONYMS

ABET	adult basic education and training
ACE	Advanced Certificate of Education
ACU	Advisory Council on Universities
AET	Adult Education and Training
ANA	Annual National Assessment
ANC	African National Congress
APPETD	Association of Private Providers of Education, Training and Development
ASGISA	Accelerated and Shared Growth Initiative for South Africa
BEd	Bachelor of Education
BEd FP	Bachelor of Education Foundation Phase
BEd IP	Bachelor of Education Intermediate Phase
BEd Sen/FET	Bachelor of Education Senior and Further Education and Training Phase
C2005	Curriculum 2005
CAPS	Curriculum and Assessment Policy Statement
CCERSA	Committee for College Education Rectors of South Africa
CDE	Centre for Development and Enterprise
CEPD	Centre for Education Policy Development
CESM	classification of education subject matter
CETC	Community Education and Training Centre
CHE	Council on Higher Education
COLT	Culture of Learning and Teaching
COSATU	Congress of South African Trade Unions
COTEP	Committee on Teacher Education Policy
CPD	Continuing Professional Development
CPTD	Continuing Teacher professional Development
CPUT	Cape Peninsula University of Technology
DBE	Department of Basic Education
DET	Department of Education and Training
DHET	Department of Higher Education and Training (also known as DoHET)
DOE	Department of Education
ECD	Early Childhood Development
ECE	Early Childhood Education
ETDP	Education, Training, and Development Practices (ETDP SETA; see SETA below)
ETDP SSP	Education Training and Development Practices Sector Skills Plan (also known as the Skills Plan)
EFA	Education for All
ELRC	Education Labour Relations Council
EMIS	Education Management Information System
EPU	Education Policy Unit
FDE	Further Diploma in Education
FET	Further Education and Training
FTE	full time equivalent
GEAR	Growth, Employment and Redistribution Plan
GENFETQA	General and Further Education and Training Quality Assurance Act
GET	General Education and Training
GETC	General Education and Training Certificate
GFETQSF	General Further Education and Training Quality Sub-Framework (of the NQF – see below)
GNP	gross national product
HE	higher education
HEI	higher education institution
HEQC	Higher Education Quality Committee
HEQSF	Higher Education Quality Sub-Framework (of the NQF – see below)
HEQCIS	Higher Education Quality Committee Information System
HEMIS	Higher Education Management Information System
HESA	Higher Education South Africa
HET	higher education and training
HOD	Head of Department
HRD	human resource development
HSRC	Human Sciences Research Council
ICT	information and communication technologies
IEB	Independent Examination Board
IEFSS	inclusive education and full-service schools

IKS	indigenous knowledge systems	PHEI	private higher education institution
IPET	initial professional education of teachers	PIRLS	Progress in International Reading Literacy Study
IQMS	Integrated Quality Management System	PPN	post provisioning norms
ISFTEQSA	Integrated Strategic Framework for Teacher Education and Qualifications in South Africa	PQM	programme qualification mix
		PRAESA	Project for the Study of Alternative Education in South Africa
ISASA	Independent Schools Association of South Africa	PSA	Public Service Act
		QCTO	Quality Council for Trades and Occupations
JET	Joint Education Trust		
JIPSA	Joint Initiative on Priority Skills Acquisition	RNCS	Revised National Curriculum Statement
		RPL	recognition of prior learning
LiEP	Language in Education Policy	RSA	Republic of South Africa
LiHEP	Language in Higher Education Policy	SACE	South African Council for Educators
LOLT	language of learning and teaching	SACHED	South Africa Council for Higher Education
LTR	learner teacher ratio	SACMEQ	Southern and Eastern Africa Consortium for Monitoring Educational Quality
MDG	Millennium Development Goal		
MRC	Medical Research Council		
MRTEQ	Minimum Requirements in Teacher Education Qualifications	SADC	Southern African Development Community
NAPTOSA	National Professional Teachers' Organisation of South Africa	SADTU	South African Democratic Teachers' Union
NCS	National Curriculum Statement	SAIDE	South African Institute of Distance Education
NCV	National Certificate (Vocational)		
NDP	National Development Plan	SAIRR	South African Institute of Race Relations
NECC	National Education Crisis Committee	SAPSE	South African Post-Secondary Education (information system)
NEEDU	National Education Evaluation and Development Unit		
		SAQA	South African Qualifications Authority
NEET	not in employment, education or training	SASA	South African Schools Act
NEIMS	National Education Infrastructure Management System	SET	science, engineering and technology
		SETA	Sector Education and Training Authority
NEPA	National Education Policy Act	SGB	school governing body
NFF	New Funding Framework	SRN	Schools Register of Needs
NFSAS	National Student Financial Aid (Assistance) Scheme	TED	Teacher Education and Development
		TEFSA	Tertiary Education Fund of South Africa
NGO	non-governmental organization	TIMSS	Trends in International Mathematics and Science Study
NMMU	Nelson Mandela Metropolitan University		
		TVET	Technical and Vocational Education and Training
NPC	National Planning Committee		
NPDE	National Professional Diploma in Education	UDF	United Democratic Front
		UFS	University of the Free State
NQF	National Qualifications Framework	UK	United Kingdom
NRF	National Research Foundation	UKZN	University of KwaZulu-Natal
NSC	National Senior Certificate (also known as Matric or Grade 12)	UNESCO	United National Educational, Scientific and Cultural Organization
		UNISA	University of South Africa
NSE	Norms and Standards for Educators	UoT	university of technology
OBE	outcomes-based education	USA	Universities South Africa
ODL	open distance education	WIL	Work Integrated Learning
PALC	Public Adult Learning Centre	Wits	University of the Witwatersrand
PBO	public benefit organization	WSU	Walter Sisulu University
PDE	provincial department of education		

This book is dedicated to the many children in South Africa whose bright and youthful minds deserve a better quality of education.

The book is also dedicated the girls and boys who continue to be damaged by the prejudice arising from teacher indifference and community ignorance of diversity with regard to race and gender in our schools and universities.

SERIES EDITORS' PREFACE

The manifold dimensions of the field of teacher education are increasingly attracting the attention of researchers, educators, classroom practitioners and policymakers, while awareness has also emerged of the blurred boundaries between these categories of stakeholders in the discipline. One notable feature of contemporary theory, research and practice in this field is consensus on the value of exploring the diversity of international experience for understanding the dynamics of educational development and the desired outcomes of teaching and learning. A second salient feature has been the view that theory and policy development in this field need to be evidence-driven and attentive to diversity of experience. Our aim in this series is to give space to in-depth examination and critical discussion of educational development in context with a particular focus on the role of the teacher and of teacher education. While significant, disparate studies have appeared in relation to specific areas of enquiry and activity, the *Cambridge Education Research Series* provides a platform for contributing to international debate by publishing within one overarching series monographs and edited collections by leading and emerging authors tackling innovative thinking, practice and research in education.

The series consists of three strands of publication representing three fundamental perspectives. The *Teacher Education* strand focuses on a range of issues and contexts and provides a re-examination of aspects of national and international teacher education systems or analysis of contextual examples of innovative practice in initial and continuing teacher education programmes in different national settings. The *International Education Reform* strand examines the global and country-specific moves to reform education and particularly teacher development, which is now widely acknowledged as central to educational systems development. Books published in the *Language Education* strand address the multilingual context of education in different national and international settings, critically examining among other phenomena the first, second and foreign language ambitions of different national settings and innovative classroom pedagogies and language teacher education approaches that take account of linguistic diversity.

Robert J. Balfour's *Education in a new South Africa: Crisis and Change* provides an informative, at times uncomfortable, in-depth analysis of the degree to which, 20 years after the country's post-apartheid constitution launched its 'transformation project', government policy has led to improvement in provision and performance in education in the country. The author examines the dynamic between the two constructs of 'crisis and change' (in counterpoint to Ken Hartshorne's earlier study of 'crisis and challenge' in schooling during the apartheid era) in relation to the state of different sectors of education as well as with regard to key themes such as gender, race, language and funding. This is a scholarly monograph that makes a strong contribution to the *International Education Reform* strand of our series and to our understanding of the scope of educational development in South Africa.

Michael Evans and Colleen McLaughlin

INTRODUCTION

INTRODUCTION

South Africa's colonial history cannot be underestimated in terms of its impact on the under-development of black people socially, culturally, educationally and economically. In areas defined as *Bantustans* (such as QwaQwa, Transkei, Ciskei or KwaZulu), the history of agricultural production was affected by two developments that have been well documented in conventional histories of the interior. First, there was depopulation and the eradication of subsistence farming through the two successive South African wars, which saw Afrikaner small farmers dispossessed of their land (Lord Kitchener's 'scorched earth' policy, 1899–1902); this was followed closely by Lord Milner's (1897–1907) efforts to concentrate labour proximally in mining cities such as Kimberley and Johannesburg. Both policies, begun in war and pursued in peace, had as their focus the resettlement of vast portions of the population and in themselves prefigured subsequent forced migration and other 'influx control measures' associated with 'grand apartheid' and the formation of the Bantustans (or 'native reserves') (Thompson 2001). The history of 'structural adjustments' and social engineering in South Africa is long. The creation of the Bantustans by the Nationalist government was pursued from the 1950s as a means of creating rural areas where population density made possible the supply of cheap labour to urban areas or mining areas; the purpose of an array of policies was never to enable the development of sustainable livelihoods.

It is clear that education in the apartheid era, in addition to reinforcing race separatism, gender and racist stereotypes, was designed to produce a relatively unskilled labour force for industrial centres. Even when, in the

1970s, colleges or universities were provided for these areas (for example, the University of Transkei, or the University of Bophuthatswana), the function of education was limited to providing sufficient numbers of teachers, workers and nurses for the schools and institutions located in Bantustans. Inevitably the quality of education was affected by lower State education spending on black people, and a curriculum that was limited and restricted in its reach (Hartshorne 1992).

It is difficult in modern-day South Africa not to see the longevity of the legacy of apartheid, despite a swathe of policy changes, economic development and systems growth. For example, the persistence to this day of agricultural subsistence farming in rural areas has had an impact on the quality and scope of education in rural areas in which just under half of South Africa's children are located. The neglect of rural areas and rural schools is the result of a constellation of apartheid initiatives to separate the races through the Group Areas Act (no. 41 of 1950), to create systems of indirect rule through the retention and consolidation of tribal authorities and identities (Black Homelands Citizenship Act of 1970), and control population movement between rural areas and cities to effect population density to supply cheap labour to industry (Influx Control Act no. 68 of 1986). As mentioned in the Special Issue of *Perspectives in Education* on 'Rural Education and Rural Realities' (De Lange, Balfour & Khau 2012), it was only after 2005 (and the *Emerging Voices* report, 2011) that a focus on the role of education in those areas most neglected by the apartheid State (the Bantustans) was explicitly articulated. At a time during which scholarship concerning rural education began to emerge in South Africa, criticisms have abounded concerning the efficacy of education, and the role of scholarship in enlightening and providing solutions to low examination performance and relevance (Jansen 2012, 1), not only in terms of university requirements, but also of what is provided by universities in terms of industry 'fitness for purpose'.

And yet, since its first democratic elections in 1994, education has been central to the transformation project of the State. Within the first six years, policy changes (in which education featured centrally) led to the redevelopment of the curriculum (in four manifestations over two decades beginning with *Curriculum 2005*, the *Revised National Curriculum Statement*, *National Curriculum Statement* and the *Curriculum Assessment Policy Statements* (see Appendix 1), the amalgamation and centralisation of 19 former departments of education, the rationalisation of the teacher-corps on the basis of post-provisioning norms for classrooms. The changes were comprehensive and far-reaching and resulted in the introduction of one higher education sector accountable to and dependent on the State for public funds, a unified secondary and primary education sector, and new curricula.

Invariably a book like this cannot focus on the detail of selected issues that distort matters concerning, for example, success in schooling. This issue relates simultaneously to the quality of education provided by teachers as well as to the quality of education provision itself (in terms of resources, of which teacher supply and demand is one contested aspect), which I will illustrate in due course.

The supply of teachers to schools has been the focus of several scholarly works and government reports. It is unclear what the 'real' supply-and-demand issues are in South Africa. Drawing from a 2005 Department of Education report, a 2012 article in the *Financial Mail* argues that South Africa will need an additional 15–20 000 teachers by 2015. These figures are forecast on the basis of vacancies likely to arise by 2015. However, a 2008 Department of Labour report argues that if the teacher/pupil ratio is 38:1, there remains a surplus of 62 852 teachers in the system. A 2010 SACE report suggests that the drive to reduce pupil/teacher ratios has been successful, but this has made the demand for teachers higher. Some academics have argued that there is no shortage in absolute terms but that between 2013 and 2015, shortages would become more evident and acute. In 2003 there were 366 000 teachers in the system, of which 36% were between the ages of 40 and 50 (DoE 2005). In 2005, the teacher attrition rate was estimated to be 5.5%. In 2007, 20 000 (just under 5.5%, 20 130 of the 366 000) teachers left employment while 6000 entered the system. If it is true that 36% of the teachers aged 40–50 will reach retirement around 2013, then approximately 131 000 teachers would need to be replaced by then. On average, 6000 teachers enter the education system annually. Between 2003 and 2013, 60 000 teachers on average would have entered the profession. Accepting that 62 852 teachers may indeed be classified as 'surplus', then 10 additional years' worth of graduates would total 122 852. The shortage in real terms is 8148, which the Department of Higher Education and Training claim will be eradicated before 2020. Universities will need to nearly double graduating new teachers to meet this shortfall. Reference to skills supply problems feature in this book.

The Department of Basic Education (DBE) and Department of Higher Education and Training (DHET) reports concerning teacher education do not address issues concerning quality. The quality of professional competence is addressed in a wide variety of published research. However, the shortages outlined above are compounded by perceptions regarding the low status of teaching, the absence of stronger State support for teacher education

(education is the lowest subsidised profession in higher education), and low quality. Perceptions of the low quality of teacher competence are reinforced by research, for example, suggesting that teacher absenteeism is related to inadequate subject-content knowledge (Carnoy, Chisholm & Chilisa 2012). Consider also that research in the USA (2003) showed that the teachers most likely to exit the profession were those who performed highest on standardised aptitude tests (Billingsley 2003). In South Africa, the HSRC (ELRC 2005) study found that 55% of teachers would want to leave the profession if they could, and that younger and newer teachers are more likely to leave the system earlier. Low status and low quality (of content knowledge especially) are thus challenges both internal and external to the profession.

Furthermore, research also shows that poor schools, or schools in rural communities and lower income areas, have the highest rate of teacher attrition. These schools are ironically the most expensive schools in the system because staff turnover is high. The combined impact of problems concerning supply, perceptions and quality of teacher education needs further contextualisation. Assuming that the last cohort of teachers (enrolled either in colleges or universities prior to the transformation of higher education) were approximately 19 years of age on entry, and graduated (given dropout and completion rates) aged 24, then teachers who enrolled for their studies in 1989 (just before the restructuring of higher education gained momentum) would have finished their training in 1994. This group (as well as teachers who trained in 1970 and 1980) will be in employment up until 2034. The first two chapters will therefore focus on the systems created for education while the quality of learning (in terms of performance and also teacher training) is addressed in chapters to follow.

Fine-grained research on teacher supply and demand has been undertaken recently in terms of the *Teachers in South Africa: Supply and Demand 2013–2025* report (CDE 2015), in which analysis of data concerning teachers in the system is carried out. In the scope of this book, however, the problems associated with analysing data that is not always reliable, concerning a sector in which employment patterns and attrition trends are not always predictable, would be insightful, but would also require a substantive engagement not suited to the overview provided here. There are other issues of equally pressing importance which similarly might have justified dedicated chapters (for example, HIV and AIDS education research concerning interventions mounted by, or in collaboration with the State; see the work undertaken by Shisana et al. (2005 and 2014) at the Human Sciences Research Council, at the University of KwaZulu-Natal, or Nelson Mandela Metropolitan University in the Eastern Cape, in relation to the role of teacher education with regard to HIV and AIDS education for children as well as student-teachers). Consider also the fact that until 2014 half of South Africa's population lived in areas typified as rural. Thus rural schools and education provided by the State in rural areas, may similarly have been not only of interest, but also of key relevance to a book such as this. These are all commendable areas of focus and scholarship, and would have merited a place here were it not for the extensive scholarship already undertaken, some of which has reached publication. In lieu of these foci, the book instead reports (in Chapters 3 and 4 on university education and technical and vocational education respectively) on education research undertaken over the first 10 years as a means of indicating those aspects emerging as areas of sustained scholarship, as well as those in which more energy and effort still needs to be invested.

The following sections provide a rationale for the book and a chapter-by-chapter description of its contents, addressing in overall terms the degree to which the State through education institutions (schools, universities and colleges) has attempted to realise its goals in terms of the transformation project as anticipated in the Constitution (1996).

PURPOSE OF THE BOOK

In 2014, South Africa celebrated 20 years of a full and participatory democracy, and this book reflects on the impact of change in relation to the longevity of apartheid's legacy. In 1992, a seminal work on education entitled *Crisis and Challenge: Black Education, 1910–1990* (Hartshorne 1992) was published by OUP (Cape Town). This book described the foundations of apartheid education as a system by exploring the quality of education provision and education performance in schooling in the apartheid era. In 2004, *Changing Class* (Chisholm 2004) brought together a series of chapters on education in South Africa in which the 10 years of change since the transition to democracy occurred in 1994 was analysed from a range of perspectives and by different authors, but as it was a multi-authored book, the coherence of the argument was lost and it rather represents reflections on a series of facets and also different perspectives in relation to the transformation project.

Having described in the previous sections the broad dimensions of social, educational and economic engineering characteristic of apartheid, and the work to date that addresses the impact of apartheid and the initial post-apartheid period, this new single-authored book responds to (and indeed draws from in its titling) these seminal works on education in South Africa to explore the following themes within a structure as outlined here.

The book explores the nature of change (of which transformation has been a key political and social component as underlined by the Constitution of South Africa, 1996) in relation to the persistence of crisis specifically in education. It does not approach this through a conventional historicised (Brannigan 1998) reading of crisis and change, but rather from the perspective of change as planned and implemented in the context of a society already functioning within systemic inequalities, inequities and social challenges.

Inevitably, reference to the transformation project (a phrase used repeatedly throughout the book to mean the aspirations to a new society, the design of policy to provide shape to values, rights and aspirations as noted in the Constitution), must touch on, and sometimes seem to defer to policy, but it is important to note that it is people (rather than documents) who create the conditions under which policies concerning education come to be experienced and lived. Thus, reference to policy documentation (at times very detailed in this book) itself predisposes the analysis to assume the State as both guardian and agent of policy development and enactment. This cannot be true, since the work of many agencies (non-governmental organisations – NGOs – and statutory bodies created independently of government control) work in collaboration with, and sometimes even in competition with government to realise the aspirations of policy (whether about equal education or language in education, for example). Thus, while I acknowledge the role of civil society in partnership with the State, the focus of this book has been fairly narrowly constructed to consider the impact of changes as effected through government itself. This is a limitation of the book. In writing it, I have drawn heavily and selectively on research already undertaken by scholars of education in South Africa. Yet, this is not intended as a history of education development since much of what is described, in terms of impact of change for example, is still the lived experience of teachers, learners, administrators or academics working in education in South Africa. As such, what is presented in the chapters that follow is not new research, but rather an overview of what changes have occurred with reference to relevant scholarship.

THEMES ELABORATED UPON IN THE BOOK

The education crisis in South Africa features prominently in serious journalism and media in South Africa (*Financial Mail* 2013; *Mail & Guardian* 2013). Analyses of spending trends in relation to students' poor performance (Jones in *Financial Mail* 2013) in annual national assessment exercises and international measures (PIRLS or TIMSS, for example) suggest three questions that are not always considered together in scholarly work and investigative journalism on the subject: what has the impact of change and transformation been on education in South Africa? Why does the crisis in education persist? And what is the likely impact of both crisis and change on South Africa's further development?

The book opens with an introduction in which a description of schooling together with an overview of the expansion of the sector since 1995 together is provided, with a sense of learner performance at selected intervals in the 20-year period. Related policy change is also referred to as illustrative of the wide-ranging transformation intentions and scope of the Mandela, Mbeki and Zuma administrations in relation to the provision of schools, teachers and curricula. At the outset this integration of reporting on change as well as its related policy dimension denies neat divisions between policy and change. It would have been more straightforward to describe policy development over time (as curriculum and policy specialists such as Chisholm, Motala and others have done), but without a concomitant illustration of what occurred in classrooms, some indications of how learners and teachers experience change, and what selected commentators have observed about those changes, it is difficult to gain a sense of the impact over time on the teaching and learning experience of change.

That said, research on policy about education change effected by post-1994 governments points to the overwhelming concern to enable South Africa to transform into a multiracial, multi-ethnic and multilingual country in which the differences between citizens (race, language, gender, belief and so on) are valued in the ways in which citizens live, work and interact with one another from a perspective of shared respect for human dignity for the common good. Understandably, education is a key instrument to effect broad societal transformation. Thus Chapters 1 to 4 concern themselves with sectoral perspectives on education, while Chapters 5 to 7 concern themselves with three issues that are key to understanding the need for transformation of education in South Africa with reference to selected foci: gender, language and funding.

These foci are justified in the following terms: the elimination of race prejudice underlies all legislation concerning education provision and opportunity in South Africa. It was Nelson Mandela who claimed that education was the most important means of changing society and a glance at the policies in which education features, testifies to this belief. The creation of a non-sexist and non-racist State implies the centrality of efforts to deal with gender and race prejudice, and also to enable freedom to participate in education given South Africa's racial and linguistic diversity. Race integration is touched on in relation to those chapters concerned with sectoral perspectives on education, while the chapters devoted to gender, language and the funding of education are concerned with addressing those barriers that prevent full participation in, or utilisation of, education opportunities.

Chapters 1 and 2 explore schooling and teacher education in South Africa since it is agreed widely in scholarship on the subject that schooling bears the burden (or opportunity) of realising the aspirations of a 'new' South Africa, while education in general (and teacher education in particular) bears responsibility for the preparation of young people for this new society.

The first two chapters are concerned also with describing factors implicated in education provision, with the transformation goal of widening access to education and participation in it. Widening participation also suggests a focus on increasing learners' chances of success within the system and so a range of policy developments enacted in the first decade were geared towards creating that enabling environment and spirit in education among both teachers and children.

It is important that this dynamic (aspirations to change) is understood, since policy is not only reactive in terms of its attempts to address past inequities around education access and provision, but also transformative in terms of the creation of provisions necessary to enable social and other forms of transformation. For example, several key education acts were passed within six years: the Language in Education Policy (1997), the Language in Higher Education Policy (2002), the National Education Policy Act (2002), and the South African Schools Act (2002) were all meant to address inequalities associated with mother tongue (now referred to as home language) education in South Africa, in addition to creating the conditions necessary for equal access and equal provision of quality education in an integrated education system. These acts also supported provisions made in the Constitution (1996) in terms of the creation of 11 equal/official languages of South Africa, and the right to receive education through any of these 11 languages. The impact on the education system was thus meant to be far-reaching not only for the primary and secondary education sector, but also for higher education where indigenous languages were meant to become the languages of teaching and learning, and to be promoted and developed as academic languages. While Chapter 2 describes the impact of teaching on the education system (and therefore links directly to the first chapter on schooling), it also provides a link to the third chapter, in which the role and performance of higher education in terms of the transformation project at universities is considered.

In Chapter 3, the impact of policy over the past 20 years, in terms of widening access and developing the conditions for students' success, is shown to have been variable and uneven. For example, only two universities (out of 23) have assumed responsibility to provide higher education through an indigenous language, which explains why so few schools in South Africa have formally supported education through the home language. If higher education (private and public, technical, vocational education and training) is meant to graduate young adults capable of advancing the economic and social well-being of South Africa, then Chapter 3 demonstrates that the institutions from which such growth and development are expected, have struggled with their responsibilities, not for lack of energy and will necessarily, but because capacity has been outstripped by demand. The sector, as it was in 1995, was relatively small with very low levels of participation especially from those groups not privileged in the race hierarchies of the apartheid period. In two decades the sector might well have expanded, but participation rates (retention, drop-out and success of students) remain problematic and the persistence of racialised profiles in terms of participation and success is worrying to say the least.

Chapter 3 describes the transformation of the higher education sector in institutional terms. The process of institutional mergers began with the Kader Asmal ministry in 2002. Most recently (2014) there has been the creation of two new universities in provinces in which no formal higher education provision had existed (Mpumalanga and Northern Cape, with the University of Mpumalanga and Sol Plaatje University, which were established in 2014). Participation rates in terms of widening access and ensuring student success are also described. The chapter goes on to provide an overview of education research in higher education during the first decade and argues that one means of understanding the impact of policy change in higher education is to examine the changing nature of education research as it responds to new needs identified by the State, and also civil society. This research has already been undertaken for the first democratic decade in South Africa and explored in part (Balfour et al. 2011 in a special issue of the South African Journal for Higher Education), but this book surveys the three major components of education in South Africa (schooling, universities and technical, vocational and education colleges; TVET). These are described in the literature as sectors (the schooling sector and the higher education sector), but chapters are devoted to parts of the higher education sector since it was split in two under the Zuma administration (towards the end of second decade of democracy). After 2012, higher education was configured as a separate government department, and then some years after that technical, vocational education and training colleges (TVET) came to be included as part of (in references to) the higher education sector.

In Chapter 4, the development of further education and training colleges (referred to after 2013 as TVET) is described. This part of the higher education sector was characterised by even more unevenness in terms of quality and participation in the apartheid period. Because of the envisaged proximity to the corporate and manufacturing industries, TVET colleges were to provide those opportunities for school learners (from Grade 10; ages 15–16) as well as school leavers (from Grade 12; ages 18–19) to engage with trades and skills development associated with intensive workplace learning opportunities (in the form of apprenticeships and learnerships). The chapter argues for the need for more sustained investment in industry partnerships with TVET colleges and points out that without careful coordination of placement opportunities (with the support of the colleges as well as support of employers) over a long period of time, the mismatch between industry expectations and college training is likely to persist indefinitely. While the skills and education training authorities (SETAs) were created with a view to effecting this coordination, the capacity of this part of the sector has been shown to be limited and itself requires investment and training development in order to operate more consistently and effectively in learnership or placement creation, monitoring and assessment.

Chapter 5 shifts the focus from the sectoral dimensions of education provision in South Africa to consider the focus on gender in relation both to higher education and schooling. The chapter argues for renewed commitment to gender equity (and by implication the need for gender education, gender interventions in terms of employment and diversity) is required if South Africa is to 'make good' on its stated commitment to non-sexism in workplace, let alone in education institutions of the agencies of the State. Presenting research on the performance of girls in schooling, or the reasons why girls who leave school early are most vulnerable in the workplace in addition to focusing on the relative absence of gender as a focus in higher education institutions (either in terms of enrolment planning, employment equity or staffing and promotion), Chapter 5 aims to provide a range of perspectives concerning gender in the broadest sense and in relation to issues of specific relevance to different education sectors.

Chapter 6 describes efforts to transform education with regard to the uses of languages for schooling as well as higher education. In higher education, English has become the language of power and the perceived instrument of upward mobility in social and professional contexts. Without sustained development of such languages at the higher education level, the language choices that can be supported by teachers for children in schools are thus still limited, largely, to English and Afrikaans in South Africa. The issue is more complex than can be dealt with here, but it is worth noting that language provision has been legally contested in at least six seminal court cases in which school governing bodies or parent bodies have opposed national and provincial departments of education in their attempts to institute dual- or parallel-medium language instruction in schools.

Chapter 7 extends the previous discussion on how the change in the education system has affected learning in relation to how government has planned for education provision in the last 20 years (whether in terms of schooling or in terms of higher education). Transformation as noted earlier has been premised on a few key ideas about enabling equal access to, participation in and success in education through schooling and higher education opportunities. The development of an enabling environment is dependent on the availability of resources (and the need for careful planning and foresight) on the one hand, and on the other, the availability of capacity to administer State resources responsibly, and the capacity of learners, teachers, administrators and academics to utilise optimally the opportunities created through such provision.

The book concludes with a series of reflections concerning the arguments put forward in preceding chapters about the relationships between aspirations, estimations and planning of capacity to deliver on ideals concerning quality education. These ideals remain powerful and there is still a collective hope that transformation will lead to opportunities for employment, development as well as further academic advancement towards a South Africa that can indeed be regarded as new, rather than as only a post-apartheid (post-colonial) State. There can be no doubt that concerted efforts have been made to shift the features of the apartheid legacy, and that more work is required, and more careful consideration needed in relation to the features, roles and anticipated outcomes of curriculum change, policy change and institutional or sectoral rearrangements.

THE STING OF UNDER-DEVELOPMENT AND THE STRUGGLE TO TRANSFORM EDUCATION IN SOUTH AFRICA

The introduction to this book concludes with a brief consideration of the legacy of apartheid as it pertains to only one aspect of national development: education. I wish to describe this legacy-implication briefly by way of prefacing the chapters that follow since I believe it is important to understand that the energy and commitment required to successfully transform South Africa is as necessary now as it was 10 or 20 years ago. Furthermore, a longer-term perspective is needed with regard to education planning in relation to the quality of teaching and learning within institutions in which regulation features less and a focus on quality content development and international benchmarking features more.

Assuming that the quality of teacher education curricula post-1994 is a radical qualitative departure from the curricula of the past towards teacher education programmes of high quality and efficiency (in terms of throughput, for example), then the crisis currently being experienced is likely to diminish towards 2040 (allowing for a six-year lag after 2034). Apartheid's long tail still has a sting for generations educated by teachers inadequately prepared for new curricula. If 30 944 Grade 12 (or 13.7% of the 511 152 who wrote the National Senior Certificate in 2012) graduates possess Mathematics scores sufficient for scarce skills/professions (engineering, medicine and so on), then large numbers of matriculants (Grade 12 graduates) are unlikely to meet the requirements for key professions for another 40 years without some 'desperate measures' being instituted. The first full cohort to emerge with the new NSC did so in 2007. On average, between 2007–2034 (conservatively speaking) South Africa is likely to produce just over 500 000 Grade 12 learners per year (in 2012 only 511 512 sat the NSC, of which 133 323 failed and 377 829 passed).

These children will be educated by teachers trained by apartheid-style institutions using teacher education curricula shown to be of variable quality, of which the consequences are still felt. For example, the 2012 DBE report on the NSC results states that students 'lack ... linguistic skills required to express themselves in simple and proper paragraphs ... across all subjects. Candidates displayed inadequacies regarding the skills of reading, comprehension, and analysing, evaluating and applying information to either make decisions or solve problems' (DBE 2012). The challenge of teacher re-education cannot be underestimated, a point that several chapters explore.

Given the above, one has to question the extent to which new generations (known as the born-frees) of South Africans are indeed 'born free', or born into a kind of bondage, a 'massive mediocrity', if freedom is also to be considered as empowerment with the skills to survive, let alone to access a relevant quality education. By 2055, the 'born-frees' will begin to qualify for pensions. The sting of under-development, while not visible after the last of apartheid's monuments have been mothballed, will be a significant factor to be addressed through supplementary means if South Africa's economic growth (which has averaged 2.1% in the last 10 years) is to be accelerated to deal both with un-employment (currently estimated at 24.6% in March 2013) and the challenges of population growth. What measures might be used to address the crisis in education comprehensively so that teaching and learning for success become features of the system, instead of variances? There are many possible answers to this question, beginning in schools with learners, or with teacher education and teachers. One thing is clear, however – the prospect of another 20 years of under-performance in higher education and schooling compels South Africa to renew its effort and commitment to change with the aim of raising the quality of teaching and learning and research geared towards visible success that enables confidence and competence to be measured in a close inter-relationship.

PART ONE:
South Africa's education sectors and performance

1   Schooling in South Africa

1.1   INTRODUCTION

South Africa celebrated 20 years of democracy in 2014. It was also the year in which the founding statesman and first President, Nelson Mandela, passed away. The new South Africa was founded on an idea of transformation as a broad social, political, education and economic project in which the aspirations of the Constitution of South Africa (1996) could be realised. It is with a degree of pride that the Department of Basic Education (DBE) can claim that 'Approximately one in every three people in South Africa is in the school system'.

Education was positioned atop the hierarchy of transformation priorities in 1994 (Chisholm & Petersen 1999; Harber & Brock 2013). But education had also been key to the apartheid policies and strategies designed to encourage segregation and a racial hierarchy that was profoundly damaging for communities in South Africa. Motala notes that 'the strategic importance and determining role of segregated and unequal education policy in disempowering the majority population previously, was now employed as an equally strategic instrument for equitable development of the population at large' (Motala 2001). In the Constitution, access to education was framed as a basic human right, and by implication, access to the support services and infrastructure to enable such access was either to be put in place anew, or restructured to serve a unitary education system. The Constitution guarantees that South Africans will not only enjoy equity of access to quality services (like housing or education, justice or due process), but that all development will seem and become commensurate with the State's aspirations to non-sexism, non-racism, equal opportunity and dignity.

It was assumed by policy-makers, intellectuals, politicians and activists alike that the systems that existed prior to 1994 were divisive, reactionary and racist, favouring the race and class privileges of the apartheid regime, and before that, of the colonial State. Prior to the demise of the apartheid State there were 19 departments of education in South Africa; each province had its own, each Bantustan (known also as homelands or 'native reserves'; see Thompson 2001) also had its own; and there were examining boards and examinations set by each authority more or less independently of each other even at the highest (pre-tertiary) level. Given that the structure of the education system was designed along race categories, the perpetuation of this system, with its structures, remained unacceptable at a political level, as well as inequitable on material and other grounds.

The preparation work for the transformation project in South Africa began with activists and intellectuals associated with progressive politics in the 1980s (for example, the National Education Crisis Committee). A number of political, academic, social and other movements emerged to resist apartheid, not least of which were the African National Congress and the United Democratic Front, both of which were linked to a variety of trade unions and other movements, including religious and social organisations (Chisholm, Motala & Vally 2003). The groundswell aimed at transformation was thus made up of a broad alliance of organisations. This history of the influence of these organisations in relation to thinking about education in a post-apartheid South Africa is touched upon in Hartshorne's book *Crisis and Challenge: Black Education, 1910–1990* (1992). Certainly, the commitment of the government to education development (schooling, further education and training, vocational education and universities) has been clear and unequivocal throughout all the administrations since 1995. In 2006 the then Minister of Education, Dr. Naledi Pandor, ascribed deficiencies in the system not to under-spending, but to the incapacity of the education system to utilise allocations to 'support full transformation' (Pandor 2005a). The evidently generous allocation on education of 9.7% of the GDP on expenditure for 2005/2006–2008/2009 needs to be contextualised in terms of the systems performance as elaborated in subsequent sections and chapters (National Budget Review 2006, 18).

This chapter takes a broad look at schooling in terms of a range of themes: the first section provides an overview of children in schools in South Africa over the new democratic period (from the perspective of the Department of Education (DoE), first in the Mandela and Mbeki administrations, and later the Department of Basic Education (DBE) in the Zuma administrations). This section demonstrates substantial growth in schooling and good discipline in terms of children enrolling for, and remaining in, schools. The second section provides two overviews of learner performance in the 20-year period and suggests that while performance appears to be indicated, the analysis of the categories has not remained stable over time and performance is undermined by routine under-performance in international comparative tests and assessments. The third section describes the numbers of teachers in the schools over the period and analyses some of the problems around the provision of teachers depending on locality, region and socio-economic class. This is followed by the fourth section, in which school infrastructural needs are described in terms of the DoE's (Department of Education or Department of Basic Education) progress towards providing for basic teacher and learner support, new schools and administrative support. The fifth section discusses curriculum reform, policy and legislative frameworks.

While the first 10 years of Democracy provided an opportunity for a series of reforms, both in higher education and schooling, that opportunity, considering the impact of the changes envisaged in 1994, and mostly implemented between 1995 and 2005, has only really become possible in the second decade of democracy. It is only in the last 10 years that the impact of the first 10 years' worth of change and reform in higher education and 20 years in schooling can be assessed.

1.1.1 The state of education in 1994

- Matriculation pass rate of 53.4%
- Adult literacy rate below 70%
- 7.1% of the population had a tertiary education
- 99% of white teachers were qualified
- 93% of Indian teachers were qualified
- 71% of Coloured teachers, and
- 54% of African teachers

1.1.2 Professional staff in the higher education system comprised

- 80% white people
- 12% African
- 4% Coloured and
- 4% Indian

  (The Presidency 2014, 40)

1.2 POLICY AND THE LEGISLATIVE FRAMEWORKS FOR EDUCATION

Schweisfurth (2013) suggests that culture plays a part in the success of education reform. South Africa's legislation, from the Constitution to various acts of parliament, has been described as among the most progressive in the world. In this section the purpose and the nature of education policy are described. It can be difficult for people living in patriarchal, traditional societies to meaningfully engage in democratic education if it does not fit with local ways of understanding learning and relationships (Schweisfurth 2013). Naidoo (2014, 70) argues that 'democratic learner-centred education was counterintuitive to teachers' previous methods and training, counter to teachers' own school experience and cultural upbringing, counter to principal-educator management styles, counter to learner home environment and counter to societies' expectations of what schooling entailed'. That there is wide recognition by South African commentators about the gaps between policy and outcomes goes without saying.

It is worthwhile providing the reader with some extracts from the Bill of Rights, from which the South African School Act (1996) and other policies, for example the Language in Education Policy (1996), are derived.

29. Education

1) Everyone has the right

(a) to a basic education, including adult basic education; and

(b) to further education, which the state, through reasonable measures, must make progressively available and accessible.

(2) Everyone has the right to receive education in the official language or languages of their choice in public educational institutions where that education is reasonably practicable. In order to ensure the effective access to, and implementation of, this right, the State must consider all reasonable educational alternatives, including single medium institutions, taking into account equity; practicability; and the need to redress the results of past racially discriminatory laws and practices.

(3) Everyone has the right to establish and maintain, at their own expense, independent educational institutions that

(a) do not discriminate on the basis of race;

(b) are registered with the state; and

(c) maintain standards that are not inferior to standards at comparable public educational institutions.

(4) Subsection (3) does not preclude State subsidies for independent educational institutions.

30. Language and culture

Everyone has the right to use the language and to participate in the cultural life of their choice, but no one exercising these rights may do so in a manner inconsistent with any provision of the Bill of Rights.

31. Cultural, religious and linguistic communities

(1) Persons belonging to a cultural, religious or linguistic community may not be denied the right, with other members of that community;

(a) to enjoy their culture, practise their religion and use their language; and

(b) to form, join and maintain cultural, religious and linguistic associations and other organs of civil society.

(2) The rights in subsection (1) may not be exercised in a manner inconsistent with any provision of the Bill of Rights.

A number of policy-makers have written about the scope and reach of policy in relation to the lived experiences of teachers, schools, communities and learners in South Africa (Vally & Dalamba 1999, Chisholm 2009, Naidoo 2014, Balfour 2009). Dadwig (1994) suggests that there are tensions inherent between policy intent, advocacy and philosophical orientation. Naidoo (2014) posits that such tensions 'make for a contradictory scenario of interpretation, practice, and attendant outcomes at the point of teaching and learning. The acknowledged disjuncture between policy objectives and praxis creates an academic conundrum in as much as the agents of interpretation of policy and distilling of practices "on the ground" warrant the consideration of an alternate yardstick for measuring policy effectiveness, per se'.

Naidoo surveys critical policy research approaches by Prunty (1985), 'policy sociology' (Ozga 1987), 'policy-scholarship' (Grace 1987), and 'policy sciences' (Deleon 1994). While several scholars have critiqued policy research and teaching in South Africa (Chisholm 2009, and Christie 2006, among others), this section describes education as it applies to schools and schooling. As noted earlier in South Africa, education is a cornerstone of the transformation project. As the DoE noted, 'It should be a goal of education and training policy to enable a democratic, free, equal, just and peaceful society to take root and prosper in our land, on the basis that all South Africans without exception share the same inalienable rights, equal citizenship and common destiny' (1995, 22). The cornerstone act for schools is the South African Schools Act (SASA, Act 84, 1996). The act allows schools to govern themselves, it defines types of schools (private and public with varieties on these two types), and the power of schools concerning admissions, language policy and maximum class sizes. The powers of schools were meant to provide a degree of autonomy in the system, and recognised that a degree of differentiation given the plethora of official languages, religious and other beliefs should be seen as part of the diversity to be celebrated in South Africa.

Despite these powers, there have been strong tendencies towards cultural and other forms of exclusion in many schools, either on the basis of language or class and sometimes even ethnicity. According to Naidoo, the SASA (1996) provision allowing school governing bodies (SGBs) to levy school fees, as a means of 'topping-up', alleviates the limited State financial allocations. A significant consequence of this provision was that formerly privileged schools were able to levy higher fees, effectively commoditising education, thereby maintaining learner enrolment drawn largely from advantaged backgrounds (Jansen & Taylor 2003; Sayed et al. 2013).

Since coming to power in 1995, the State has also banned corporal punishment and from time to time cases in which teachers have been found guilty (either by departmental hearings or through lawsuits) have formed the substance for outrage as expressed in the popular media (see Appendix 2). This, in line with the RNCS (Revised National Curriculum Statement) (2002, 8) 'making schools safe to learn … with the expectation of ridding schools of violence. Despite policy enactments forbidding violence of any sort in schools, corporal punishment is still employed widely, particularly in rural schools' (Maphosa & Shumba 2010; Vally, Porteus & Ruth 2001; Morrell 2006; Naidoo 2014, 44). Simply put, legislation at the national level about schools has focused on the twin aspirations of access and redress with the explicit intention of developing one system of quality education accessible to all people in South Africa, regardless of class or socio-economic capital. These aspirations have been undercut by commentators who suggest that in time South Africa has in fact developed two education systems: the first system is state-controlled and consists mostly of working class children and communities in which post-provisioning, low-fee or no-fee State schools exist (Tikly & Mabogoane 1997). The second system consists of well-funded private and public schools that provide education to a largely middle class elite.

1.3 CHILDREN IN SCHOOLS

To be sure there is a wealth of information available from the DoE, the DBE and the Department of Higher Education and Training (DHET) concerning the quantitative dimension of the changes implemented throughout the education system. This overview of schooling thus considers the impact of changes made to legislation, and the impact on the effectiveness of the system itself. Typically, measuring impact is assessed in quantitative forms dealing with, for example, teacher attrition rates, teacher supply and demand rates, and learner throughput and learner success rates. However, in order to assess the magnitude and scale of the changes anticipated, it is useful to consider, initially, the growth in education over the last twenty years.

Table 1.1: Girls' Enrolment 1995, 2005, 2013

Level of education	1995	2004	2013
Primary	3 028 826	3 627 631	3 639 211
High School	1 349 259	2 256 852	2 362 230

Table 1.2: Boys' Enrolment 1995, 2005, 2013

Level of education	1995	2004	2013
Primary	3 611 390	3 816 511	3 639 211
High School	1 862 345	2 061 051	2 362 230

Or:

Table 1.3: Total learner enrolments by gender in primary, high school and tertiary education

Level of education	1995			2004			2013		
	Males	Females	Total	Males	Females	Total	Males	Females	Total
Primary	3611390	3028826	6640216	3816511	3627631	7444142	3639211	3424638	7063 849
High School	1862345	1349259	3211604	2061051	2256852	4 317903	2362230	2231267	4593497

Sources: DBE, School Realities 2013/School realities 2004/
Education statistics in South Africa at a glance 2004

Enrolment in Grade R (a pre-school year at primary school) has more than doubled, increasing from 300 000 to 705 000 between 2003 and 2011, nearly reaching the level of universal access. By 2012, 87.8% of learners in Grade 1 in public schools had attended Grade R (The Presidency, Twenty Year Review 1994–2014, 47).

In 1999 there were 123 138 991 learners at ordinary schools in South Africa. Over 56% of these learners were concentrated in three largely rural provinces (the Northern Province, the Eastern Cape and KwaZulu-Natal). However, in 1999 the teacher-learner ratio was lower than it had been in 2014 (almost 34 learners per educator in South Africa, according to Education Statistics SA) and even lower in KwaZulu-Natal (30.1%), and yet those indicators cannot be relied upon to have correlational value for the quality of education. In KwaZulu-Natal and the Eastern Cape, despite lower teacher/learner ratios, learner throughput and success rates are among the lowest in South Africa. This can be explained by the fact that the majority of under-qualified and non-qualified teachers in the system are concentrated in these two provinces. It is therefore unsurprising that in addition to the above, the same three low-performing provinces also have the highest rates of over-aged and under-aged learners in the system. Thus, Education Statistics SA report that the 'gross enrolment rate' for the Eastern Cape was 20.14%, to over 100% in KwaZulu-Natal and Mpumalanga. Five years into a new democratic dispensation, the system in these provinces had to be geared to address the challenges outlined above, and as might be expected, the turnaround needed in such contexts would be unlikely to occur within the first decade of the new dispensation. Simply put, teacher education, curriculum redesign and teacher qualification upgrading, while being national priorities, would not be felt at a provincial level with any urgency.

Ten years into the new democracy, the number of learners in the system was lower, with little over 10 000 000 learners in the system (7 681 324 learners in primary schools and 3 828 705 learners in secondary schools) (see Table 1.3). Combined and intermediate schools accounted for 707 736 learners and 29 229 educators. How is the reduction in learner numbers to be viewed? On the one hand, the reduction of schools regarded as unsustainable explains also the reduction in student numbers. However, school dropout figures in this period remain high. This is illustrated from the data concerning school dropout and retention rates. According to Education Statistics of South Africa (2005), 'Of every 100 learners in ordinary schools in South Africa, more than 31 learners were in the Foundation Phase, slightly fewer than 24 were in the Intermediate Phase, slightly more than 24 were in the Senior Phase, 20 were in the FET (Further Education and Training or secondary school, Grades 10–12) band, and less than one was in the pre-Grade-R Phase and 'other' combined. Roughly then, only a third of an initial cohort might finish their schooling on time, and of this group, ten learners (i.e. 10% of the cohort itself) would have exited school without completing'.

The introduction of Grade R and pre-Grade R means that families now have the option of enrolling children into ECD centres in South Africa.

The most recent available data for 20 140 registered sites was supplied by DSD for June 2012 and is given in Table 1.4. The largest numbers of sites are located in Gauteng (3520), KwaZulu-Natal (3398), Free State (3002) and the Eastern Cape (2938) respectively (see Table 1.4).

Table 1.4: **Number of registered ECD sites, subsidised children, total receiving services and estimated number of practitioners**

Province	Registered ECD sites	Number of children receiving subsidy	Total number of children receiving ECD services	Estimated number of ECD practitioners (registered sites)
Eastern Cape	2938	76 000	83 613	3741
Free State	3002	43 700	98 172	4739
Gauteng	3520	57 473	160 241	3354
KwaZulu-Natal	3398	73 291	131 260	5067
Limpopo	2442	56 040	206 728	2810
Mpumalanga	1402	46 558	109 386	2404
North-West	1033	32 890	66 265	2600
Northern Cape	580	25 976	30 839	927
Western Cape	1825	72 601	98 020	4350
TOTAL	20 140	484 529	984 524	29 992

Source: National DSD ECD Statistics March 2012. Provided by Louise Erasmus Social Work
Policy Manager: Partial Care and ECD

The 2010 audit of unregistered sites (Biersteker & Hendricks 2012) found that 32% of principals and 58% of practitioners have no qualifications. Levels 1 and 4 qualifications are the most common levels of qualification achieved as shown in Table 1.5.

Table 1.5: Percentage of Staff with ECD Qualifications in Unregistered ECD sites in the Western Cape

Level	ECD Qualification	Principals (%)	Practitioners (%)
None		32	58
Level 1	Basic Certificate: ECD	16	13
Level 4	National Certificate: ECD/FETC: ECD	21	13
Level 5	Higher Certificate: ECD	11	4
Level 5	National Diploma: ECD	4	2
Other	(e.g. N1 - 6, Diploma in Education, Pre-primary Teachers' Certificate, Nursery School Teachers' Certificate)	16	9

Source: Biersteker and Hendricks (2012)

These figures need also to be understood in terms of a growing awareness among communities and families of the qualitative dimensions of education provision. The apartheid era was characterised by stringent population movement controls which were linked also to schools. All groups were compelled to access the schools in their immediate residential areas. Given the differential spending associated with different groups in South Africa on education (historically black children received the lowest proportion of government spending on education when compared to Indian, coloured and white children (see Hartshorne 1992; Gustafsson & Patel 2006), this meant that children of black families could access only those schools located in the areas in which they lived. In these urban and also rural areas (associated especially with the Bantustans, rural and farm schools) the schools, thanks to the low standards of education curricula, the low quality of teachers prepared for the schools, and the low government spending on schools, were abysmal. With the changes after 1995, the Group Areas Act was revoked, with the effect that parents could begin to consider access for their children in areas where they did not reside. Obviously those most mobile (financially at least) were able to take relative advantage of the better quality of education throughout the apartheid era, as offered by private and mostly 'church' schools (in other words, those schools founded, supported and staffed by clerics or religious staff). Between 1995 and 2014 the growth in private education institutions and consortia of private schools and colleges has accelerated. In South Africa, the Crawford Schools and the Curro Schools are all private for-profit organisations offering salaries to teachers that are usually higher than State schools, and a quality of education that is usually better than that offered in the public education system. With greater choice and variety in the system has come a more differentiated market for schools. This has had a logical but odd effect on the schooling system as it has begun to outgrow its apartheid past.

A report by Mafisa and Malingo (2014) shows that over the 20-year period in Gauteng, more than 250 schools have been closed down, while in the Eastern Cape, 220 schools closed in the past three years alone. There has been a similar trend in Limpopo Province, forcing many pupils to travel long distances to schools outside their areas. The closures are confirmed by a report released by the DBE in which it has been revealed that the number of public schools had decreased from 25906 to 25826 nationally between 2009 and 2012, even though the population of pupils and teachers increased during the same period. The growth of private schools in this period cannot be said to bear a direct relation to this phenomenon, but it certainly does indirectly. In other words, as economic mobility has improved for the black middle class in particular, so access to suburban areas and thus also suburban schools has become possible. Invariably this has meant that the supply of children to township and rural schools has decreased, while the demand for better-quality schools and education has increased.[1] While it might not be true to suggest that all schools located in rural areas or townships offer a lower quality in education, it is almost certainly true that the teachers associated with suburban schools in South Africa are mostly better qualified and better resourced than their counterparts in township or rural schools located in impoverished areas. How and why is this the case? Hartshorne (1992) has shown that there is a clear pattern of differentiated spending on education in the period leading up to the 1994 elections. While this changed with almost immediate effect in 1995 with the creation of a single Department of Education, the legacy of differential treatment is long-lived and solidly entrenched. Better-quality schools (in other words, those historically advantaged in the apartheid period) were associated with former white suburban areas in which a mostly already economically privileged race group (and after 1995 a more racially diverse but nonetheless privileged middle class) made up the majority. These schools have always been staffed mostly by well-qualified and experienced teachers, and so the new South Africa continues to perpetuate class privilege through a range of means, not least of which is the class filter which limits admission to those able to afford school fees, or limits access through the language policy of the school (thus retaining class and race segregation in the case of Afrikaans medium schools). The rights to levy fees on the basis of the needs of the families subscribing to the schools, and those rights associated with the language policy or school admissions policies, are defined in the Language in Education Policy (1997) and South African Schools Act (SASA 1996).

Thus, when the DoE reports that an estimated 2400 schools closed nationally between 2000 and 2011, and further that Soweto schools are among the worst affected, the unarticulated narrative here has much to do with the newly-acquired mobility of the black middle class to access other areas of residence and thus an education also associated with area and class. In Soweto, residents living in affected areas were reported by Mafisa and Malingo (2014) to have said that 'the reason for the decreasing numbers of township schools was the poor quality of education'.

The Twenty-Year Review 1994–2014 notes the problematic issue concerning international measures of performance in relation to South African children:

> International comparisons through the Southern and Eastern Africa Consortium for Monitoring Educational Quality (SACMEQ) confirm that South Africa fares poorly in terms of learner performance in Grade 6 and teacher content knowledge when compared with countries that spend the same or less on education per capita. In terms of the SACMEQ tests, South Africa experienced no statistically significant change in performance between 2000 and 2007. In contrast, Lesotho, Mauritius, Namibia, Swaziland, Tanzania and Zanzibar experienced improvements in both Mathematics and reading. The 2011 Trends in International Maths and Science Study (TIMSS) points to improvements for Grade 9 learners between 2002 and 2011, especially for learners attending the poorest schools. These improvements start on a very low base and South Africa still has a low average in Mathematics and Science performance, well below the level expected for Grade 9 learners, as indicated by the recent ANA test results. (The Presidency 2014, 49–50).

Given that even the best schools in South Africa do not measure up particularly well in the international TIMSS and PIRLS measures, the perceptions of quality need to be mediated somewhat, as noted earlier, but remain powerful determinants for the realisation of parents' aspirations for their children. Furthermore, as the former townships have witnessed a migration of middle-class families into the suburbs, so too has the class stratification become clearer as township areas have become more visibly working class. The legacy of apartheid spending in township schools thus remains alive and well for two reasons. The first is that these schools are already staffed by teachers who, though minimally qualified, are not necessarily as well-qualified as their counterparts in 'suburban' middle-class schools, and the second reason is that the lower economic catchment areas (typically township, but also rural poor areas) have fewer resources to draw upon in terms of school fees or other forms of income to be derived from the local communities. The ironies of education in this area are plentiful. All over South Africa, former township areas became centres of social and cultural activity in which the solidarity of people oppressed by the regime found expression in writing, art, music and religious life. As these areas have become impoverished, arising from the gradual shift as classes stratify in communities (mostly gated and sometimes cordoned off depending on what is permitted under local municipal regulations), the quality of community life, of which schools are a fundamental part, is changing. From the media report by Mafisa and Malingo (2014) parents suggested the following:

> Stella Putsoa from Dube in Soweto said that in some of the local public schools there was virtually no teaching at all.
>
> 'I used to teach maths to my kids while they studied at our local school because they only had eight pages filled with work in their exercise books for the whole year,' she said.
>
> A longtime community member of Soweto's White City, known as Bab'Gambu, said most schools in the area were closed and the consequences of the closures were being felt by their children.
>
> 'Our children now travel long distances because as parents we want them to study but there are a few schools close by now, unlike in the old days,' he said.

That said, church schools have long been perceived as offering a superior education even in impoverished areas and they continue to be in high demand, and because these are mostly low-fee paying private schools, they are able to attract children from a variety of class backgrounds. This is unlike the new consortium type schools mentioned earlier, which even if values-based (for example, the Curro schools are all Christian schools), are high-end fee-paying schools (see also Chapter 7 on funding education). In rural areas the problems associated with depopulation also have a negative effect on schools and hence the high numbers of school closures in mostly rural provinces such as the Eastern Cape and Limpopo. Bloch (2014) has noted that this places a great strain on children in rural areas, who (as rural schools close) are required to walk longer distances to those that remain viable. In view of the drift to cities (2013 was the first year in South Africa's history where the scales tipped in terms of 49% of learners being located in rural areas), one might imagine that the demand for education even in the townships would increase, but the perceptions as regards quality are backed up by statistics which show that: 'The pass rate in former Model C schools is over 98%, while the pass rate in township schools is about 50 or 60%.'

1.4 TYPES OF SCHOOLS

Schooling is the joint responsibility of the Department of Basic Education (DoE or since 2012 the DBE) and Provincial Departments of Education (PDEs). The DBE is responsible for national policy, norms and standards. The PDEs are responsible for the implementation of the national mandates.

There are two main types of school in South Africa, namely public and independent schools, and collectively these are known as 'ordinary schools'. Public schools are controlled by the government through the education departments, while independent (private) schools are controlled by privately-owned individuals and/or structures. Although independent schools are privately controlled, they all have to be registered with the provincial departments where they reside, and also must comply with the various education regulations and policies that are prescribed to all learners, teachers and schools. There is, however, some flexibility and freedom granted to independent schools.

These schools are further complemented by a specialised type of schooling known as 'inclusive education and full-service schools' (IEFSS 2010, 3), which are aimed at reducing barriers to learning and participation to all learners, not only for those with impairments or are categorised as 'having special education needs' (IEFSS 2010, 3).

According to the Education Statistics 2013 (DBE 2014), ordinary schools can be classified as primary, secondary and intermediate. According to the DBE EMIS section there has been a phasing out of combined schools in the education system. There are two other separate categories of schools, namely early childhood development centres, which include those institutions who have pre-primary classes at primary schools, and special needs schools, which include standalone special schools and those attached to ordinary public and independent schools (see Table 1.6).

Table 1.6: Number of categories of schools in South Africa (2013)

Type of school	School category	Number of institutions
Public School	Primary	14 206
	Secondary	6 411
	Combined + Intermediate	5 209
	Total (Public)	25 826
Independent School	Primary	
	Secondary	
	Combined	
	Intermediate	
	Total (Independent)	1544
Total Public and Independent Schools		**27 370**
Other Education Sector	ECD	4 699
	Special Needs School	442
	Total (Other)	5 141
Grand Total of Public, Independent and Other Schools		**32 511**

Source: Education Statistics 2013 data WEB published by DBE, January 2014

1.5 LEARNERS WHO EXPERIENCE BARRIERS TO LEARNING (INCLUDING LEARNERS WITH DISABILITIES) IN SPECIAL AND IN ORDINARY SCHOOLS

With the introduction of the Policy on Inclusive Education, as published in the 'Education White Paper 6' (2001), the DoE made a commitment to enable and ensure that all children are welcomed in all schools. It indicated that children with special needs would be supported and developed regardless of their background, culture, abilities and disabilities, gender or race.[2] The introduction of the Convention on the Rights of Persons with Disabilities, ratified by South Africa in 2007, commits government to ensuring the introduction of an inclusive education system at all levels and making reasonable accommodation available to all children and youth with disabilities (Article 24).

The concept of 'full-service and inclusive education' schools was introduced to show how ordinary schools can transform themselves to become inclusive centres of care and support. Existing special schools would be strengthened to provide quality specialised teaching and support to learners with a high level of support needs, while at the same time being converted into resource centres capable of providing outreach services to ordinary schools. The DoE claims that by 2025 all ordinary schools would be required to be inclusive in their policies, cultures and practices. As part of this process, District-based Support Services must be capacitated to provide universal quality support to schools.

The strategy for Inclusive Education has been approved and implementation targeted for 2014. The following key areas have been incorporated in the strategy:

- Implementing the Policy on Screening, Identification, Assessment and Support (SIAS);

- Operationalising Full Service/Inclusive Schools;

- Improving Quality Education and Support in Special Schools and Special School Resource Centres;

- Institutionalizing Curriculum Differentiation;

- Quality Curriculum Delivery in Schools for Learners with Visual Impairment; and

- Introduction of South African Sign Language and improvement of curriculum delivery in Schools for the Deaf. (DBE Annual Report 2013, 64).

Table 1.6 shows that Gauteng has consistently been the province with the highest enrolment of learners from 2011–2013, with 36% of the total learners in special needs schools. Western Cape is the next highest with 17% followed by KwaZulu-Natal. The province with the least number of enrolments is the Northern Cape, which reflects 1.4% between 2011 and 2013.

The numbers of educators in special needs schools between the period 2011 and 2012 follow a similar pattern to the number of learners per province. Gauteng leads with the highest number of educators and this correlates with the highest number of learners, followed by Western Cape and KwaZulu-Natal. The province with the lowest number of educators is the Northern Cape (see Table 1.7). The data for number of educators for 2013 was not available from the DBE at the time of writing.

Table 1.7: Number of Special Schools with Educators and Learners per Province (2011-2013)

	2011	2012	2013	2011	2012	2013
Province	Learners	Learners	Learners	Educators	Educators	Total number of Special Schools
Eastern Cape	9031	9117	9165	878	854	42
Free State	5514	5801	6036	602	625	21
Gauteng	39 283	41 184	42 958	3182	3396	133
KwaZulu-Natal	15 955	16 264	16 811	733	1393	73
Limpopo	8360	8524	8598	706	684	34
Mpumalanga	3639	3549	3818	269	355	20
Northern Cape	1644	1646	1691	160	165	10
North-West	5634	5437	6764	236	465	32
Western Cape	19 180	20 076	20 689	1853	1802	79
South Africa	**108 240**	**111 598**	**116 530**	**8619**	**9739**	**444**

Source: DBE, Annual Special School Survey 2011, 2012, 2013

Table 1.8: Number of Schools per Province

Province	Public Schools						Ave Schools	As % Total
	2008	2009	2010	2011	2012	2013	08–13	08–13
Eastern Cape	5686	5668	5588	5589	5558	5562	5613	22.9%
Free State	1614	1547	1422	1371	1351	1327	1439	5.9%
Gauteng	1989	1970	2013	2040	2045	2056	2019	8.3%
KwaZulu-Natal	5783	5907	5927	5957	5955	5937	5911	24.2%
Limpopo	4023	3988	3965	3931	3935	3924	3961	16.2%
Mpumalanga	1873	1844	1838	1821	1807	1768	1825	7.5%
Northern Cape	602	600	597	591	560	553	584	2.4%
North-West	1730	1716	1646	1614	1591	1551`	1641	6.7%
Western Cape	1451	1453	1455	1451	1453	1458	1454	5.9%
South Africa	24 751	24 693	24 451	24 365	24 255	24 136	24 447	100%

Source: DBE, School Realities 2008–2013

There were 1584 independent schools in 2013 compared to 1 124 schools in 2008 (see Table 1.9). This represents a steady increase of 460 independent schools over the past five years. Independent schools have been increasing at an average of 77 schools per year. Gauteng has had the biggest net increase of 177 schools between 2008–2013, followed by the Western Cape, which has seen a net increase of 98 schools, and thirdly KwaZulu-Natal, with a net increase of 64 schools. All other provinces showed a net increase of less than 45 schools; Limpopo had a net increase of 44 schools, while the Eastern Cape and Mpumalanga had a net increase of 32 and 31 schools respectively.

Table 1.9: Number of Independent Schools, by Province, 2008–2013

Province	Independent Schools						Ave Schools	As % Total
	2008	2009	2010	2011	2012	2013	2008–13	2008–13
Eastern Cape	139	140	154	166	196	171	161	11,6%
Free State	61	64	66	66	68	69	66	4,7%
Gauteng	416	420	472	519	566	593	498	35,8%
KwaZulu-Natal	155	159	220	223	221	219	200	14,4%
Limpopo	99	117	141	142	143	143	131	9,4%
Mpumalanga	86	89	101	110	113	117	103	7,4%
Northern Cape	15	17	20	20	20	20	19	1,4%
North-West	54	52	55	55	54	55	54	3,9%
Western Cape	99	116	170	185	190	197	160	11,5%
South Africa	1 124	1 174	1 399	1 486	1 571	1 584	1392	100%

Source: DBE, School Realities 2008–2013

School libraries are intended to provide learners with access to learning materials such as books, periodicals and audio-visual media. International studies have revealed that a functional school library will add between 10% and 25% (Equal Education 2010, 6) to average learner outcomes, all other things being equal. A strong correlation and causal relationship have been found between the presence of a staffed library and higher academic performance in research conducted locally.

Education Statistics SA (DBE 2013, 3) stated that in 2011 there were 30 992 established public and registered independent education institutions. 25 851 of these were ordinary schools comprising 14 339 primary schools, 6 407 secondary schools and 5 105 combined and intermediate schools. The other 5 141 schools were defined as 'other education institutions', namely, Early Childhood Development (ECD) centres and special schools (ETDP SETA Skills Plan 2014, 81).

1.6 LEARNING AND PERFORMANCE: QUERY AND QUANDARIES

Not unexpectedly, if international trends are to be considered, girls perform better in terms of completing their school time within the normal cycle, with fewer dropouts and better grades. In 2005, Education Statistics SA (DBE 2005) showed that although there were fewer females than males in Grades 1–7 (less than 50%), the opposite was true for Grades 9–12. In Grade 12, females (54.4%) accounted for the highest female enrolment in all the primary and secondary-level grades. Dropout and poor success rates for boys in South Africa within the first 10 years of the changed system remained high and worryingly so, especially in the context of the global financial downturn that began to be experienced by 2005 and onwards. At that stage, the DoE noted that in schooling, the highest under-enrolment was experienced in Grades R and 12, which reflected an enrolment of 40.5% and 55.1%, respectively, of the appropriate school age population, claiming that while 'the data in this case do not necessarily indicate under-enrolment, but merely reflect the fact that about half of the population of this age was not in the formal schooling system' (2005, 13). In hindsight, such claims need to be treated with caution, given that the dropout rates in schooling, let alone higher education, provide a skewed picture of success in the system; those who remain in the system to be counted are precisely those most likely to leave with some form of education; for the many other children exiting the system earlier, the statistics remain deafeningly silent – a growing, seemingly mute and restive proportion of school-leavers too uneducated for skilled work, and too unskilled for anything but unskilled labour. With the economy visibly slowing down by 2007, and an upturn in labour unrest particularly among unskilled labour associated with the mining industry, political and higher education leadership expressed concerns about the increased unemployment of youth.

In 2014, unemployment was estimated by Statistics SA as standing at 25.4%, with an additional 1.3 million South Africans in long-term unemployment. The official term for such persons as a group is NEET: not in education, employment or training. Access to, and success in, education continued to be configured along racial lines, and more lately class lines, with Statistics South Africa confirming that, in 2014, whites were still among the group most likely to complete their schooling, followed by Indian and Asian groups. According to Bhorat et al. (2001), intra-black inequality has also increased dramatically in recent times. In addition to concerns about the low performance and retention of black learners in the system, it is also evident that performance in certain subject areas (typically those scarce skills such as Science, Mathematics and Languages) is similarly skewed along race and class lines. In every year in which the improvement in NSC pass rates is celebrated, critics routinely point to the fact that even the best of the school leavers do not in general complete their degree studies in time and are widely regarded as 'unfit' for higher education. Spaull (2013) notes that 'the more serious problem is widespread dropout before Grade 12, and that over time more pupils seem to be choosing less demanding exam subjects. Regarding the latter, it is revealing to note that over the four-year period between 2008 and 2011, the proportion of pupils taking mathematics (as opposed to maths literacy) has fallen from 56% to 45%, as more pupils opt for the easier maths literacy' (Spaull 2013, 5).

The South African government is acutely concerned with the performance of children in the system. Speaking to learners at the launch of the Nedbank Back to School project in January 2014 in Pretoria, Education Minister Angie Motshekga noted publicly the low ranking of the system, especially in Maths and Science, saying: 'South Africa has ranked its maths and science education as second last in the world, ahead of Yemen, according to a World Economic Forum Report'.

The Global Information Technology Report (2013) added that South Africa's costly access to Information and Communication Technologies (ICT) is hampering its competitiveness:

> Going up two positions, South Africa is in 70th place. Despite a sharp improvement in the development of its ICT infrastructure (59th) – notably in terms of international Internet bandwidth capacity (66th) – and a strong uptake by the business community (33rd), the ICT impacts (92nd), particularly the social ones (112th), remain limited.

The World Economic Forum's Global Competitiveness Report (2012–2013) notes that the lack of clear government vision (SA ranked 105th worldwide) to orchestrate and implement a holistic ICT strategy for the country, coupled with deficiencies in the educational system for some segments of the population (SA ranked 102nd), play negatively in this process and outweigh a rather positive political and regulatory framework for ICT development (SA ranked 21st) and pro-business environment (SA ranked 55th). It is the latest indictment of South Africa's education system since the 2011 Progress in International Reading Literature Study (PIRLS) which indicated that most South African Grade 5 learners have not yet acquired basic literacy skills:

> In the World Economic Forum's Global Competitiveness Report, 2012–2013, South Africa ranked 132nd out of 144 countries in quality of primary education, even below some of the poorest countries in Africa, such as Mali, Chad, Tanzania and Malawi. For the quality of the educational system as a whole, it ranked 140th out of 144 countries, and for the quality of maths and science education, South Africa ranked 143rd out of 144 countries, having the worst provision of maths and science education in all of Africa. (Naidoo 2014, 6)

Two decades after the celebrated implementation of the new national curriculum, South Africa continues to occupy the lower echelons of international education achievement rankings (140th out of 144 countries in the quality of education provision) vis-à-vis considerably less resourced, impoverished nations. Jansen (2014) makes the following points about the pass rates and policy concerning the promotion of children who fail in the system:

> 'The fourth, and arguably most serious dimension of this crisis, is the institutionalisation of low standards and low expectations in the school system. The problem is not the low standards, it's that we accept them,' he said.

> 'What message do you give when in 2012 your Minister of Basic Education says: "30% for a slow learner is fine," or, "when someone has achieved 30%, it means that person has been able to master the basic skills."'[3]

> 'It's human behaviour – if you tell a child to jump this high, that's what they will do,' he added. 'We need to give the message that this is not good enough. Yet our government is happy with this.'

> As if a 30% pass is not bad enough, South Africa is the only country in the world where learners in Grades 10 to 12 are automatically promoted after failing a year.

> The fifth point he made is that the resolution of the crisis does not require more resources, but a more efficient use of existing resources. 'Why is it that some schools can achieve something different, given the same resources?' (Jansen in Planting, 2014)

Spaull (2013) summarises South Africa's achievement in the two decades. Using the SACMEQ II (2000) and SACMEQ III (2007) test results, he argues that it is evident that there has been no improvement in South African Grade 5 literacy or numeracy performance over a seven-year period. Sadly, this performance is worse than countries much poorer than South Africa (South African pupils ranked 10th of the 14 education systems; 12th for reading and 8th for mathematics, behind much poorer countries such as Tanzania, Kenya and Swaziland).

Spaull also considered the TIMSS 1995, 1999, 2002, 2011 Trends in International Mathematics and Science Study (Grade 8/9 Mathematics and Science) and found that tests for mathematics and science showed that there had been no improvement in Grade 8 Mathematics or Science achievement between 1995 and 2002. However, when these same tests were applied to Grade 9 learners (who wrote the Grade 9 test), there was marked improvement between 2002 and 2011 in Maths and Science performance amounting to approximately one-and-a-half grade levels of learning. This shows that there has been some improvement over the period. But, as Spaull (2013, 4) notes, 'While this is hopeful, it is difficult to celebrate when one considers how low the post-improvement level of performance really is'. For example, in 2011 a third of pupils (32%) performed worse than guessing on the multiple choice items (i.e. no better than random). Furthermore, three-quarters (76%) of Grade 9 pupils in 2011 still had not acquired a basic understanding about whole numbers, decimals, operations or basic graphs, and this is at the improved level of performance. Thus improvement can only be read as such because of the low base from which it was charted in 2002. To place this in perspective, South Africa's post-improvement level of performance is still the lowest of all participating countries, with the average South African Grade 9 child performing between two and three grade levels lower than the average Grade 9 child from other middle-income countries.

Other measures of school success are determined by the DBE through the Annual National Assessments, but year-on-year the questions in these tests change and so without any control items in the tests, there is a question concerning their validity. Unfortunately, the credibility of the results is thrown further into doubt by South African learners' low performance in international testing measures already described. This chapter does not consider performance in the annual national assessment because of the mismatch between claims made regarding this data and the international benchmarks that can demonstrate both validity and reliability over time.

1.7 TEACHERS AT WORK IN SOUTH AFRICA

Pendlebury (1998) suggested that South Africa's accession to membership of global organisations after a long period of relative isolation required that it implement radical and key reforms in education in a short period of time. A focus on values and policies (whether macro-legislation or micro-policy in terms of the curriculum, for example), has ultimately, as its aim, people as well as places in which education as a practice is situated and conducted. This section describes the teaching corps in South Africa in terms of where they are located, how they are supported, and how ready they have been to embrace and enact new curriculum initiatives after 1995.

1.7.1 Politicisation of the profession

At the outset it has to be stated that the teaching profession is an embattled one in South Africa, in part because apartheid focused on education as a means both of the repression and under-development of black people. Thus the area identified as a site for coercion and repression became also a site for contestation and confrontation, as noted by Govender (in Chisholm 2004), Hyslop (2003), Chisholm (2003) and Motala (2006). Teacher unions, as they developed in their resistance to the apartheid State, became political entities capable of mobilising resistance and confrontation with the State as seen for example in the schools boycotts of the 1950s (Hyslop 1987) and in cataclysmic Soweto Uprising of 1976 (Hyslop 1985 and 1990).

Given the poor quality of teacher professional development in the apartheid period, it is thus not surprising that high levels of unionisation have not been accompanied by high levels of commitment to professional development through the unions. Where unions have been very successful is in the ongoing politicisation of teaching and instead of partnership with government, there has developed a tradition of contestation between government and the unions, almost always in terms of teachers' conditions of service. Strikes such as those that occurred in 2008 (when most members of the largest union, the South African Democratic Teachers' Union, embarked on a go-slow, limiting the hours of teaching in schools, and increasing levels of teacher absenteeism), have been highly damaging to the professional image of teachers, and have had an observable impact on the quality of learners' experience in schools. As Jansen notes:

'The second "critical fact" is that there is no system of accountability for what happens inside schools,' Jansen said. 'Unless we hold teachers to account, we will perform at the bottom of the ladder. And we can't do that because the South African Democratic Teachers Union (SADTU) will have us for breakfast.'

With every year that goes by the greater the educational and social inequality between our two school systems becomes. We are in trouble.

In a school – as in any functioning organization – rhythm and routine are essential. 'This is absent in most SA schools,' Jansen said. 'On average five teachers in every school are absent every day – and SAFTU is motivating for more sick leave'. (Jansen in Planting 2014, 1)

SADTU members are drawn mostly from former DET and Bantustan schools, whereas the National Association of Professional Teachers of South Africa and the South African Teachers' Union (SATU) draw their members from formerly white, Indian and coloured schools. The race politics so typical of the apartheid era unfortunately and very damagingly remains a consistent theme in teacher protests in the new democratic period.

The struggle to develop a culture of a professionally-focused teachers' corps has been a persistent cause for concern. The South African Council of Educators (SACE), which was created as the statutory professional body for teachers in 1995, has been tasked with developing a mechanism to institute, promote, recognise and accredit continuous teacher development for teachers in schools.

1.7.2 The under-development of the education system

Scholars have noted the deleterious effects of the apartheid curriculum in schools: not only was content suited to the race classification of people, but, for example, Prinsloo (2000) compares the examination papers of the late apartheid period for English Second Language (termed 'English as an additional language' after 1995) and isiZulu First Language (termed 'home language', for example), and showed that the curriculum for black schools (bantustan schools as well as Department of Education and Training in the apartheid era) was not only less challenging in terms of intellectual stretch, but also less demanding in terms of content when compared with examination papers set by the 'white' education departments. Implied, even in this documentary analysis, is that the teacher training associated with different race groups was different also in terms of quality and standards and expectation.

The department (DoE/DBE) in its reporting has tended to focus primarily on the quantitative data concerning teachers and learners in the system. Thus, in 2005, the department could claim that the 'national learner-to-educator ratio trend line, as reflected in Table 1.7, stayed fairly consistent between 2001 and 2004, but decreased between 2004 and 2005' (2005, 15). Six provinces (the Eastern Cape, the Free State, Gauteng, KwaZulu-Natal, Mpumalanga and the Western Cape) showed a net decrease from 2001 to 2005, while Limpopo indicated the highest net increase, of 7.3%.

According to departmental statistics, there were, in 1999, 27 461 ordinary public and independent schools in South Africa. These figures exclude special needs schools or pre-primary ones (Early Childhood Development centres, or pre-primary care schools or centres). Just over 97% (26 644) of these ordinary schools were public schools and less than 3% (817) were independent schools. The distribution or concentration of schools bears no correlation to the achievement of the regions named. Thus, while the Eastern Cape in 1999 had the largest number of ordinary schools (6 190), and the Northern Cape had the smallest number of ordinary schools (493), it was the Western Cape and Gauteng that outperformed other regions in terms of learner results in the 20-year period. This suggests different levels of complexity to the analysis. On the one hand, while the Eastern Cape had the highest number of ordinary public schools (6 145), KwaZulu-Natal (5 578) and Mpumalanga (4 035) together accounted for almost 60% of all ordinary public schools in South Africa in 1999, but their year-on-year learner performance remained among the lowest in South Africa. These three provinces account for the highest concentrations of schools and learners from rural areas, confirming the *Emerging Voices Report* (Chisholm and Porteus 2005) that rural education remains the most neglected dimension of education for almost half of the school-going population.

In 1999, there were 365 447 educators (teaching the 12 313 899 learners in ordinary schools in South Africa, as mentioned in the previous sections). KwaZulu-Natal had the highest number of educators in ordinary schools (74 719), while the Northern Cape had the lowest (6773). It would not be unusual to expect that a lower teacher–learner ratio would enable a better quality of teaching (well-qualified teachers prefer to engage with smaller numbers of learners as this enables teachers to identify learners' styles of learning and barriers to learning experienced by the learner and identified by the teacher). However, in 1999 the teacher–learner ratio was lower than it had been in 2014 (almost 34 learners per educator in South Africa, according to Education Statistics SA), and even lower in KwaZulu-Natal (30.1), and yet those indicators cannot be relied upon to have correlational value for the quality of education. In KwaZulu-Natal and the Eastern Cape, despite lower teacher–learner ratios, learner throughput and success rates are among the lowest in South Africa. This can be explained by the fact that the majority of under-qualified and non-qualified teachers in the system are concentrated in these two provinces. Spaull (2013, 5) notes further that:

> in the Eastern Cape only 20% of Grade 2 pupils from the 2001 cohort went on to pass the NSC exam in 2011, compared to 60% in Gauteng and 50% in the Western Cape. These 'conversion rates' provide a good indication of the quality of education offered to pupils in these provinces. While one should be aware of

the differing socio-economic profiles of the provinces, the fact that equally poor provinces with similar geographical, sociological and historical profiles have different conversion rates is testament to the fact that schools and provincial administrations can make a difference.

It is thus unsurprising that in addition to the above, the same three low-performing provinces also have the highest rates of over-aged and under-aged learners in the system. Thus, Education Statistics SA reports that the 'gross enrolment rate' for the Eastern Cape was 214%, and in KwaZulu-Natal and Mpumalanga over 100%. Five years into a new democratic dispensation, the system in these provinces had to be geared to address the challenges outlined above, and as might be expected, the turnaround needed in such contexts would be unlikely to occur within the first decade of the new dispensation. Simply put, teacher education, curriculum redesign, teacher qualification upgrading, while national priorities, would not have much immediate impact at provincial levels.

The question of why schools become unsustainable, and why they close, has been touched on earlier in this chapter, and is a complex one. By 2005 the number of schools had been reduced to 26 592 as part of a rationalisation of ineffective and small (and thus unsustainable) schools located mostly in rural areas (typically farm schools, or multi-grade schools in villages). Education statistics show that of the 26 592 ordinary schools, 19 260 were primary schools and 5851 were secondary schools.

Ten years into the new democracy the number of learners in the system was similarly lower with a little over 10 million learners in the system (7 681 324 learners in primary schools and 3 828 705 learners in secondary schools). Combined and intermediate schools accounted for 707 736 learners and 29 229 educators. The overall number of teachers in the system had also been reduced from over 370 000 in 2005, to a little over 350 000 in 2005 (228 957 primary school teachers and 123 947 secondary school teachers). How is the reduction in learner numbers and teachers to be explained?

On the one hand, the reduction of schools regarded as unsustainable explains also the reduction in student numbers. However, school dropout figures in this period remain high. This is illustrated by the data concerning school dropout and retention rates. Education Statistics SA (2005) indicates that of every 100 learners in ordinary schools in South Africa, more than 31 learners were in the Foundation Phase, slightly fewer than 24 were in the Intermediate Phase, slightly more than 24 were in the Senior Phase, 20 were in the FET band, and less than one was in the pre-Grade-R Phase and 'other' combined. Roughly then, only a third of an initial cohort might finish their schooling on time, and of this group, ten learners (i.e. 10% of the cohort itself) would have exited school without completing any kind of qualification.

In 2005, the DBE had started to count the number of teachers employed by schools in a private capacity. This had not been the practice in 1995. In other words, this is where schools with access to substantive privately raised funding, through class fees or community assistance, were able to employ additional teachers. This had the simultaneous effect of bringing down the overall national pupil–teacher ratios, but creating the wrong impression of more equity of access to teaching in the system. In fact, already enabled communities, mostly urban and middle class by nature, simply circumvented the post-provisioning norm, and employed additional teachers in particular in subjects defined as 'scarce skills' (Arts and Culture, Science and Mathematics and Languages).

For schooling, which includes both independent and public schools, according to the 2013 School Realities data, there were 25 720 schools (24 136 public and 1584 independent), served by 425 023 educators and servicing 12 489 648 learners. Independent schools comprise 1584 schools, with a staff of 33 194 educators, teaching 513 804 learners which translates to 4.1% of the entire learner population in SA (DBE School Realities 2013).

In 2011 in South Africa there were 30 992 established public and registered independent education institutions that submitted the survey forms. Of these, 25 851 were ordinary schools and 5141 were other education institutions – namely, ECD centres and special schools. The ordinary schools comprised 14 339 primary schools and 6407 secondary schools. In comparison, this represents an increase of a little over 3000 additional schools in the system over a 20-year period. By 2011 there were a little over 12 000 000 learners in the system comprising 5 980 939 learners in primary schools, 3 966 838 learners in secondary schools and 2 340 217 learners in intermediate or combined schools.

By this time the primary there were 187 065 school teachers, 146 434 secondary teachers and 87 109 educators for the combined and intermediate schools. Comparatively, there were fewer teachers in the system in 2011, for the same number of children, roughly, as recorded in 1999 (in 1999, there were 365 447 educators teaching 12 313 899 learners in ordinary schools) in South Africa. While the detail concerning numbers in the system is interesting, what is especially revealing in the 20-year period since 1994 is the persistent trend towards high levels of participation in schooling in the early years, tailing off in the later years of senior school. The loss of approximately 10% of children going through the system remains a worrying phenomenon, at once complicated by the fact that the changes to the curriculum over the period have been frequent and substantial. The Twenty-Year Review 1994–2014 of South Africa (The Presidency 2014) suggests that progress in education is measurable and definite.

The learner-to-teacher ratio improved from 33 to 1 in 2000 to 30 to 1 in 2012. As a result of improved infrastructure, a higher proportion of younger children are accessing classroom facilities. Overall, South Africa is achieving gender parity in school enrolment with a Gender Parity Index of 1 in 201223, and is on track to meet the Millennium Development Goal (MDG) of achieving universal primary education by 2015. Progress has also been made in increasing access to schools for children with disabilities, with more public special schools being built. More work is required in this regard because access is still limited, with less than 40% of children with disabilities accessing formal education, either through special schools or mainstream education. The improvements in access have resulted from a number of interventions. The burden of school fees for poor households has been reduced by introducing no-fee schools" (The Presidency 2014, 48).

But, as noted by Harber and Mncube (2012), access to schooling is the single most important issue in the developing world, where a significant proportion of children of school-going age remain outside the schooling system in their respective countries (Harber & Mncube 2012). Furthermore, critics of the system (notably Bloch 2009) observe that a conspicuous number of (historically) black schools continue to be ineffectual, despite changes in education policy, constitution and schools legislation notwithstanding. As Jansen notes:

> The third fact is that the government has tried to resolve the crisis through reforms that do not address the core of the problem. Their approach is, if you don't know what to do, develop a new policy. (Jansen in Planting 2014, 1)

The comments above suggest that measures of system-efficiency are complex, relating not only to the degree to which schools are able also to support adequately the good performance of teachers, but also to infrastructure, learner support and success. Reading data is equally complex since assumptions made with regard to efficiency cannot be sustained in an environment where so many systemic inequality issues associated with apartheid continue to have an impact on present-day success or failure in education.

In terms of support, for example, data concerning administrative support is available to learners and teachers in provinces in South Africa. Unfortunately, though, because of the deep-seated nature of the problems associated with apartheid's legacy, neat deductions are seldom supported by the data. The table below, taken from Education Statistics SA (2001) is illustrative of this phenomenon. The department (DoE/DBE) provides data on administrative support in regions, but those associated with top performance in terms of schooling (typically Gauteng, North-West and Western Cape) bear no relation to the other provinces either in terms of population density, learners in the system or education performance (as associated with the quality of teaching and education in these areas).

Table 1.10: Learner-administrative staff ratio (LAR), in the ordinary schools, by province, in 2011

Province	Administrative	Learners	LAR
Eastern Cape	3226	1 963 578	609
Free State	1815	658 010	363
Gauteng	8 220	2 022 050	246
KwaZulu-Natal	5 352	2 847 378	532
Limpopo	1 531	1 695 524	1107
Mpumalanga	2 701	1 046 551	387
Northern Cape	678	274 745	405
North-West	1 915	765 120	400
Western Cape	3 513	1 015 038	289

Source: 2011 SNAP Survey

Furthermore, impressive progress has been made in terms of providing access to education in the form of no-fee, or low-fee schools (see Heystek in Chapter 7). Thus, the Twenty-Year Review 1994–2014 (The Presidency 2014) noted that by 2012, 78% of learners (more than 8 million) in 80% of public schools (close to 20 000 schools) benefited from the no-fee policy. In addition to this, the government had introduced school meals in all no-fee schools through the National School Nutrition Programme and has claimed that this initiative 'has contributed to regular and punctual attendance by learners and enabled them to attend school without being hungry' (48).

By 2012, about 9 million learners in 20 905 primary and secondary schools – virtually all the learners from poor households – were receiving a government-funded school lunch. Notwithstanding the sincere and dedicated efforts of the government to provide for children and thereby better support them in their learning, the critical issue concerning success in schools has to do with the quality of teaching. Jansen (2014) argues that:

The performance of the good schools masks the crisis in the system. Growth in the pass rate does not reflect improvements in the system. The international and comparative tests of achievement do not lie – we should not be interested in how we perform inside SA but how we compare internationally.

How, when it comes to global rankings, can we come first in auditing and accounting standards and dead last in science and mathematics, along with Guinea-Bissau. It's because the auditing and accounting profession is held to account by a standard that is set outside the country.

Unfortunately, when it comes to education, that standard is set by the government, and it's been declining since 1954 (when the government took the responsibility for black education away from the Catholic and Anglican churches). (Jansen in Planting 2014, 1).

What is important in either a centralised or decentralised system is the nature of leadership, 'precisely one of the scarcest resources in developing countries, and even in developed countries' (Carnoy 2008 in Chsholm 2012, 21). The bottom line 'is that decentralisation of management can work well in counties where there is already sufficient capacity at the local level to allocate resources efficiently and produce effective education' (Carnoy 2008, 22, in Chisholm 2012, 23). The Twenty-Year Review 1994–2014 notes that the identification of 'problem areas' necessitated that the government establish in 2009 the National Education Evaluation and Development Unit (NEEDU). NEEDU published a comprehensive report on the state of literacy teaching and learning in the Foundation Phase in 2012. Findings in the report included the fact that learning time is being lost due to the late-coming of learners, abuse of leave by teachers and daily school disruptions. Furthermore, it was found that learners' performance is affected by the limited subject knowledge of teachers, heads of department and subject advisors (The Presidency 2014, 49–51).

It has taken over 10 years to reach agreement about the need for relative uniformity in relation to the provision of standardised and good education facilities, and even today this remains an area of annual reporting in DBE (former DoE) reports. The Minimum Norms and Standards for Public School Infrastructure (2013) regulations were legislated to describe minimum uniform norms and standards for public school infrastructure. The Norms and Standards also served to ensure that there was compliance with the minimum uniform norms and standards in the design and construction of new schools and additions, alterations and improvements in schools, timeframes within which such infrastructure backlogs has to be eradicated.

1.8 SCHOOL INFRASTRUCTURAL NEEDS

The NEIMS Report (2011) shows that out of 25 783 schools in South Africa, 3544 schools do not have electricity; 2402 have no water supply; 913 do not have any ablution facilities; 11 450 are still using pit latrines; 22 938 do not have stocked libraries; 21 021 do not have any laboratory facilities; 2703 have no fencing at all; and 19 037 schools have no computer centres.

In the 20 years since Nelson Mandela came to power, the government has consistently devoted resources to the improvement of facilities such as those listed above, but even after these two decades, mud schools, lack of clean running water and electricity, and even security, textbooks and school furniture, continue to be challenges for the DBE (NEIMS Report 2011). Naidoo (2014) argues that the persistence of these issues belies the persisting notion of the celebrated 'education transformation and democratic citizenship' programme. The proportionately high budgetary allocation for education – Mandela's 'great engine of growth and development', has materialised, apparently, in a 'trickle-down effect', minimally mitigating chronically debilitating infrastructural conditions in a substantial constituency of schools – a far cry from the 'safe (pedagogic) environments conducive to democratic education' (Dewey 1916; Lipman 2003; Naidoo 2014, 42–43).

Against the backdrop of political change in the country, acclaimed as the 'last bastion of colonialism' in Africa, the stark paucity of achievement in the classroom (since 1994) remains a major concern (Nugent 2004). South Africa's ranking at the bottom of the international education index understandably is an anomaly in a portfolio that commands the lion's share of the national budget (DoE 2010), notably in a climate of intense competition for priorities in terms of scarce financial resources and stringent budgetary allocations (Harber & Brock 2013). In this regard, resource allocation for the education sector is the unlikely culprit in being considered solely responsible for the low level of achievement in education.

Spaull (2013) argues that 'apart from the 25% of schools that are mostly functional, South African schools as they currently stand do not, and arguably cannot, impart to pupils the foundational knowledge and skills they should be acquiring at school'. Improving pass rates against the backdrop of post-provisioning norms which guarantee abnormally large classes for all children other than those from middle-class families (whose parents can afford to subsidise additional posts in schools) does not guarantee quality education in terms of the individual attention children need in the early years of schooling. It is for this reason that claims made by the DBE concerning improvements are met with scepticism: 'While the NSC pass rate has been increasing in recent years, this measure should not be seen as an accurate indication of the quality of education in the country. It is flawed because it only reflects the achievement of the best-performing 50% of a cohort, i.e. those that make it to Grade 12, and it does not take into account subject combinations and the fact that more pupils are opting for easier subjects like mathematics literacy, compared to more challenging subjects like mathematics' (Spaull 2013, 7).

One of the issues in relation to the increasing number of learners in the system and the obvious needs this has created both in terms of the creation of new schools and a new generation of teachers to educate young people, relates to teacher supply-and-demand. Because South Africa's education system was designed in the apartheid period to develop differential and unequal access to education of unequal levels and quality, it is not surprising that teacher supply-and-demand is closely linked to issues of quality in education (see Hyslop 1989).

1.9 CURRICULUM REFORM

When the new government took power in 1994, a priority was the standardisation of education curricula. Unsurprisingly this was a cornerstone of the transformation project and in the early years the emphasis was both on teacher education and on school, viz. outcomes-based education (OBE; Spady 1994). OBE espoused many of the aspirations of equal education, democratic education, as well as the methodologies associated with learner-centred approaches to teaching, communication competence, collaboration and self-directed learning. However, as Chisholm (2004) argues, this policy shift, while important in signalling how the State envisioned the role of education as a means of emancipation and development with a view to progress, was not accompanied by a radical shift in teacher education policy or reform. The first five years of democracy in South Africa saw school curricula change without changes being effected either to teachers coming into the system, or teachers already in it. That there ought to have been a major process for education as well as re-education goes without saying. Instead, a new curriculum was developed which required that teachers change methodologies, assessment techniques and learning strategies. The Twenty-Year Review 1994–2014 (The Presidency 2014) notes that OBE 'proved to be difficult to implement and was subsequently replaced by various revisions, including the

National Curriculum Statement Grade R–12 and the National Curriculum and Assessment Policy Statement (CAPS) between 2011 and 2014' (48).

Scholtz (2008) argued that OBE was 'based on cooperation, critical thinking and social responsibility, thus enabling individuals to participate in all aspects of society. Concomitant with this is the need for teachers to change their pedagogy from one that is more didactic and teacher-controlled to one that [encourages] … active learner participation' (22). Naidoo (2014) suggests that the 'the new policy was categorical in its progressive aims, democratic vision and the newly defined role of the teacher as vanguard of the new pedagogy in South African classrooms':

> The kind of teacher that is envisaged … contributor to the transformation of education in South Africa … teachers who are qualified, competent, dedicated and caring … mediators of learning, interpreters and designers of Learning Programmes and materials, leaders, administrators and managers, scholars, researchers and lifelong learners, community members, citizens and pastors, assessors and learning area/phase specialists. (RNCS 2002, 9)

OBE was widely critiqued on the basis of three important points: the language of OBE was alien and new to most teachers in the system and even the roll-out of OBE through country-wide workshops was problematic. Trainers were contracted by government to train teachers on how to use OBE, without accounting for the various levels of awareness of English as a lingua franca, and in the context of highly complex pedagogical terms (guided learning, self-direction, problem-based learning, integrated assessment and so on), the very model used to roll out the new curriculum was itself considered as top-down. Many prominent educationists (for example, Jansen (1998) (and Bloch 1999; Chisholm 2003) noted that the new policy (known as *Curriculum 2005*) was in fact incommensurate with teachers' existing knowledge and required a new way of teaching that not only assumed essentially middle-class and urban values, but also assumed a resource and capacity base (equipped classrooms, media centres, libraries, functioning schools and facilities) that were at best fragile and at worst non-existent. *Curriculum 2005* was revised by a committee led by Linda Chisholm (2002) at the end of the century and resulted in a new document: the *Revised National Curriculum Statement* (2002), as based on the recommendations of the *Chisholm Report*. In essence, the revisions entailed an affirmation of the progressive and democratic language of the curriculum, but also a refocusing on the content on the understanding that progressive education methodologies were fairly useless without a sound knowledge base.

Nevertheless a number of radical departures from the past call for comment here. The first concerns the place of official languages in the curriculum. The Constitution made provision for the use of 11 official languages in education. The legislation framing this is known as the Language in Education Policy (LiEP), in which additive bilingualism was promoted with the idea that the home language was introduced to children first in primary school and that additional languages would be gradually scaffolded later in the curriculum. In these terms schools could choose, through the School Governing Body (SGB), the language of instruction as derived from the language(s) spoken by the community. Initially, this seemed to become operative only in those schools where English[4] had never been a language of instruction to begin with, but in the last five years, more schools have been opting for a language policy in which English features at least as an additional language, or as the language of instruction.

A second feature of the new curriculum was the creating of phases associated with the schooling years beginning with Grade 0, Early Childhood Education (also known as reception year or pre-school), and Grades 1–4, known as the Foundation Phase, to be followed by the Intermediate Phase or Grades 5–7, a Senior Phase, known as Grades 8–9, and a Further Education and Training Phase known as Grades 10–12. In this system students are able to exit the school at the end of Grade 9 and request to be admitted to a Further Education and Training college (FET; now TVET), should they seek to pursue vocationally oriented education (typically the trades, hospitality, tourism and other forms of vocational training, for example, agriculture and so on). All school leavers would ideally be able to leave the system after 13 years of education with a National Senior Certificate (NSC), which replaced the old provincial departments' (19 all in all) matriculation examinations.

A third defining feature of the new curriculum occurred within the Intermediate Phases in which students no longer chose individual subjects but rather subjects from a selected groupings of what was termed 'learning areas': for example, Arts and Culture, Life Sciences, Languages, Social Sciences. This differed from the OBE curriculum in which there were more choices available and fewer groupings.

In 2011, in recognition of the growing sense of confusion and discord with regard to the content and levels appropriate to the learning areas, let alone phases, a third round of revisions (known as the *Curriculum and Assessment Policy Statement*; CAPS) was enacted. The Twenty-Year Review 1994–2014 (The Presidency 2014) notes that 'The CAPS spelt out what teachers should teach and assess, how lesson plans should be prepared, and how teaching should take place. This was crucial for addressing gaps that were apparent in the outcomes-based curriculum. CAPS also introduced English as a subject in the early grades to ease the transition to instruction in English for learners who are not first-language English speakers' (The Presidency 2014, 48). While curricula have become more content-focused in the last 20 years, it is important not to lose sight of the original intention of OBE: learner-centred education designed to develop self-directed learning. This is still regarded as an influential idea and concept derived from the OBE documentation introduced in 1995, and its relevance extends beyond subsequent revisions to the curriculum. As Boehm notes:

> Learner-centered attitudes can be regarded as an important prerequisite for life-long learning in an ever changing world of work. This is supportive of the ability to adjust to new job requirements. Current jobs too require more self-initiative and flexibility from employees so that the ability to learn is as important as the readiness and motivation to take initiative. (Boehm 2000, 9)

According to Naidoo (2014), this round of revisions contained an 'even stronger focus on curriculum content, adopting the previously eschewed traditional, cumulative approach to learning and knowledge acquisition'. The OBE terminology and jargon associated with earlier policies were removed and a straightforward common-sense approach to teaching was described in relation to a set of prescribed minimum content with 'teacher-proof' guides. This demonstrates the State's increasing awareness of the generally low competency levels of teachers in South Africa. Rogan and Macdonald (1985) argue that the introduction of innovative pedagogies is unlikely to succeed if teachers are not confident in their own subject-content knowledge. Naidoo (2014) suggests that the majority of non-white teachers in South Africa had experienced the limited apartheid education curriculum and were now expected to teach the comprehensive national OBE curriculum. Like Chisholm, Naidoo (2004, 16) suggests that the immediate reforms of the system should also have focused on the upgrading of knowledge content, but without policy reform this could not have occurred or be guided. On the other hand, policy reform without re-education was the equivalent of form without substance, and the absences in knowledge substance became evident after five years, highlighted by the patchy and confused implementation of *Curriculum 2005* (as based on OBE).

With successive curriculum reforms (of which there have been at least four in the last 20 years), the focus narrowed at times so that by 2011, with the introduction of CAPS, it was evident that the national focus on assessments (known as the annual national assessment) that CAPS (2011) had moved away from group to individual work; it decreased flexibility and creativity of the teacher and reinstituted annual national testing of Grades 3, 6 and 9. Naidoo argues that 'The combined effect of these four major changes, along with the changes in terminology and renewed content (rather than skills) focus can be interpreted as an effective about-turn in government education policy strategy, signalling a change of intent' (Naidoo 2014, 50).

1.10 REFLECTIONS

The aim of education-related directives, policies and strategies has been to widen access, develop quality and create success. Mother-tongue education has been a central feature of initiatives at policy level that relate to access and success. But, as Naidoo argues, the policy that prescribes that children be taught in their mother tongue (in the first three grades), does in some instances prevent race integration in the early years. Thus the language policy could be used both to enable success and straitjacket access along race lines (Soudien & Sayed 2003). The new constitutional right to choice of language of learning was overtly democratic in its intention to ensure a learner-centred approach to teaching. Naidoo suggests that this has been a double-edged sword. Arguments rest on two problematic areas: the first is the relative absence (especially between 1995–2004) of indigenous language materials for use in Grades 1–3, while the second has to do with the fact that the overwhelming majority of teachers were not themselves trained to use indigenous languages for teaching and learning. This latter aspect was another 'legacy factor' from apartheid, but its long-term effects countered the positive intentions of the curriculum as well as the language policy itself both of which aspired to 'develop the full potential of each learner' (RNCS 2002, 8). What impact have successive waves of curriculum reform had on learning in South Africa over the 20-year period in question? The Minister of Basic Education instituted a Maths and Science task team in 2013 which found that '43% of South African Grade 5 learners failed to reach the lowest international benchmark, in contrast to 5% of Grade 4 learners internationally. This means that they have not yet mastered the basic reading skills required to access and retrieve information for reading comprehension purposes', the PIRLS report (Howie et al. 2011) stated. It further revealed that about 90% of the Grade 4 learners tested in English or Afrikaans attained the lowest international benchmark, while between 24% and 57% of children writing in all nine official languages did not achieve it. Learners tested in Sepedi and Tshivenda achieved the lowest results, according to the study (Evans 2013).

The data suggests overwhelmingly that change via policy redevelopment had had a disappointingly small impact on performance either of learners or of teachers. In part, factors such as these are receiving the attention of the DHET through its teacher education bursary scheme (where languages are defined alongside Mathematics and Natural Sciences as 'scarce skills').

This chapter has surveyed a range of factors that affect learner performance and the quality of education received in South African schools. The pressure for curriculum change at the outset was complicated by the capacity of the system (not only in terms of schools or teachers, but also district and area officials such as subject advisors) to deliver on the promise of improvement in the conditions of teaching and learning, and also to meet the need for a national and new curriculum designed to foster enquiry, collaborative learning and a love of reading. These pressures were evidently greater than the system's capacity to deliver on them, and the resulting levels of frustration, and sometimes even confusion and fatigue, detract from the equally significant gains made in terms of universal primary education, the improvements in school infrastructure, the provision of nutrition to the poorest of the schools and learners, and the improvements made in teacher qualification levels. Should an overall assessment be that the schooling provided has failed learners, then it is clear that more will need to be done to improve the quality of teachers and teaching in schools, and it is towards that end that the next chapter will address itself.

NOTES

1   The issue of how and why schools come to close is complex. As children migrate with families to urban centres, rural schools lose numbers, making the post-provisioning norm (the ppn as discussed in Chapter 7) difficult to sustain. Teachers are thus reduced and then schools become multigrade and unable to cover the curriculum.

2   www.thutong.gov.za/inclusiveeducation. Retrieved August 2014.

3   In 2012–2013 there was an outcry over the apparently low standard (30%) required to pass the NSC. According to Wilkinson and Rademeyer (2015), pupils are required to take a minimum of seven subjects. These include three compulsory subjects – usually a first language, a first additional language, mathematics or mathematical literacy and life orientation: 'Pupils need 40% in three subjects (one of which must be your home language), and 30% in 3 other subjects' (1). Furthermore, there is no averaging of marks

in the National Senior Certificate exams: 'No learner will be awarded a [National Senior Certificate] if s/he attained an average of 30%.'

4   In secondary school a range of other languages, for example, Hindi, Urdu, Tamil, Telegu, Greek, Hebrew, Mandarin and the like, could be accommodated.

2 Teacher education in South Africa: Part of the problem or part of the solution?

2.1 INTRODUCTION

The role of schools, and thus also of teachers (and therefore higher education institutions generating teachers for schools), cannot be over-estimated in terms of providing an integrated solution to the challenge of unlocking South Africa's creative and innovative potential as a developing economy. Frustrations of teachers, academics and political leaders at the quality of education in South Africa have long been expressed – in fact, ever since before the democratic transition in 1994. In other words, the performance of the schooling sector is not a post-apartheid problem as noted by Morrow (2007) and Christie (1994) alike. From 1995 onwards there was a rush of policy and legislation from the 'White paper on Education and Training: First Steps Towards a Democratic Society' (Department of Education 1995) to, among others, the 'White Paper on the Organisation, Governance and Funding of Schools' (Department of Education 1996), the South African Schools Act (Republic of South Africa 1996), the Further Education and Training Act (Republic of South Africa 1998b); the Employment of Educators Act (Republic of South Africa 1998); the Skills Development Act (Republic of South Africa 1998a); the Language in Education Policy (Department of Education 1997), and the 'White Paper 7 on the Transformation of Learning and Teaching for the Information and Communication Technologies (E-Education)' (Department of Education 2004). In addition, during this period, on the international front, the United Nations articulated the *Millennium Development Goals* (United Nations 2000), and South Africa committed itself to implementing the relevant goals in the education sector.

The challenges affecting schooling as a sector, arising from the different ways in which teachers were trained, and for different purposes, have left the profession scarred. The chapter thus begins with a brief description of the fragmentation of education in South Africa, the consequences of which have meant wildly different learning experiences for children depending on their gender, class and race. The fragmentation provides a context for understanding the low morale of teachers and negative perceptions of teaching as a profession. Changes to the curriculum have been motivated by a strong desire to bring about the better performance of schools and the quality of teachers, and thus to restore confidence to the profession. Part of what that restoration must achieve for schools and teachers themselves is a commitment to provide for an equitable distribution of teachers across South Africa's schools. Thus the third part of the chapter considers the problematic situation of teacher supply and demand, a problem that has preoccupied the profession since 1995, when the first unified Department of Education was created. Whilst issues concerning confidence, morale and perception speak to the need for better teachers in more schools, there is also a need to understand what progress higher education institutions have made in terms of research in and about education. The chapter concludes with this overview of research, which itself illuminates the priorities and gaps that have been identified and addressed since the transition to democracy in 1994. The argument traced throughout is that while there has been structural change coupled with concerted efforts to raise the qualifications levels of teachers, the quality of in-service teacher education, particularly, remains challenging, affecting the performance of schools and the prospects for out of school youth. Having understood something of the nature of teacher education in South Africa, this chapter provides a basis for understanding the higher education landscape.

Contemporary critics such as Jansen ascribe the problems experienced in higher education, and indeed in education generally, to the levels of expectations (standards) associated with schooling and the curriculum. While the Department has celebrated the shift from pass rates like 61% in 2009 to 78% in 2013, Jansen and others (for example, Bloch 2009) have doubted the credibility of the results, even though Umalusi, the standards generating body responsible for assuring the validity of national senior certificate examines, has year-on-year certified that the results are reliable.

In 2014, 688 660 young people wrote their National Senior Certificate examinations (of these, 550 127 were full-time students and 138 533 were part-time). Jansen summarises the problems in the following terms:

'The foundation of any society depends on the quality of education in our schools. And the first point we have to acknowledge about our education system is that it is in a crisis.'

[Jansen] explained that the crisis remains unresolved because of political denial.

'South African schools are working for one third of our children, but social development and stability depend on what happens to the other two thirds,' he said.

'The sixth point to understand ... is that the large-scale turnaround of South Africa's schools will not happen in the foreseeable future. 'This will only happen with large-scale change in the system – there are political obstacles – and this needs governmental intervention and leadership'. (Jansen in Planting 2014, 1)

Jansen's argument is that there is insufficient acknowledgment by the profession and the state of the poor quality of teaching, and too little coordinated effort to address the challenge systemically. Teacher education is thus a useful place to begin this second chapter, having described schooling in Chapter 1. Higher education in South Africa has been subjected to radical organisational changes since 2004, and has continued to form the focus of national attention in relation to the under-performance of learners and teachers in the schooling sector.

The purpose of such reforms in higher education (with reference to teacher education) was twofold: the first was to provide under-qualified and unqualified teachers in the system with basic qualifications in order to enable them to teach in schools, and the second was to upgrade those qualifications (mostly diplomas and certificates issued by the former colleges of education) held by teachers already in the schools. Concerns over teacher education have been well-documented. In 2003, the Education Portfolio Committee of the Parliament of South Africa noted their concern with the poor levels of productivity among educators (Petjé 2002), and the 'low quality of the average educator' (Education Portfolio Committee 2003), citing ineffective teaching methodologies and administrative inefficiencies. The socio-economic status of pupils is also acknowledged as exerting a significant influence on educational attainment. Where do these problems originate? Some studies suggest that low literacy and educational levels among the adult population create circumstances in which learner performance is undermined, and that the way to develop literacy is through cultural and other non-governmental organizations. Other commentators suggest that schools, and particularly teachers, ought to be sufficiently literate in languages as to be able to teach not only subject content, but also the discourse associated with different school subjects in the curriculum.

2.2 TEACHER EDUCATION: THE FRACTURED MIRROR TO FRAGMENTED LEARNING

Coherence in teacher education had not been a feature of State policy or organisation in the period prior to 1994. Up to 1910 (when the four colonies in South Africa came together to form the Union), various colonial governments oscillated between education provision that was voluntary or mandatory for white children up to the end of primary school, allowing missionary schools a degree of autonomy from the State. By 1948, increasing shifts towards centralisation, even of control of independent schools, became a feature of organised administration to be set up along racial lines, in which differential education spending was a key feature (Hyslop 1990 and 1999).

The colleges of education were similarly disjointed and of variable quality prior to 1994. By 1994 there were 104 colleges, 83 of which served mostly black students (over 70 000 students, with just over two-thirds of these – 48 672 – enrolled for primary school qualifications). In total in South Africa at this time there were 150 higher education institutions providing teacher education, with approximately 200 000 enrolled students (32 universities, 120 colleges). Not all the colleges offered education of a low standard, but given that the curricula and nature of education offered were so widely disparate, it is understandable that the first few years of the new democracy were characterised by a swathe of policy changes without the commensurate focus on the capacity development, or facilities development to contain, and materialise (or operationalise) the changes. Chisholm suggests that 'despite some pockets of excellence, institutional failure, marked by high turn-over rates, vacancies, dysfunctionality and incapacity, are characteristic of State institutions' (Chisholm 2009, 20). One of the features of this failure was the disproportionate focus by analysts on developmental policies rather than on the internal functioning of the profession (20). In some instances, this mirrors the emphasis within the State, the unions and bureaucracy on elaboration of development strategies and coordination mechanisms that ultimately have little effect (20).

The government after 1995 embarked on a process of reassessing the worth and maintenance of the teacher education institutions (as well as universities) and concluded by 2003 that the retention of colleges of education was not aiding in the production of teachers characterised by quality in education or consistency of curricular approach. By 2004, most of these colleges had either been closed or incorporated into universities. Universities thus were provided with a mandate to reform and undertake teacher education on behalf of the State.

During the pre-1994 era there were also no uniform national regulations to govern initial teacher education provision (IPET). The Department of Education and Training (DET for black education), the provincial departments of education associated with the House of Assembly (white), the House of Representatives (coloured), and House of Delegates (Indian), had different regulations and specifications for IPET, while colleges in the former homelands (or Bantustans) were not subordinate to any of these authorities. In the early 1980s, the Committee on Teacher Education Policy (COTEP) was formed to govern IPET in the former white institutions through a set of minimum standards. During the late 1980s and 1990s, under the influence of the Committee of College of Education Rectors of South Africa (CCERSA), this set of minimum standards began to exert an influence on IPET programmes across a broader spectrum of providers. With the promulgation of the Norms and Standards for Educators (NSE, 2000), a uniform set of standards was set for all IPET programmes. That there has been substantive change in the size and shape of schooling as a sector, or the size and shape of teacher education after the demise of apartheid, is well-researched (see Jansen and Taylor 2003; Chisholm 1992; and Bloch 2009).

Though substantial reorganisation of the sector occurred in 2004, the actual curriculum content associated with various disciplines received very little, and then very patchy attention. In some institutions (notably the University of KwaZulu-Natal), there was a deliberate attempt to Africanise the curriculum with the introduction of indigenous knowledge systems (IKS). This arose from the leadership of the University of KwaZulu-Natal, which endorsed a particular perspective on context as illustrated by a comment by the Vice-Chancellor Makgoba, who argued that '[a]n African [higher education] institution's fingerprint should be African and it should exude Africa even as it honours universal knowledge' (Makgoba 1997, 141–42). While similar initiatives may have been adopted symbolically in the post-apartheid era, Africanisation of higher education has been characterised more by slogans than by substantive review or change. The reasons for this are few and mostly arise from the fact that indigenous knowledge (whether of African languages or culture) has yet to be inscribed into curricula from sources that exist mostly outside formal higher education (Le Grange 2007 on science education, for example). It is thus still rare to find IKS specialists working in Science or History in the curriculum, for example. That said, some education policies (notably the Languages in Education Policy and Languages in Higher Education Policy) have provided the grounds for a focus on indigenous languages in education, and some re-writing of apartheid history textbooks has occurred.

Further to this, and specifically in terms of understanding the relationship between curriculum content knowledge and the economy, it is doubtful that content knowledge contributes sufficiently to the needs of either higher education and training (including technical and vocational training) or the economy. Vally and Motala (2013) suggest that the framing of curriculum reform and qualifications frameworks occurs within the context of late twentieth-century capitalism, neo-liberal economic policies and globalisation. The State formed a series of statutory bodies (the Council on Higher Education, and its Higher Education Quality Committee (HEQC) in 1998; the South African Qualifications Authority (SAQA) in 1995, the South African Council of Education in 2001), and established a national qualifications framework (NQF 1997) to describe articulation routes and academic levels for post-school qualifications (more about these initiatives is provided later in the chapter).

Suffice it to say that as a result of these initiatives a degree of standardisation was brought to teacher education qualifications. Within the NQF, new teacher education qualifications were legislated and a series of qualification reviews (or audits) were conducted of universities offering teacher education qualifications. The purpose of these reviews was not only to ascertain the capacity of institutions to offer teacher education programmes, but also to bring a desired degree of consistency in design and approach to teacher education qualification (programmes) between the years 2007–8. Determining the extent to which new programmes (in institutions mostly merged with, or incorporating, teacher training colleges) could thus offer quality programmes to a new generation of student-teachers, was a focus of this review process.

In post-apartheid South African higher education institutions, the curricula design and basic 'models' for teacher education remain the same as those that existed prior to 1995, though responsibility for the quality assurance and quality of education received has changed radically.

2.3 PERCEPTIONS OF TEACHING AS A PROFESSION IN RELATION TO PERFORMANCE IN SCHOOLS

The low status and quality of teachers remain compelling issues in South Africa. Judging by the recent National Senior Certificate (NSC) results, the quality of teachers (skills and knowledge) is especially problematic:

the professional development of teachers as associated with the Advanced Certificates in Education and National Professional Diploma in Education did not compel teachers to improve their subject content knowledge competencies, but focused rather on the attainment of higher qualifications, many of which were in fields not related to the subjects that teachers teach. Perceptions of the low quality of teacher competence are reinforced by research, for example, suggesting that teacher absenteeism is related to inadequate subject-content knowledge (Carnoy, Chisholm & Chilisa 2012). Taylor notes the link between the low quality of teaching and low expectations of learners.

> Teacher educators' low expectations of the academic quality of students (including weak subject content knowledge, lack of proficiency in English and generally poor reading and writing skills) are not always counterbalanced by any structured attempt to transform poor quality entrants into good quality 'reflective' practitioners. (Taylor 2015, 4)

Some research suggests that teacher absenteeism in South Africa is related to inadequate subject knowledge (Carnoy & Chisholm 2012). Unable to meet the requirements of new curricula, teachers stay away. Frequent changes to the curriculum have been noted as contributing to teacher fatigue, and a further loss of confidence as the curriculum has changed, and so too have expectations of teachers' knowledge of subject content altered. Other scholars (for example, Cosser 2011a and Samuel 2009) have pointed out that conditions of service, better salaries and more differentiated promotion routes in the profession for teachers, would provide for better recognition of the profession in the public view.

Taylor (2015) suggests that there are three dimensions to definitions of professionalism in the workplace. The first concerns the social trust invested by the public in the profession in question, and this social trust derives from public confidence in the profession's abilities 'to demonstrate that its theories and practices are more effective in providing a particular service than those of competing groups':

> However, it is one thing to achieve this first marker in one or more institutions, but it is quite another to achieve it as part of a collective endeavour, across the entire sector. This is the second mark of a profession: there is consensus on best practices. The requirement is not uniformity – which would allow no possibility of innovation, even revolt, or progress – but at least there should be broad convergence on a limited number of minimum sets of practice protocols and how they can be understood in relation to the underlying theory.

A third condition of professionalism is that the knowledge and practice standards are maintained and jealously guarded by practitioners within the occupational field, not by government. This is professional quality assurance, as opposed to bureaucratic managerialism. It could not be any different, since only adepts within a field have the expertise to judge the value of new knowledge claims and to certify novice entrants into the profession. This is one of the most important characteristics of the strong professions. (Taylor 2015, 2)

Thus, whilst change in the curriculum, especially in relation to certain subjects and content areas, has had a discernible positive impact on what is taught (for example, the promotion of African languages has shifted perceptions of these as being of low status, to high status and desirable in employment and social cohesion), more also needs to be done in relation to developing the credibility of the profession itself.

Despite the changes that have altered the 'look' of higher education and teacher education in South Africa, changes in teachers' salaries, and recognition in terms of national awards that have been effected since 2004, the profession itself continues to suffer nationally from low esteem. Perceptions concerning the value of teachers are associated with the embattled nature of schooling. Until recently low salaries, poor conditions of service, high learner-teacher ratios and the low status of childcare (especially noteworthy in the training of Grade R and pre-Grade R) have affected the profession negatively. Cosser (2008) notes that teaching is not regarded by university entrants in South Africa as the profession of choice:

A cross-tabulation of learner perceptions of choice with enrolment in different academic programmes reveals that Education occupies position 16 out of 21 programmes in the Department of Education programme list (DoE, 2001) in terms of the extent to which students enrolled in Education feel they have been able to choose their present life situation. (Cosser 2008, 5)

Until such time as the quality of the education received by children is shown to have a demonstrable and credible impact on learner performance in the scarce skills in particular, and until such time that South Africa performs better in international and comparative measures of learner performance, it is the teaching profession that will bear the brunt of public impatience and scepticism with regard to the value of teaching and its positive contribution towards young people's prospects of finding worthwhile employment.

Taylor (2015) and others have noted that greater regulation of teacher education might provide the basis from which a focus on the achievement of better quality becomes possible, but in itself regulation does not guarantee quality. Unfortunately, one of the consequences of frequent change in the school curriculum is that higher education institutions tend to focus more closely on new curriculum requirements rather than on 'raising the bar' in two particular areas of teacher education curricula: *subject-content knowledge* and *pedagogic-content knowledge*. The following section describes approaches to curriculum design in relation to these two areas of teacher education and development.

2.4 TEACHER EDUCATION CURRICULA CHANGE: IN-SERVICE AND PRE-SERVICE HIGHER EDUCATION QUALIFICATIONS

Despite the reorganisation of institutions to incorporate teacher training colleges, and the subsequent curriculum reforms associated with various acts of legislation (for example, the Minimum Requirements for Teacher Education in South Africa (2008), the content and foci of higher education teacher education curricula have remained under-examined after 1994. This fact is sometimes overlooked in discussions concerning teacher competence or performance, and yet it remains the single most unexamined dimension of debates concerning schooling and teacher education in South Africa. In part this gap can be explained due to the fact that in 2001 it was determined that as many as 65 000 teachers were either unqualified or under-qualified (Keevy 2006). The substantive focus for teacher education in the first decade (1995–2004) was on the upgrading or re-skilling of this group of teachers through a series of new qualifications legislated as requirements for (in-service) teachers after 2001. These qualifications were known as the National Professional Diploma in Education (NPDE), to be followed by an Advanced Certificate in Education (ACE). Notwithstanding these requirements, initial teacher education and the curricula associated with Bachelor degrees in education remained configured in terms of three models.

The three models for initial (undergraduate) teacher education in South Africa are the *consecutive*, the *integrated* and the *concurrent*. In the first model, students typically undertake their degree studies in faculties other than education and then complete their training with a one-year diploma (typically the Postgraduate Certificate in Education or PGCE, the successor to the old Higher Education Diploma). This was the model associated with university education during the apartheid era, bearing in mind that universities primarily offered teacher training for secondary school teachers, and that students entering undergraduate bachelor degrees would therefore have selected at least two major subjects to follow through from year 1–3, and thereafter either would complete either the postgraduate diploma, or a further degree. Within this model the student teachers would have been provided with an in-depth exposure to subject content knowledge over three years and would have received exposure to pedagogic content knowledge in the postgraduate diploma (through the offering of teaching methodology modules and teaching practice, or Work Integrated Learning as it is known in South Africa).

Primary school teacher training would, in the period prior to 2004, have been offered in the teacher training colleges and sometimes certified by regional universities. The point, however, is that in apartheid South Africa, teacher training as undertaken by the colleges would not have involved university academic staff, even if curricula were approved or endorsed by universities. Since the closure of the teacher training colleges in the transformation exercise led by Kader Asmal (which reached its apogee in 2004), universities assumed direct responsibility for not only the qualifications offered to teachers, but also for the actual provision of teaching in terms of legislative requirements fixed for teacher training by the State.

The second model associated with teacher training is known as the 'concurrent' model whereby students would have pursued their methodology, curriculum and pedagogy modules within a school or faculty of education, whilst pursuing their major subjects at the same time in faculties associated with those subject choices (Sciences, Humanities and Social Sciences, for example). Within this model the focus would have been on the development of subject-content knowledge in concurrent development with pedagogic-content knowledge, but without the necessary dialogue between the pedagogy specialists and the subject specialists. The student teacher would thus have gained experience in the subject knowledge together with the teaching methodologies (hopefully) relevant to the subject (and these methodologies will have been specific to the field), as well as the generic methodologies associated with assessment. Debates concerning the value of this model are ongoing, with pedagogy specialists suggesting that the focus is too strongly on the subject at the expense of, for example, an understanding of which pedagogies are suited to learning styles development associated with different age groups.

The third model for teacher education in South Africa is known as the 'integrated' model. This involves students undertaking modules within education in which subject-content knowledge is integrated with pedagogic-content knowledge. Within this model, teacher education is conducted entirely within schools or faculties of education and student teachers are developed by subject specialists who have become, primarily by virtue of their scholarship, education specialists within their original academic fields. As one might expect, subject specialists who are not in education sometimes tend to regard such specialists as 'applied', and thus not in touch with developments within the field and not able to apply understandings of 'academic depth or rigour' in terms of subject-content knowledge. There is wide-ranging research on subject-content knowledge, pedagogic-content knowledge and even specialised subject-content knowledge internationally (Shulman 1987, Boyer 1990 and others) as well as in South Africa, and these three models, and their sometimes vociferous proponents, contribute to the debates about which is most efficacious. However, research to support one over the other is not substantively developed as yet.

Nonetheless, as a consequence of the poor performance in the system over the last 20 years, there has been considerable debate concerning which models are likely to generate teachers who are able not only to implement and communicate the curriculum content in classrooms, but also to innovate and lead curriculum design with schools (in other words teacher competence in pedagogic-content knowledge and subject-content knowledge).

What teachers should know of the subject matter or content that they are to teach is an important issue in their IPET. How this issue is examined affects the design and development of pre- and in-service teacher education programmes and is crucial for constructing curriculum materials that can be a resource for teacher learning. Content knowledge or knowledge of a discipline itself is insufficient, since it is important to know how to make this content or subject matter knowledge available to others. Curricular knowledge is represented by the full range of programmes designed for the teaching of particular subjects and topics at a given level. Strategic knowledge is activated when a teacher is confronted with situations or problems where no simple solutions are possible.

There is no evidence to suggest that better schooling is provided by graduates from universities with an undergraduate degree in the area of a major subject. On the other hand, the adoption of new models of teacher education (in which undergraduate students undertake their major subjects in faculties of education with a stronger methodological focus on pedagogy) is too new to determine its impact on the quality of teaching or learner performance in schools. The absence of large-scale studies with evidence to advise higher education institutions on best practice in terms of impact on learner performance remains problematic. It was only in 2014 that the government commissioned a large-scale study (undertaken by the Joint Education Trust; Taylor 2014) on the nature and aspects of the quality of teacher education at universities.[1]

That aside, most universities in South Africa offered bachelor's programmes through the concurrent and integrated models by 2014. In general, higher education institutions in the apartheid years offered a series of higher diplomas (sometimes referred to as University Education Diplomas, or Higher Diplomas in Education). In fewer instances an entire bachelor's programme was offered (usually known as the Bachelor of Primary Education at the more robust teacher education colleges).

Since 1995 the emphasis has shifted from the one-year higher education diploma (or postgraduate certificate in higher education) to the full four-year professional degree in education divided into specialisations: the Foundation Phase (Grades R–3, Intermediate Phase (Grades 4–6), Senior (Grades 7–9) and FET Phases (Grades 10–12). This represents a change in emphasis, but not necessarily a real change in curriculum content. That a shift has occurred does nevertheless suggest that confidence in the ability of relatively short diplomas and certificates to prepare teachers adequately for the complexities of schools, not to mention the complexities of learning, has diminished.

What is clear is that despite interventions at the level of higher education, the absence of support and openness to new ideas and pedagogic approaches within the teaching profession accounts in part for the minimal impact of new curriculum changes on actual teaching in classrooms. This begins with teaching practice. Chisholm et al. (1999) noted that the negative features of teaching practice have proved resilient, often in spite of progressive and learning-centred policy changes. As Ono and Ferreira (2010) also note, teachers do not change their teaching practice too easily and any form of development would require protracted support in order to effect change. Naidoo states that it 'is arguable that the new education transformation policy failed to recognise that the work culture of officials entrusted with custodianship of the democratic education programme, was likely to have been consistent with that of the previous order' (Naidoo 2014, 41). The gap between policy intentions and the capacity to deliver on these, is perhaps the most consistent theme describing the relationship between change and continuity in education between pre-apartheid and post-apartheid South Africa. Readers of the history of this period cannot help but notice the high expectations associated with the belief in the State to deliver on the promises of liberation (in the form of the transformation project). Of equal importance is the State's self-confidence in believing that institutional change could be effected through policy and legislation. This combination of expectation and confidence explains the tremendous energy with which government leadership and the intellectual elite of the new South Africa, affected the swathe of policy and institutional reform associated, not least, with education. The under-estimation of the capacity of teachers to implement, let alone exceed the expectations of new curriculum developments such as OBE and the NCS, remains one of the most profound disappointments of the period under review, exceeded perhaps only by the evident incapacity of the civil service to maintain, or extend, delivery of basic services, particularly in relation to the infrastructural needs of a growing economy and population. In this sense the story of South Africa's transition to a post-colonial State echoes those stories associated with Eastern European and indeed African transitions after the breakup of the Soviet Union, and during the demise of colonial empires after the great wars.

Capacity exists in relation to considerations concerning supply and demand. This applies both to economics and to the knowledge economy concerned mostly with the development of knowledgeable and skilled school leavers by a cohort of dedicated and competent teachers or academics. Not only did it become evident in time that teachers remained singularly underprepared for the new interventions, but that that unpreparedness was and is a consequence of apartheid architecture, the implications and longevity of which can never be underestimated. The sections that follow explore this challenge from a range of perspectives, beginning with teacher supply and demand, then focusing on the capacity of higher education to meet supply and demand expectations, together with the planning capacity of the Departments of Higher Education and Training and Basic Education as the primary employers of knowledge workers (teachers and academics) in the education sector.

2.5 TEACHER TRAINING AND SUPPLY AND DEMAND

Issues concerning supply and demand cannot be considered in the absence of an understanding of the historic context for education leading up to 1994. Scholars such as Crouch and Lewin (2003) and Chisholm (2009) argue that the shortages need to be considered in two ways: first, in terms of the growth in population in South Africa, and second, in terms of the damaging consequences of apartheid policies that included not only systemic under-spending on education for people of colour, but also a long period in which there were serious limitations placed on missionary and other organisations not in sympathy with the racist policies of the day. The limitations placed on churches and non-governmental organisations saw the closure of many institutions providing quality education to South Africans before 1950. As these pressures increased, expenditure on education for black people remained so low that in 1998, after a period of ten years of political unrest and instability, the Department of Education and Training (DET) was obliged to create 10 338 new posts. There were only 6032 teachers, according to Hartshorne (1992, 245), to fill the posts (thus a shortage of 4306 existed in those years). Another reason why this shortage could not be addressed in the immediate aftermath of 1994 was that the education system itself was so fragmented that understanding the shortages was no simple task. It was noted that 17% of the primary teachers and 3.7% of the high school teachers employed directly by the DET had no formal qualifications. In the Bantustan areas, up to 27% of the primary school teachers had no qualifications and 12.7% of high school teachers similarly were unqualified. These findings are significant for two reasons: first, the actual shortfall in terms of vacant posts changes depending on whether or not a reader considers unqualified teachers to be occupying vacant posts; second, that the DET was obliged to employ unqualified teachers meant that the post-apartheid administrations would inherit not only the enormous task of addressing shortages (especially in black schools), but also of re-training teachers who had either no post-secondary qualifications, or who were teaching in posts for which their qualifications were unsuited. The Twenty-Year Review 1994–2014 (The Presidency 2014) claimed that 'University enrolment has almost doubled since 1994' (15), which is also to suggest that teacher education has similarly had to expand.

The demand for teachers is commonly understood as being shaped by three main issues: pupil enrolment, PTRs (pupil-teacher ratios), and teacher turnover (burn-out, stress, illness, death) (Chisholm 2009, 21). Policy-driven changes to expand access to education will increase the demand for teachers, as will curriculum reforms and conditions in teaching relative to other professions (Cooper & Alvado 2006).

It is important to understand that the systems inherited from the apartheid regime were never intended to develop education for equal access or equal opportunity. It is thus not surprising that one of the first challenges faced by the new government was simply to ensure equity of provision in the system through the establishment of norms concerning teacher supply and demand at the level of districts, regions and provinces. According to Chisholm (2004), education debates in South Africa have since 1994 been characterised by 'supply panics related to the poor image of teaching, teacher attrition rates and the threat of HIV/AIDS'.

Teacher shortages were a legacy bequeathed by apartheid. Teacher education after the missionary period was haphazard in part because of the state's insistence on separation of races. Teacher education, along with nursing and policing, was one of the few ways to obtain an education for black people. The colleges of education in the pre-apartheid period were initially over-subscribed; throughput was weak, and qualification differentiation problematic. These colleges were part of a corrupted system; Chisholm (2014) notes that many rural institutions were administered by white Afrikaans-speaking officials removed from, and at odds with, young militant students. The consequence of this was that, as a sector, teacher education institutions had little voice in the re-thinking of teacher education by the mid-1990s (26).

In 1992, Hartshorne wrote that:

> South Africa had reached a point at which it simply cannot afford to continue present approaches to the education and training of black teachers, or any of its teachers. The present system marked on the one hand by growing numbers of colleges for black teachers struggling to cope with this demand, and on the other hand by unused and underutilised facilities in the white sector, cannot be justified ... (1992, 25).

In an era marked by huge wastage of national resources provincial departments of education preferred to close colleges and retrench staff rather than to admit students; this was a consequence of the Group Areas Act, which would have been transgressed if black and other students had been admitted to formerly 'white' institutions. Never has such a manifestly evil dispensation endured for so long at the cost of so many, than has apartheid. Perceptions with regard to the quality of teacher education have similarly deep roots in education in South Africa. In 1998, according to Hartshorne (249), 93% of Grade 12 graduates from schools had an F aggregate (33–39%). With such an aggregate, colleges could admit students to train to be teachers. The indifferent quality of education thus made for graduates who were not only below university standards, but who also would have entered colleges in order to study rather than out of commitment to the profession. Universities at this stage in general made little or no contribution to the education of teachers for black schools, let alone of black teachers. And even at black universities, scholars such as Ndebele et al. (2013), and Taylor and Jansen (2003) note that the throughput rates were generally very, very weak.

The longevity of the apartheid legacy is acknowledged in its impact on the quality of teaching and teachers in the Twenty-Year Review 1994–2014 (The Presidency 2014): 'The poor ANA results can be attributed to inadequate teacher competency, subject and curriculum knowledge (26), as well as weaknesses in school and district management.'

To strengthen the quality of education, the Funza Lushaka bursary scheme was introduced to tackle teacher shortages by encouraging more learners to study to become teachers. From 2007 to 2013 a total of 62 804 bursaries were awarded to student teachers at a cost of over r1.9 billion.

Table 2.1: Funza Lushaka Graduate Placements in 2013

Province	Vacancies as at 28 February 2013	Number of Funza Lushaka graduates placed as at 31 March 2013
EC	5454	0
FS	812	156
GP	1279	365
KZN	2212	860
LP	2512	141
MP	2940	71
NC	953	74
NW	1499	80
WC	1328	279
Grand Total	18989	2026

Source: DBE Parliamentary Report May 2013

Over the past three years, 1 696 students graduated in 2009, 2 588 in 2010 and 2 634 in 2011. Of the students who graduated, 1 083 of the 2010 cohort were placed in 2011, and 946 of the 2011 cohort were placed in 2012, and 2026 in 2013 (DBE 2013).

However, in general there has been a decline in the number of teacher graduates for a variety of reasons. Firstly, universities have a limited capacity to enrol large numbers of students compared to the teacher training colleges. Then there are considerable financial constraints in terms of fee increases and the costs of teacher training (in terms of work-integrated learning, for example). Thirdly, the status of the profession itself, in addition to the conditions of service in schools, makes for an unattractive image. Job placement and competition for talented students from other high-wage sectors such as engineering, financial services, mining and medicine, alongside challenging working conditions, also make teaching seem less appealing to young people (ETDP SETA Skills Plan, 2014, 124–25).

Finally, the length of time it takes to place Funza Lushaka bursary graduates in some provinces is a concern that needs to be addressed. For teachers already in the system, a teacher development plan with a multipronged approach has been introduced, especially in the worst-performing schools. Through the Teacher Union Collaboration initiative, 80 000 existing teachers had been trained by the end of the 2013 academic year. In future, minimum competency requirements for teachers, coupled with strengthened teacher-support programmes, may need to be introduced to complement initiatives to increase teacher competence (The Presidency 2014, 49–50).

> For ordinary schools, including public and private, there has been a 6% (24 070) increase in the total number of educators employed from 2008 to 2013. The public schooling sector has seen an increase of 3.6% (13 769) in the number of educators employed by the State but there has been a substantial increase of 45% (10 301) employed in the private sector between 2008 and 2013. The system is still experiencing educator shortages, especially in the fields of Foundation Phase, Mathematics, Science, Accounting and Language Teachers. The Education Labour Relations Council (ELRC)/HSRC 2006 study estimated that between 18 000–22 000 educators need to be replaced annually. A positive trend across ordinary schools is that the majority of educators are qualified. (ETDP SETA Skills Plan, 2014, 20)

The ETDP SETA (2014) describes the following causes of teacher attrition in 2014: attrition due to retirement (rates vary from 5%–12% of educators who are likely to retire by 2015); the incidence of HIV and AIDS is estimated to affect 80 000 by 2015, resulting in the need for replacements; teachers who leave the profession early, estimated by the HSRC at between 18 000–22 000 annually; major shortages in indigenous languages and mathematics and science teachers. As mentioned in the introduction to this book, the loss of young teachers from the profession creates a drain on the vitality of the teaching force.

The Integrated Strategic Planning Framework for Teacher Education and Development (ISPFTED) indicates that there is no certainty regarding the exact number of teachers leaving the profession annually. The DBE conducted substantial research in preparation for the drafting of such estimates which range from 3.8% to 6.0%. In deciding on projections for the ISPFTED, three different attrition rates were used (4.0%, 4.5% and 5.0%) to compensate for the uncertainty around this matter (DBE 2011, 59; ETDP SETA Skills Plan 2014, 113).

Table 2.2: Scarce Skill Demand identified by SGB Schools, 2013

OFO Code	Scarce Skills	Demand
232123	Maths teachers Grades 10–12	Immediate
233101	Maths teachers Grades 4–9	Immediate
232126	Physical Science teachers Grades 10–12	Immediate
234101	Foundation Phase school teachers	Immediate
233102	Natural Science teachers Grades 4–9	Immediate
531201	Teachers' Aides	Immediate
232119	Language teachers Grades 10–12	Immediate
232118	ICT teachers	Immediate
2322101	Accounting teachers	Medium-Term
235201	Special Needs teachers	Medium-Term
134501	School Principals[2]	Medium-Term
235301	Teachers of English to speakers of other languages	Medium-Term
143105	Sports administrators	Medium-Term

Source: ETDP SETA WSP Submissions from SGB Schools for 2013/2014, 119

2.6 RESEARCH ON CHANGE IN EDUCATION: REVIEWS AND OVERVIEWS IN SOUTH AFRICA

This section has outlined challenges affecting the teaching corps in South Africa, arising not only from the restructuring of the sector, but also from the need to develop quality within the sector itself in relation to teacher education (pre- as well as in-service). Teacher supply and demand factors are key to government planning in relation to how schools come to be provisioned and higher education coordinated in relation to teacher supply and demand. The following sections illustrate, this time from the perspective of research, the needs in higher education with regard to teacher development (professional development, content areas as well as other areas of need).

Two major surveys of education research were conducted in the period 2007–2009. The first was a survey (undertaken by Deacon, Osman and Buchler 2009) of all published research on education in South Africa between 1995–2005 as commissioned by the National Research Foundation (NRF). The second survey of the same period, commissioned by the Ford Foundation and the National Research Foundation, was of education research undertaken by graduate students of education at all South African universities (undertaken by Balfour, Moletsane and Karlsson 2009). This is alluded to in the first section of this part of the chapter and deals with the first survey of research as undertaken in a reorganised higher education sector.

For some scholars such as Jansen (2004), the changes in higher education include increasing regulation to promote accountability and order autonomy, shifting models of delivery, the nature of the workplace and changing notions of higher education. He refers to this as 'between free trade and the public good' (Jansen 2004, 293), articulating the uneasy relationship between the role of higher education in relation to the provision of a skilled labour force for the State. Teacher education lies at the intersection between higher education and the generation of skilled labour, making it part of the market politics in which accountability with regard to performance (in schooling and higher education alike) is expected. As Hart (2002, 3) suggests:

> Political liberalisation had coincided with a moment of intense market triumphalism, and powerful political pressures were gathering force from within and beyond to press South Africa to conform to free market neoliberal orthodoxy.

The impact of 'market triumphalism' is evident inside the ideational space (as had been evident in the *Growth, Employment and Redistribution Strategy* or *GEAR*, and later in the *Accelerated and Shared Growth Initiative for South Africa* or *ASGISA*). Although critics of the neo-liberal enterprise (for example, Nicholson, 1994) have long articulated a distrust of its impact on South Africa's developing economy, policy-makers and industrialists have appeared to endorse a perspective that is at odds with the socialist ideology long entrenched in the liberation movements. The impact is also evident outside the ideational space, as exemplified in the creation of universities of technology, the combined resources of which were meant to provide not only increased access to learning (a transformation imperative), but also the increased provision of skilled labour (a market imperative). The capacity of higher-education institutions to deliver on the mixed bag of expectations has become a source of disappointment and friction as further regulation of the sector has not yielded significantly in terms of pace of provision, or the anticipated change in demography of the skilled workforce. One such area, unsurprisingly, is teacher education and related to that, teacher supply and demand.

Within HEIs, that friction is replayed in what Jansen (2004) has described as the 'growth of managerialism', which has internalised the drive towards the transformation of institutional governance, demographics and curricula (the threat to disciplines regarded as marginal in purpose and value to the State: for example, indigenous language departments, fine arts, and drama).

Arguments regarding the autonomy of institutions to determine these have been met with the logic of the balance sheet, and the need for institutions to demonstrate contributions to the transformation of the State both in their internal organisation and functioning, and in terms of delivering on the promise of the skilled graduate. In view of the context described above, one might expect research to have been broadly responsive to the new needs of the developing State after 1995, especially since teacher education and provision were identified immediately as priorities.

However, conversely, Deacon, Osman and Buchler (2009, 1073) noted that in terms of disciplinary specific research, almost half (48%) of education research from 1995 to 2006 has been concentrated in four disciplinary areas, namely, higher education studies (13%), education policy (13%), educational theory (13%), and teacher education (9%). The majority (64%) of education research is small-scale and eclectic, 28% is case study research, and 8% is large-scale research (Deacon, Osman & Buchler 2009). Almost a third (30%) of education research focuses on the higher education sector (second only to research focused on the formal schooling sector, at 42%). Within the higher education sector, most research (42%) takes place at the systemic level, with 32% of research at the institutional level and 26% at the classroom level. In terms of scale, 7%, 37% and 56% of research in the higher education sector is large-scale, case-study and small-scale research, respectively. The uneasy coexistence of political idealism and educational realism in higher education was evident from the start, with the National Commission on Higher Education's 1996 discussion document emphasising equity, democratisation, development, quality, academic freedom and efficiency, being applauded by an international workshop as 'one of the best tertiary education documents ever written', and simultaneously questioned regarding the availability of the capacity and of the resources needed to implement it (Hartshorne 1996, 272–3) (Deacon, Osman & Buchler 2009, 1074).

Policy studies in higher education have focused on four overlapping areas: the policy values of access, equity, democratisation, development, quality, relevance, academic freedom and efficiency; the need for greater social responsibility and accountability; institutional cooperation and the internationalisation of higher education; and the need for strategic planning amidst funding constraints (Deacon, Osman & Buchler 2009, 1075–76). Two opposing camps have been identified: the 'developmentalists', who argue that higher education must be driven by State objectives and local relevance, and the 'institutional autonomists', who emphasise that higher education must be autonomous and critical (Ekong & Cloete 1997, 10; Muller 2005, 89). These were done in the context of the country's 'dual development imperative' of having to simultaneously address basic needs and engage in global competition (Muller & Subotzky 2001, 163). Change in higher education has been driven not only from the centre but equally by institutions themselves, which have exhibited a wide range of often unexpected responses (ranging from aggressive self-marketing, to waiting for redress, to flexibly, or 'going with the flow'), while global and market trends have turned out to be more important than originally anticipated (Cloete et al. 2002, 4, 116, 286).

The country has a skewed distribution of social and cultural capital, and inadequate general or basic education, and this has resulted in the inability of higher education institutions to render their staffing complements substantively more equitable in terms of either race or gender. This problem has been exacerbated by declining rates of participation in higher education, inadequate levels of support for postgraduate students, perceived racial discrimination, and competition from the public and private sectors which offer higher salaries (Mkhwanazi & Baijnath 2003, 107–9).

Other camps have called for 'differentiated access' to higher education, which could allow both well-prepared students, and those who are disadvantaged but exceptional, to be fast-tracked (Luckett 2001, 31). On the other hand, others have been disquieted by the counterproductive and inconsistent yet widespread tendency to see RPL as a merely technical 'mass access mechanism rather than as a strategy for individual development' (Moll & Welch 2004, 160 1077).

These misperceptions and blunders do not solely depend on poor proficiency in the language of instruction (usually English), but also rest with inadequate immersion in the discourse of the specific academic discipline. Henning et al. (2001, 110–13) suggest that one possible solution is to encourage students to 'link early learning and present understanding' by starting from their existing cognitive models, permitting the use of first languages and code-switching, and eventually converting to English and then to discipline-specific language. Practically using languages other than English in higher education causes several obstacles, including the limiting effects this might have on cross-cultural communication at the expense of translating high-level concepts and textbooks (Horsthemke 2004). Despite the situation, if such problems are addressed it would go a long way towards validating local cultures and indigenous languages (Cele 2004). Online and distance modes of education demonstrate, furthermore, that the question of using 'mother-tongue or English' is not only a problem in South Africa or for South Africans (Dahlgren 2006, 75). There are also difficulties in determining an appropriate language of instruction in a context of multi-ethnic societies and growing international migration. However, there are also non-language-related factors behind students' learning difficulties, including their feelings, the degrees to which they are empowered or powerless, and their under-standing of institutional cultures (Hutchings 2006, 253). Therefore, student learning is in part a result of the extent of investment, or identification with the academic identities and roles valued by the institution and its function-aries (McKenna 2004, 272; Deacon, Osman & Buchler 2009, 1078).

Notwithstanding good intentions, Pretorius (2003, 130) indicated that the implementation of both transformation and quality assurance in higher edu-cation is 'hampered by a focus on accountability rather than on improve-ment'. Thus it is likely to be slow and halting, and will face varied forms of resistance (ranging from individual insecurities through group and struc-tural inertia to opposition from intellectual, economic and political vested interests), In order to solve this it will require adequate planning, adequate information and staff buy-in (Strydom et al. 2004, 210–13; Bitzer 2004, 29). Researchers warn that over-regulation can be demoralising, and that forcing professionals to 'live under the presumption of being lazy unless proven pro-ductive' can actually undermine productivity (Enslin et al. 2003, 86).

In almost every school and higher education context there is the phenom-enon of under-preparedness, which ranges from arguments against 'deficit' conceptions of education to debates over whether constructivist principles can address the phenomenon and how they can do so. It also arises from criticisms of the elitism of academe and its disciplinary knowledge, or of the principle of government policies, to the challenges of learning through the medium of a second language. This is perhaps one of the most consistent and yet least directly examined themes in education research in South Africa, and not only in higher education. Closely related is the acquisition of aca-demic literacy, which brings into focus issues of languages of instruction and learning, of cognition and achievement, of institutional and individual expectations, cultures and power differentials, and of the need to delve fur-ther into the complex nature of learning. Deacon, Osman and Buchler (2009, 1081) warn that in terms of assessment, issues of consistency and fairness are not well-practised, and that institutions and academics are not being held accountable for their practices in a more appealing and inclusive way so as to avoid quality-cheapening resistance.

If academics have been concerned with the challenges that affect perform-ance in the sector, then higher-education students (almost always teachers themselves) have been equally concerned with the performance of learners and teachers in schools. Sometimes this research has occurred in response to the challenge of curriculum change, often also in relation to the need for teachers to prepare for such changes and to translate them meaningfully into learning and teaching activities for children.

From the survey conducted by Balfour et al. (2011), the database shows a discernible difference in the volume of knowledge generation between the first five years (1995–1999) and the second five years (2000–2004) of the first decade of democracy. There has been an increase in the number of post-graduate education theses in the latter period (see Table 2.3).

Table 2.3: Theses produced in the periods 1995–1999 and 2000–2004

Period	Number
1995–1999	1708
2000–2004	2066
Not known	0
Total	3774

Notably, within this decade most research was produced by female researchers and is located at the master's level (see Table 2.4 and Table 2.5).

Table 2.4: National gender profile of thesis authors across institutions

Gender	Number
Female	2076
Male	1646
Not Known	52
Total	3774

Table 2.5: Disaggregation of theses by degree

Degree	Number
Master's	3082
Doctorates	692
Total	3774

The racial identification of the author is not declared in a thesis. Although names are not a reliable indicator of racial identification and their interpretation is susceptible to the researcher's and data capturer's limited association of names, the team used names as a proxy to determine the postgraduate researcher's racial identification. On this basis, the 1995–2004 survey reveals that the largest group undertaking postgraduate research is the 'white' racial group, with the number of African students increasing incrementally over the decade. Although the 'white' racial group constitutes a minority in the South African population, it continued to feature significantly in postgraduate education research (see Table 2.6), still reflecting the legacy of preferential access to quality education and resources in the decades of apartheid.

Table 2.6: Approximate race profile of thesis authors

Racial profile	Number
Not Known	14
White	1786
African	1477
Coloured	112
Indian	374
Other (e.g. Chinese, Korean, etc.)	11
Total	3774

In their survey of published education research during the same period, Deacon et al. (2009, 1073) report that 'much of this scholarship is diffuse, small scale and individualized, with a dearth of large scale research projects that could consolidate knowledge about issues of national and global importance'. They assert that 41% of research focuses on the systemic level, 35% on the classroom level, and 22% on the institutional level. In addition, they state that 64% is small-scale research, 28% case studies, and 8% is large-scale. The survey of postgraduate education research included some of these same categories, but also explored categories that might be applied to descriptions of education research. The aim was to provide a detailed description of the methodological framing of postgraduate education research in South Africa. Table 2.6 represents and confirms in broad strokes the findings of Deacon et a.l (2009), that the vast majority of education research is qualitative.

Table 2.7: Quantitative and qualitative postgraduate research

Approach	Number
Qualitative	2130
Quantitative	811
Mixed	706
Theoretical	113
Not known	14
Total	3774

Furthermore, just under a third of postgraduate education research (or over 50% of the qualitative research) follows a case study design. The next largest methodological design (863 theses) is described as being a survey, followed by phenomenological studies (328 theses), and thereafter ethnographies (117 theses) and 'model development' (114 theses).

What is evident in the analysis of the range of qualitative work surveyed is the predominance of methodological choices that are influenced by psycho-social accounts of experience. In relation to the first decade of democracy, perhaps this emphasis is not unexpected; the social, psychological and material experience of apartheid on education, educators and learners needed to be described and understood. That research would have had its origins in South Africa in the 1970s, when resistance to Bantu Education gained momentum and some formerly 'white' universities began to admit black people into these institutions, thereby defying the race legislation of the period.

As with the survey provided by Deacon et al. (2009), the survey of education research undertaken by students sought also to understand which areas of education research typically were receiving attention and then to determine whether there were any links to policy development and social issues to which these developments often applied. The survey suggests that education sectors identified by government (Department of Education 1995b) as its concern in the first decade of apartheid received significant attention in education research. Thus, two-thirds (2 650) of the surveyed theses are about schooling and the next largest category (497) consists of theses about tertiary education (see Table 2.8).

Table 2.8: Composite representation of sectors in Master's and Doctoral theses

Sectors	Number
Adult Basic Education and Training	92
Civil Society	55
Early Childhood Education	36
Government bureaucracy	60
Post-Secondary Education	61
Tertiary Education	497
Continuing Education	93
Parastatal Organisations	3
Schooling	2650
Service Providers	70
Private Sector	37
Mix of Sectors	72
Nil (e.g. theoretical)	48
Total	3774

These trends are expected to become more fully developed in the second decade of democracy. The issues that feature minimally in the first decade of knowledge generation by postgraduate students in education are those relating to gendered identity for educators and learners, gender and violence, HIV and AIDS education in schools, rural education, issues affecting identity in education in rural areas, adult basic education and training (ABET), and early childhood education (ECE). The survey showed a leap in research being undertaken in these fields (especially in ECE and ABET), and a close reading of the data also shows that the majority of this research (up to 80%) is produced at the Master's degree level. That there is a dearth of doctoral research suggests that there has not yet been a more sustained engagement with these new areas of work. That, in turn, contributes to the perception that postgraduate research has had and is having little impact on education in South Africa.

The survey also showed a decline in research associated with subject-content areas in the first decade after 1995. Thus, for example, areas such as History Education declined in the first decade of democracy (for example, as seen in Table 2.9), probably because History as a school subject was for a period of time removed from the FET curriculum. A similar decline in research activity could be noted in relation to theses about democracy and power. This may be because researchers, perceiving that the systemic struggle for democracy had been achieved, moved away from such broader questions to research issues that were more context-specific and oriented to implementation such as legislation, and institutional organisation and practice (see

Table 2.8). What Balfour et al. (2011) point to in drawing these possible connections between data and political history is a purpose whereby the research is illuminating for the researcher as well as for decision-makers. This is because it demonstrates not only the causes and effects of action, but provides an element of reflection that may be theoretically mined as well as educationally purposeful in the curriculum and the quality of teacher education.

Table 2.9: Sector trends for theses over the ten-year study period

	Special Needs/Remedial Education/Inclusive Education	Academic (development/literacy etc)	ABET/Adult Education	Distance Education	Research	Values	History	ECE/ECD/Foundation	Law/Legislation	Community/Communities	RPL	Democracy/Power	Racial/Desegregation	Violence/Bullying	HEIs/Institutions	Independent Schooling
1995–9	113	15	65	28	3	11	56	45	10	67	4	50	12	4	407	9
2000–4	111	32	88	25	10	14	33	62	29	74	6	41	11	25	545	11
1995–2004	224	47	153	53	13	25	89	107	39	141	10	91	23	29	952	20
Master's 1995–9	93	12	48	19	1	8	38	38	7	51	2	39	10	2	313	7
Master's 2000–4	96	21	76	21	5	9	25	50	21	64	2	32	10	23	442	9
Master's 1995–2004	189	33	124	40	6	17	63	88	28	115	4	71	20	25	755	16
Doctoral 1995–9	20	3	17	9	2	3	18	7	3	16	2	11	2	2	94	2
Doctoral 2000–4	15	11	12	4	5	5	8	12	8	10	4	9	1	2	103	2
Doctoral 1995–2004	35	14	29	13	7	8	26	19	11	26	6	20	3	4	197	4

These issues and factors contributing to the development of education research and the nature of such development are addressed later in the book. Preceding sections have described postgraduate research from the first post-apartheid decade, linking scholarly works, albeit schematically, to the plethora of policies emerging in the first blush of social transformation. Unsurprisingly the patterns of knowledge production reflect the apartheid landscape, with most of the research in education being generated by those institutions characterised as previously advantaged.

Table 2.10: Post-graduate education theses per institution[3]

Institutions	Provincial base	Number of theses
University of Johannesburg	Gauteng	712
University of South Africa	Gauteng	552
University of KwaZulu-Natal	KwaZulu-Natal	416
University of the Witwatersrand	Gauteng	408
University of Pretoria	Gauteng	302
North-West University	North-West	221
University of the Free State	Free State	202
University of Cape Town	Western Cape	172
Stellenbosch University	Western Cape	171
Rhodes University	Eastern Cape	138
University of the Western Cape	Western Cape	134
Nelson Mandela Metropolitan University	Eastern Cape	125
University of Zululand	KwaZulu-Natal	117
University of Limpopo	Limpopo	33
Tshwane University of Technology	Gauteng	29
Durban University of Technology	KwaZulu-Natal	18
Cape Peninsula University of Technology	Western Cape	9
University of Fort Hare	Eastern Cape	8
University of Venda	Limpopo	7
Vaal University of Technology	Gauteng	0
Total		3774

In terms of knowledge generation, the table above suggests also that those institutions that generate the least amount of research on teacher education and the performance of schools are located in precisely those regions where the performance of schools is the weakest (KwaZulu-Natal, Eastern Cape and Limpopo).

This section demonstrates the nascent nature of education research as conducted by academics on the one hand, and teachers who are themselves students in higher education, on the other. What becomes evident immediately is that it is a minority of teachers who undertake higher education studies, and then most often in the context of minor case studies for which there is little meta-reading of research available. In terms of higher education itself, research on education, when compared to other broad fields (sciences, humanities) is under-developed, reflecting historical emphasis on the production of teachers often in isolation of the universities (through the erstwhile colleges of education). In relation to the challenges concerning education in rural schools, Foundation Phase education, HIV and AIDS education, it is clear that much more investment and work needs to be done.

2.7 REFLECTIONS

This chapter has considered some of the implications that apartheid had for teacher education in South Africa after 1994. What becomes evident is that higher education institutions have not been able to respond to the supply-and-demand issues regionally with any amount of ease. In part this might be explained by the fact that those universities that were located in rural areas, or in regions far from industrial centres, tended also not to have the capacity to train and produce teachers of quality for the local schools. This deduction is supported by the data gathered by the ETDP SETA, in which it is shown that the provinces with the most vacancies in schools (Eastern Cape at 5454, Mpumalanga at 2940, and KwaZulu-Natal and Limpopo at 5212) are those provinces in which there either are no universities, or universities with histories of neglect and disadvantage. The challenge here is to develop new institutions (as has already occurred in Mpumalanga and the Northern Cape in 2014 with the creation of two new universities there), or to rejuvenate and better support those institutions (such as Fort Hare in the Eastern Cape) damaged by apartheid neglect. KwaZulu-Natal and Limpopo both possess large universities where the ostensible focus must be wider access, together with the investment of further resources in teacher education, with a view to improving the quality of the teacher training received there.

Those universities located in urban areas (such as UJ, UP, US and Wits) were also those institutions that were formerly racially segregated and therefore would not have trained high-quality teachers for rural (or indeed urban) schools where most, if not all, children were black. Furthermore, the universities characterised by fairly high levels of research generation tended to focus on small-scale case-study projects that formed the basis of students' research work, thus making it difficult to extrapolate from these studies those findings with the potential to add value to the system in terms of the challenges concerning education as a whole. In terms of methodological preferences the emphasis on qualitative research methods parallels the choice of case studies and might be ascribed to the fact that postgraduate students for higher degrees are usually teachers in employment. Schools at which such teachers are employed become natural sites for research.

Thus, whilst Deacon et al. (2009) noted the systemic challenges addressed by researchers in publications, the survey of theses generated on education show promising signs, the first of which is that teachers are doing most of their research on schooling, and the second of which is that the majority of the students (teachers) undertaking such research are black. This suggests that the transformation aspirations with regard to wider access are being realised.

However, the other side to the increase in postgraduate work on schooling as undertaken by teachers is the lack of impact generated by the introduction of the new qualifications designed to enable teachers to meet the minimum requirements of teacher qualifications. It is widely accepted in South Africa that the advanced certificates (ACEs) and national professional diplomas (NPDEs) have not yielded the expected improvement in learner performance in the schooling sector. This in itself suggests that the effectiveness of higher education has come into focus. It is at universities that teacher education is provided and with the closure or incorporation of teacher training colleges in 2002, the role of universities in addressing the poor performance of schools would come into sharper focus in terms of delivering not only graduates capable of adding quality to the education system, but also to meeting the needs of a new South Africa in terms of economic growth and prosperity and adding energy and commitment to the transformation of society. The following chapter provides an account of higher education in terms of change and capacity development in relation to the success and participation rates of students entering higher education after 1995.

NOTES

1   Lewin, Samuel and Sayed (2003) have undertaken a policy-practice related review of change in education in South Africa as part of the MUSTER (multisite teacher education research) project at Sussex.
2   It must be noted that school principals are paid by the Department of Basic Education.
3   Note again, that Walter Sisulu University declined to participate in the study.

3 University reform: Access, integration, success and research

3.1 INTRODUCTION

This chapter considers the role of higher education as a means of enabling South Africa to advance the interests of its people through quality education that can lead to meaningful skilled employment. The sector is complex and by 2015, not yet stable. In the past 20 years it has seen multiple shifts in terms of size and shape (through the merging of institutions, the incorporation of teacher training colleges into universities, and the addition and redevelopment of further education and training colleges into technical and vocational education and training colleges), and also in terms of policy frameworks for qualifications (for example the National Qualifications Framework or NQF, and its later iteration, the Higher Education Qualifications Strategic Framework or HEQSF), and the legislation affecting teacher education (for example, the Norms and Standards for Educators and the subsequent Minimum Requirements for Teacher Education Qualifications or MRTEQ) (see Appendix 2).

The chapter describes first the broad features of the sector in relation to institutions, enrolments and performance, and then focuses specifically on performance in the sector. This emphasis links closely with the focus of the previous chapter in which the role that teacher education plays in relation to under-performance and problems in schooling (the focus of Chapter 1) was described.

A study concerning the relationship between schooling and the transition to higher education was concluded by Spaull in 2013, who noted the following six key observations from a survey of studies about school-to-work and school-to-tertiary institutions transition:

1. Poor quality schooling at the primary and secondary level in South Africa severely limit the youth's capacity to exploit further training opportunities. As a result, existing skills deficiencies among those who are the product of an underperforming school system (predominantly black youth) are likely to persist.

2. South Africa's narrow youth unemployment rate of 50% is staggeringly high, both in the context of far lower average global and sub-Saharan youth unemployment rates and in terms of the country's already high aggregate narrow unemployment rate of 25 %.

3. The percentage of 18–24-year-olds who are not in education, employment or training (NEET) has increased from about 30% in 1995 to 45% in 2011, while the percentage enrolled in education has decreased from 50% to 36% and the percentage of youths in employment remained fairly constant at between 17% and 19%. As such, there appears to have been a shift away from participation in education in favour of either economic inactivity or unemployment among the youth.

4. Youth unemployment in the country is not only high, but has risen precipitously since 2008, following a national trend of worsening unemployment. Moreover, the nature of unemployment experienced by the youth appears to be becoming more severe in terms of an increase in the proportion of unemployed youths that have never worked and the proportion that have been looking for work for more than a year.

5. For the youth, passing the NSC exam does not provide sufficient assurance against becoming unemployed, nor does it markedly increase one's chances of procuring employment relative to 18–24-year-olds who have lower levels of educational attainment. Instead, the value of passing the NSC exam lies in opening up the opportunity to acquire some form of tertiary education qualification.

6. Though the unemployment rates for 18–24-year-olds with tertiary qualifications are much lower than those for youths with the NSC or less, they are nevertheless high in relation to South Africa's overall unemployment rate (Spaull 2013, 6–7).

As described above, the percentage of 18–24 year-olds who are not in education, employment or training (NEET) has increased from about 30% in 1995 to 45% in 2011, while the percentage enrolled in education has decreased from 50% to 36% over the same period. The unemployment rate for the youth has also increased from 36% in 1995 to 50% in 2011, standing at twice the national unemployment rate in 2011. Furthermore, of those unemployed in 2011, more than 70% had never been employed before.[1]

A range of reports analysing the career or employment prospects for out-of-school youth express concern about the need for the education system to better prepare young people either to access higher education institutions (including FET colleges) or for work itself. School education is often referred to in such documents as 'sub-standard', and the quality of education received is linked in the argumentation to economic consequences or implications for those in receipt of substandard education. It needs to be noted, however, that some scholars such as Vally and Motala (2014) and Allais, have challenged the view that education is a simple panacea for unemployment and economic problems.

Statistics suggest that the prospects for youth in these circumstances are not improving, but instead seem to be deteriorating over time. The percentage of 18–24-year-olds who are not in education, employment or training (NEET) has increased from about 30% in 1995 to 45% in 2011 while the percentage enrolled in education has decreased from 50% to 36% over the same period. The unemployment rate for the youth has also increased from 36% in 1995 to 50% in 2011, standing at twice the national unemployment rate in 2011. Furthermore, of those unemployed in 2011, more than 70% had never been employed before.

Spaull (2013, 8) notes that 'Perhaps most disconcertingly, for the youth, completing Grade 12 does not markedly increase one's chances of finding employment relative to 18–24-year-olds with less than the NSC. Rather, the value of matric lies in opening up opportunities to acquire some form of tertiary education, an opportunity available to only a small minority'.

3.2 HIGHER EDUCATION AT A GLANCE

Since 1994 there have been various stages of transformation, differentiation and restructuring in the South African university landscape. A key component of the restructuring process was the merger of the 36 universities to form 23 public Higher Education Institutions (HEIs). As of 2015, the public higher education and training sector now consists of 25 public HEIs, and these universities can be classified into four broad categories:

• Eleven traditional universities, inherited from the pre-1994 era;

• Six comprehensive universities, resulting from mergers of previous universities and technikons;

• Six universities of technology, which are upgrades of former technikons;

- Two new institutions of higher education, namely the Sol Plaatje University in the Northern Cape, and the University of Mpumalanga, both of which started enrolling students in 2014.

These institutions function as administrative hubs, partnering with other universities to coordinate the provision of higher education. In 2015, Sefako Makgatho will open in Gauteng, bringing the total number of universities to 26.

The traditional universities offer theoretically-oriented university degrees, including a range of undergraduate and postgraduate degrees in faculties such as humanities, science, commerce, pharmacy, law and education. The comprehensive universities offer a combination of academic and vocational diplomas and degrees, which include practical programmes as well as theory. The universities of technology focus on vocationally-oriented education such as internships. Universities of technology (UoTs) originated from the former technikons of South Africa. UoTs were established post-apartheid to develop research alongside teaching. Prior to the transformation of higher education, technikons focused on training 'technologists' or 'application-oriented professionals' (later broadly conceived beyond the engineering fields). Research was conceived narrowly around the idea of 'applied research' (CHE 2010; Johnson et al. 2010). Johnson and Cooper (2014, 98) state that there are six UoTs across South Africa.

In relation to enrolment and participation, the Council on Higher Education (CHE Report 2013) noted that:

> ... in the period since the transition to democracy in 1994, there has been substantial growth in higher education enrolments. The higher education system has grown by over 80% since 1994, to a total enrolment of over 900 000. Significantly, this growth has contributed much to redressing race and gender inequalities in admissions, with African enrolments reaching 79% and female enrolments 57% of the total by 2010. The 'graduation rate', that is, the number of graduates as a percentage of head count enrolments in a given year, has also grown, though only marginally from 15% in 1994 to 17% in 2010. In terms of population groups, the number of African and coloured graduates, and their proportions in total graduate output, have increased substantially: for example, the number of African first-degree graduates grew by 50% between 1995 and 2010, to some 31 000. (Ndebele et al. 2013, 12 and 39)

Participation rates in higher education in South Africa have increased from 15% in 2000 to 18% in 2010. Ndebele et al. (2013, 41) note that '... although significantly higher than the average GER for sub-Saharan Africa, which is 6%, it is well below the average for Latin America (34%) and Central Asia

(31%) (UNESCO 2010). In line with such trends, the Green Paper (DHET 2012a) has revised the participation rate target to 23% by 2030, which is still modest'. Thus, while there has been discernible growth, it is clear that the 'low participation rate continues to act as a brake on social and economic development and is a key factor in explaining the shortage of high-level skills' (Ndebele et al. 2013, 41).

Having provided an indication of the sector in overall terms, the sections to follow describe efforts to regulate the sector with the purpose of providing a degree of confidence not only in the quality of education provided, but also the size and shape of the sector in relation to the needs of the economy and society in general.

3.3 STATUTORY BODIES AND THE REGULATION OF HIGHER EDUCATION IN SOUTH AFRICA

The key role players in the public higher education and training (HET) landscape are the 25 universities, including students and lecturers, Unions, the Department of Higher Education and Training (DHET), the Council on Higher Education (CHE), Higher Education South Africa / Universities South Africa (HESA / USA), the National Student Financial Aid Scheme (NSFAS, discussed more fully in Chapter 6), the South African Institute of Distance Education (SAIDE), and the South African Qualifications Authority (SAQA). The Education, Training and Development Practices Skills Authority (ETDP SETA, described more fully in Chapter 7) is also a key role-player as it is responsible for data about public HEIs as a sector.

All HEIs (public and private) are required to have their qualifications approved by the Department of Higher Education and Training and accredited by the Council on Higher Education (CHE). The Council on Higher Education is responsible for ensuring a degree of consistency of shape and form (minimum number of credits associated with each qualification in terms of what is made possible through the National Qualifications Framework) for the standards of prorgammes. The quality of the programme is facilitated through the Higher Education Quality Committee of the CHE, through an academic peer review process in order to assure the public and the State of the quality of programmes offered to students. Every HEI maintains its own Programmes and Qualifications Mix (PQM), on which are listed all qualifications offered by the respective institutions. The PQM differs from institution to institution in relation to whether the institution is defined as a comprehensive, technical or conventional university. In South

Africa, only universities are granted institutional autonomy, as defined by a legislative act passed by the Parliament of South Africa, which takes the form of a statute designed to guide the university's governance arrangements. Technical and vocational colleges (TVET; see Chapter 4) are controlled directly by the DHET. A similar arrangement exists for private higher education institutions, irrespective of whether these are universities, further education and training (FET) or TVET colleges. The DHET maintains a list of recognised and accredited institutions and possesses the legislative powers to de-register an institution and thus prevent it from offering qualifications to members of the public. Private higher education student enrolments, organisational arrangements, students and staffing data are reported annually to the Registrar for Private Higher Education Institutions in South Africa.

The South African Qualifications Authority (SAQA), also established by an Act of Parliament in 1995, is an organ of the government which takes responsibility for the maintenance of the National Qualifications Framework. All qualifications and programmes accredited by the DHET and CHE are lodged by institutions of higher education (public and private) with SAQA, where a registration number is provided. The SAQA website is often the first point of reference for prospective students looking to establish that a qualification offered by an institution has been registered with SAQA. SAQA also advises institutions on issues concerning qualification equivalence, especially in relation to the recognition of foreign programmes or qualifications that may be taken into account when determining whether students can access further qualifications with institutions offering these in South Africa.

Universities South Africa (USA; formerly known, until 2015, as Higher Education South Africa, or HESA) is a representative organisation, similarly set up by Parliament through an act, to operate as a lobby and advisory group to the department (DHET) and Parliament on higher education matters. USA takes responsibility for the organisation of representative constituencies associated with higher education institutions (for example, USA convenes and facilitates meetings, as well as developmental workshops, colloquia and conferences on issues of relevance and concern to the sector). USA defines such constituencies as 'communities of practice' (examples of which are the Registrars' Imbizo, the Education Deans' Forum, the Vice-Chancellors and University Principals' Forum, the Science Deans' Association and so on). The facilitation role played by USA in relation to such groupings is an important part of leadership development in public South African universities.

There are no statutory bodies associated with private higher education in South Africa. Private higher education institutions (PHEIs) have a representative association which was established in 1997 (the Association of Private Providers of Education, Training and Development of South Africa or APPETD). The association provides a similar role to that of USA for PHEIs, although it is not supported by the State. The need for such support is nevertheless widely acknowledged as a gap since members of APPETD do not form part of the developmental initiatives provided by USA for public higher education constituencies and yet documentation concerning the role of higher education in South Africa speaks often of PHEIs as 'partners' in education. More about this need is outlined later in the chapter.

3.4 CAPACITY FOR TEACHING AND RESEARCH AT SOUTH AFRICA'S PUBLIC HIGHER EDUCATION INSTITUTIONS

Universities can be categorised in terms of their enrolment. Close to half of all public HET institutions have more than 2000 employees. A minority (22%) of institutions have fewer than 1000 employees. One in approximately every three institutions has between 1000 and 2000 employees.

According to the DHET data for 2013 there were 65 862 permanently appointed staff at public HEIs in 2013 (Table 2.24). The HEMIS personnel categories show that 31 707 (48%) of the 65 862 members of staff were categorised as professional staff. Professional staff, as per the DHET definition, comprise instruction and/or research and/or support staff who spend more than 50% of their official time on duty on instruction and research activities. Support staff in this context would be academic development specialists appointed to lecture and provide specialist support to academic and research staff.

Employees in the public HET sector are relatively young, with close to 1 out of 2 employees falling within the 35–55 years of age range, and less than 1 in 5 over 55 years. Approximately one-third of all employees are less than 35 years of age. For the period 2014–2015, compared to 2013–2014, the number of employees between the ages of 35 and 55 has decreased, whereas employees older than 55 years have increased. This still reflects an ageing workforce (especially in relation to the professoriate), which presents potential challenges to the sector regarding skills retention as older staff members approach retirement. The sector is concerned about reduction in its workforce over the coming years, and is considering succession planning and other means of addressing this issue (ETDP SETA Skills Plan Focus Groups 2014).

Figure 3.1: Employee Age Ranges

(2011-2012: n=22725, 2012-2013: n=36104, 2013-2014: n=29553, 2014–2015: n=55514)

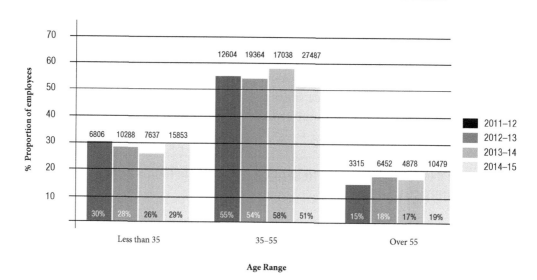

Source: ETDP SETA WSPR (2011–2012, 2012–2013, 2013–2014)

There are 17 267 (31%) of the total number (55 514) of HEI employees who fall into the category of lecturers and professors for the 2014-2015 period. The majority (53%) of these employees fall into the 35–55 age range and only 23% are over 55 years, which supports the notion of an ageing lecturer workforce.

Figure 3.2: Age Ranges of Lecturers and Professors (n=17267) at public universities

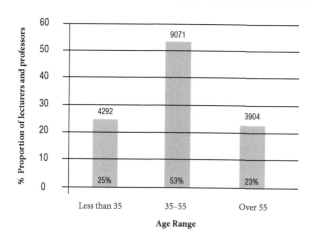

Source: ETDP SETA WSPR (2014–2015)

Figure 3.3 describes, from the perspective of race categorisation, the head-count participation of race groups in higher education staffing. From the graph it can be seen that black academic staff participation in higher educa-tion has increased, but this figure shows the total of staff and closer inspection reveals that black people are retained mostly in support and administrative functions, with especially poor representation in the professoriate.

Figure 3.3: Headcount overall staff members by race from 2007–2012

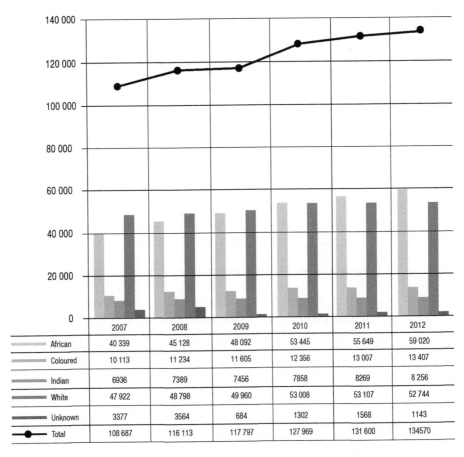

	2007	2008	2009	2010	2011	2012
African	40 339	45 128	48 092	53 445	55 649	59 020
Coloured	10 113	11 234	11 605	12 356	13 007	13 407
Indian	6936	7389	7456	7858	8269	8 256
White	47 922	48 798	49 960	53 008	53 107	52 744
Unknown	3377	3564	684	1302	1568	1143
Total	108 687	116 113	117 797	127 969	131 600	134570

Source: Council on Higher Education (2014). VitalStats: Public Higher Education, 2012

The gradual increase of black academic staff in higher education is not matched in university management positions. As Figure 3.4 shows, white managers continue to be heavily represented, even though there has also been a gradual increase in the representation of black people among this category.

Figure 3.4: Headcount senior management staff members by race from 2007–2012

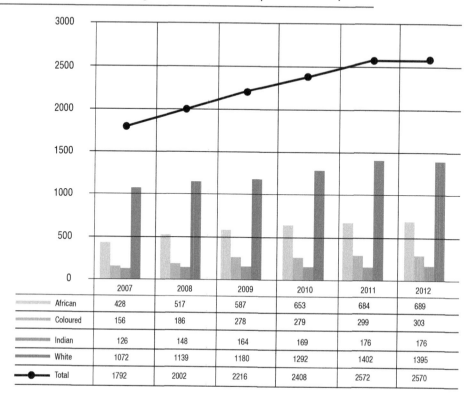

	2007	2008	2009	2010	2011	2012
African	428	517	587	653	684	689
Coloured	156	186	278	279	299	303
Indian	126	148	164	169	176	176
White	1072	1139	1180	1292	1402	1395
Total	1792	2002	2216	2408	2572	2570

Source: Council on Higher Education (2014). VitalStats: Public Higher Education, 2012

Figure 3.5 outlines the qualification level of personnel employed in Public HEIs. Staff members are broken down into three categories, namely management, academic and support staff. As expected, close to 100% of management staff have obtained university qualifications, with only 4% of management staff obtaining a technikon qualification or a qualification from another institution. Just over 8 out of 10 academic staff members have obtained a university qualification, 1 out of 10 has obtained a technikon qualification and a minority (5%) have obtained a qualification from another institution. The majority of support staff has a university qualification, with one-third of support staff obtaining a technikon qualification or a qualification from another institution.

Whilst the management staff component has more university-qualified personnel, it is important to note a significant increase of 42% in the percentage of support staff with university qualifications in 2014. Figure 3.6 shows the qualification levels of members of staff classified according to race from certificate through to doctoral level.

Figure 3.5: Staff Qualifications: Permanent Staff (2012: n=17251, 2013: n=17838)

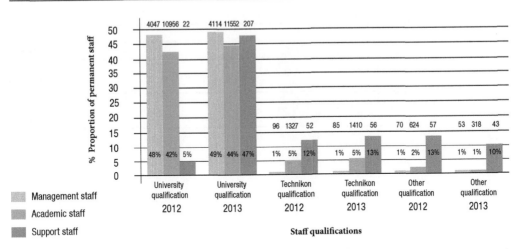

Source: DHET (2012), DHET (2013)

Figure 3.6: Headcount of permanent academic staff by race and qualification from 2007–2012

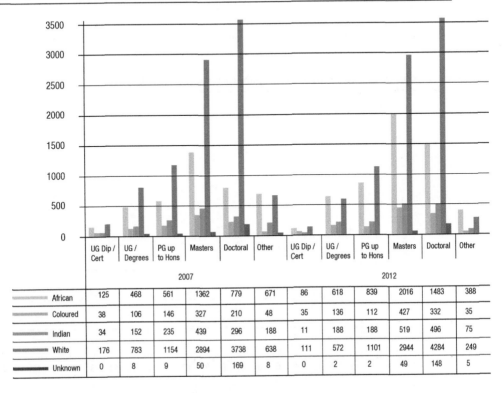

	UG Dip / Cert	UG / Degrees	PG up to Hons	Masters	Doctoral	Other	UG Dip / Cert	UG / Degrees	PG up to Hons	Masters	Doctoral	Other
			2007						2012			
African	125	468	561	1362	779	671	86	618	839	2016	1483	388
Coloured	38	106	146	327	210	48	35	136	112	427	332	35
Indian	34	152	235	439	296	188	11	188	188	519	496	75
White	176	783	1154	2894	3738	638	111	572	1101	2944	4284	249
Unknown	0	8	9	50	169	8	0	2	2	49	148	5

Source: Council on Higher Education (2014). VitalStats: Public Higher Education, 2012

Figure 3.7: Percentage research outputs by all publication types in four broad fields from 2010–2012

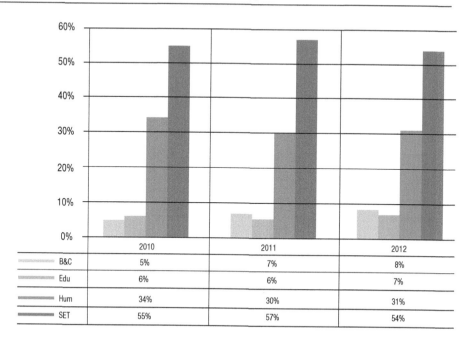

	2010	2011	2012
B&C	5%	7%	8%
Edu	6%	6%	7%
Hum	34%	30%	31%
SET	55%	57%	54%

Source: Council on Higher Education (2014) VitalStats: Public Higher Education, 2012

Figure 3.8: Percentage research outputs by all publication units (CESM), 2012

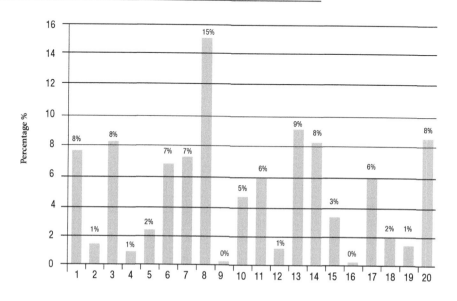

Source: Council on Higher Education (2014) VitalStats: Public Higher Education, 2012

In terms of research, Figure 3.7 describes publication types. These data confirm the research undertaken by Deacon et al. (2009) and Balfour et al. (2011) (with respect to education research in the 1995–2004 period, see Chapter 2), in which research generation in education is shown to be small in comparison with Science, Engineering and Technology (SET), and Humanities.

Figure 3.8 describes research generativity associated with categories of study (classified and described in Chapter 7).

There is a substantive body of research on higher education itself in South Africa. In addition to the many CHE commissioned reports on quality assurance and curriculum development in the sector, scholars such as Marock (2000), Ntshoe, Higgs, Wolhuter and Higgs (2010), Van Koller (2010), and Soudien (2007) have written on the complexities of quality assurance in relation to the many challenges concerning historical redress and change in the last 20 years. Such studies point to the tensions between the need to create capacity to offer scarce and critical skills on the one hand, and the need to develop a new leadership as well as citizenry capable of realising the transformation ideals of the State, on the other. Given the legacy of structural inequalities between race groups, and also between genders, it has often been thought that the affirmative action or employment equity drives can be used as an effective means of achieving redress in South Africa. Balancing these dimensions with the commitment that higher education institutions must display towards quality in teaching and learning as well as research, has been very difficult to sustain. Unfortunately there are too many examples where good governance, quality research, student success and throughput have been sacrificed to the detriment of the sector as a whole (see Appendix 2). Nonetheless, the commitment to transform South African society needs to be especially strong and evident in (higher) education if real change is to be made real over time.

Sehoole (2005), Jansen (2004) and Makgoba (1997) have commented on the impact of transformation on the sector, both from an access and success perspective. Other scholars, such as Van Damme (2001), have commented about the influence that internationalisation has on the diversity and experience of students in higher education. The drive to internationalise the student body, whether through Africa co-operation agreements such as those entered into in the Southern African Development Community (SADC) region, or those created through international staff and student exchange, have had a positive impact not only in research development, but also student experience at many South African higher education institutions.

Other researchers have described the impact of changed funding models on research generation and the culture of managerialism (or accountability) associated with it (see Strydom & Fourie 1999; Wolhuter 2014). In relation to this latter dimension, Odhav (2009), for example, has explored the extent to which policy failure is a feature of the sector.

In relation to the above, other researchers, for example Mkhwanazi and Baijnath (2003), and Soudien (2010) have explored the impact of changing policies on employment equity, or affirmative action on higher education employment trends and quality. Mubangizi (2004) and Robus and Macleod (2006) have explored contentious matters concerning race relations between students and staff at universities, while Francis and Le Roux (2011) have described the social justice issues associated with change.

There have been a number of contributions made concerning the culture of higher education institutions during this period of change (see Strydom, Zulu & Murray 2004; Thaver 2009). Mgqwashu (2007), Balfour (2011), Narismulu and Dhunpath (2011), Van Louw and Beets (2008), and Webb (2012) have all undertaken research on diversity in relation to the development of indigenous languages for learning at higher education, or in relation to the protection and representation of gender sexual minorities (for example, Balfour, forthcoming; Soudien et al. 2008; Rothman 2014). Other scholars have explored diversity from the perspective of religious beliefs and the impact these have on perceptions of diversity, tolerance and acceptance (Le Roux 4014; Du Preez & Roux 2010).

With respect to studies on gender (addressed more fully in Chapter 5), the research shows concerted effort over the 20-year period to increase the representation of women in the academy and particularly in management positions. Every higher education institution's employment equity policy contains reference to the need to promote and develop the capacity of women to lead in research and administration at universities, but progress has been slow as described in paragraphs to follow.

In relation to women in management positions in higher education (see Figure 3.9), there has also been a gradual, though not significant, increase in representation. This needs to be considered in relation to the instances of racism and sexism reported in South Africa as affecting women and black people (noted also in relation to student life on campuses as described in the Soudien Report, 2008, in Chapter 5).

Figure 3.9: Headcount senior management staff by gender from 2007–2012

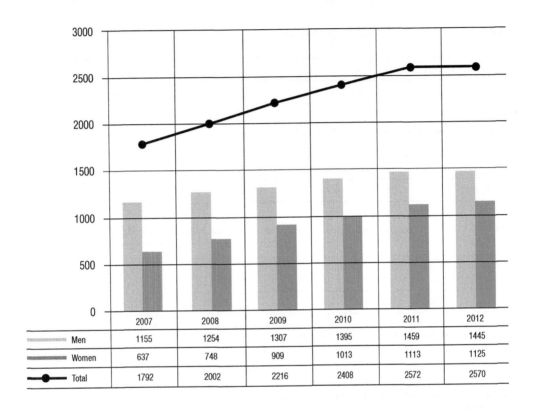

	2007	2008	2009	2010	2011	2012
Men	1155	1254	1307	1395	1459	1445
Women	637	748	909	1013	1113	1125
Total	1792	2002	2216	2408	2572	2570

Council on Higher Education (2014) VitalStats: Public Higher Education, 2012

Having described staffing and the progress made to transform universities in terms of their human resources, the following sections provide data concerning the participation and success of students accessing universities in South Africa.

3.5 ACCESS TO HIGHER EDUCATION IN SOUTH AFRICA: UNIVERSITY ENROLMENTS

The Twenty-Year Review: 1994–2014 (The Presidency 2014) claims that 'University enrolment has almost doubled since 1994, and there have been huge increases in enrolments at further education and training (FET) colleges'. The race and gender composition of the student body has been markedly transformed since 1994. The South African government has been working on challenges in the FET sector, including very low throughput rates and industry perceptions of problems with the quality of FET (TVET) colleges (see Chapter 4).

Table 3.1: Females' Enrolment 1995, 2005, 2013

Level of Education	1995	2004	2013
Tertiary	312 597	450 651	591 066

Table 3.2: Males' Enrolment 1995, 2005, 2013

Level of Education	1995	2004	2013
Tertiary	285 667	348 814	347 134

Table 3.3: Students' enrolments by gender in primary school, high school and tertiary education

Level of education	1995			2004			2013		
	Males	Females	Total	Males	Females	Total	Males	Females	Total
Tertiary	285 667	312 597	598 264	348 814	450 651	799 465	347 134	591 066	938 200

Sources: Education statistics in South Africa at a glance 2004

Table 3.4: Number of higher education institutions

Years	1995	2004	2013
Public FET		50	50
Private FET	155	864	536
Public University	21	23	26
Private University	15	11	11

Table 3.5: Enrolments in higher education institutions

Institution	1995	2004	2013
Public FET		406 144	657 690
Private		706 884	115 586
Total		1 112 028	773 276

Continued over page

Public University	385 221	569 384	953 373
Private University	190 191	171 873	94 478
Total	575 412	741 257	1 050 851

Sources: South African Higher Education open data
South African Transformation Monitor (SAT Monitor)
Statistics on Post-School Education and Training in South Africa: 2012

The data above are also represented in Figure 3.10 below in which the gradual increase in enrolments at universities as represented by the four 'race' groups is demonstrated. White and Indian enrolments have remained consistent over a seven-year period, whilst Black enrolments show a marked increase. Women also far exceed men in higher education in enrollment terms.

Figure 3.10: Headcount enrolments by race from 2007–2012

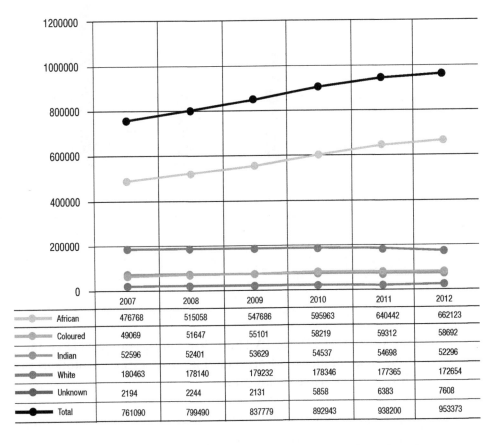

	2007	2008	2009	2010	2011	2012
African	476768	515058	547686	595963	640442	662123
Coloured	49069	51647	55101	58219	59312	58692
Indian	52596	52401	53629	54537	54698	52296
White	180463	178140	179232	178346	177365	172654
Unknown	2194	2244	2131	5858	6383	7608
Total	761090	799490	837779	892943	938200	953373

Source: Council on Higher Education (2014) VitalStats: Public Higher Education, 2012

After the major transformation which resulted in the merging of universities and universities, the enrolments of universities increased as the conditions in terms of funding became more and more favourable to the majority in public universities. Research on private higher education (see Badroodien 2002; Mabizela 2003) has noted that the relationship between public and private institutions is tenuous, as also is the relationship between State agencies (the Department, CHE and others).[2]

Figure 3.11 disaggregates gender and broad fields of study. These data confirm that education as a field is dominated by women, and that women have increased in participation in areas conventionally associated with men (Business and Commerce, and SET).

Figure 3.11: Headcount of graduates by gender and field of study from 2007–2012

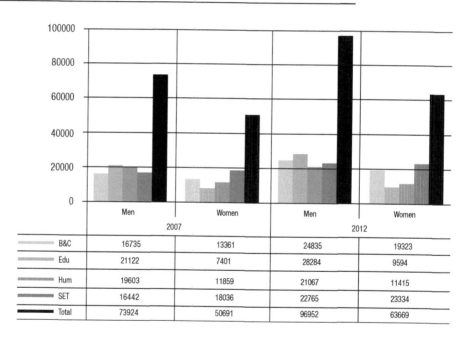

	Men 2007	Women 2007	Men 2012	Women 2012
B&C	16735	13361	24835	19323
Edu	21122	7401	28284	9594
Hum	19603	11859	21067	11415
SET	16442	18036	22765	23334
Total	73924	50691	96952	63669

Source: Council on Higher Education (2014) VitalStats: Public Higher Education, 2012

Data from the ETDP SETA Skills Plan (2014, 136) provide an indication of the concentrations of learners in higher education institutions in South Africa as described in Figure 3.12.

Figure 3.12: Provincial Spread of Students (2012: n=953373, 2013: n=998382)

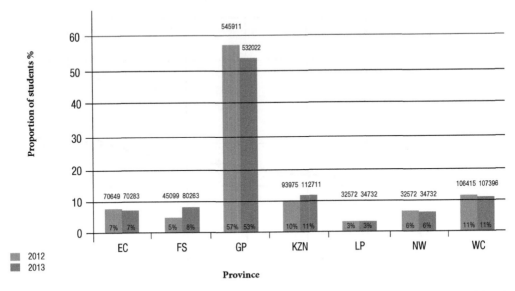

Source: DHET Data (2012), DHET (2013)

Figure 3.13: Top Ten National Student Qualifications (2012: n=953374, 2013: n=983698)

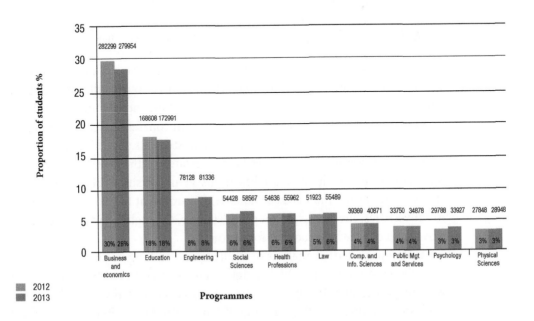

Source: DHET Data (2012), DHET (2013)

Figure 3.14: Course success rates by race from 2007–2012

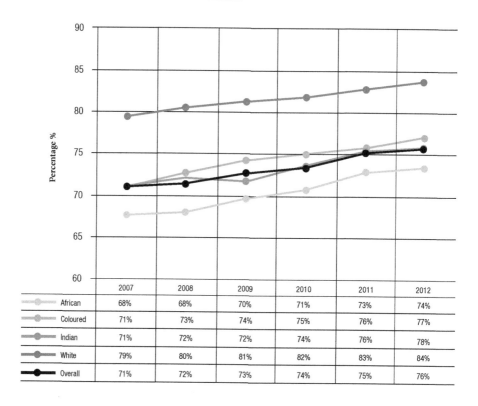

	2007	2008	2009	2010	2011	2012
African	68%	68%	70%	71%	73%	74%
Coloured	71%	73%	74%	75%	76%	77%
Indian	71%	72%	72%	74%	76%	78%
White	79%	80%	81%	82%	83%	84%
Overall	71%	72%	73%	74%	75%	76%

Source: Council on Higher Education (2014) VitalStats: Public Higher Education, 2012

Figure 3.13 above depicts the various CESM qualifications that students are enrolled in at Public HEI institutions. The top three courses that students are enrolled in are Business and Commerce, Education and Engineering (SET).

Figure 3.14 describes student success rates in courses and shows improvements over time in terms of the percentage of students obtaining their qualifications successfully, but this needs to be related to the longer time it takes for students to finish their qualifications at universities. Figure 3.14 also shows that, despite the marked increase in enrolment terms of black people in universities, the participation rates (success, throughput and retention) of this group are the lowest of the four groups.

Having provided an analysis of students and staffing in higher education, the following section provides insights into data collected by ETDP SETA with respect to identifying scarce or critical skills needed within the sector. Such information is collected annually in South Africa, but only the most recent is provided here to complement observations concerning the relative state of higher education in universities (please see Chapter 4 for information concerning technical and vocational colleges).

3.5.1 Demand and supply gap analysis

The delivery mechanisms for training and education of staff include formal qualifications (for example, PhDs), continuous professional development, involvement in research, support provided by mentors and attendance at conferences.

The extent of international partnership and collaboration at public HEIs indicates that some training is conducted at international universities. Skills demand is affected by public HEIs' inability to retain staff even though they might invest in and provide their training. This situation is exacerbated by low remuneration, employment conditions, lack of specific skills, training changes and the increase in staff retirement rates. The ETDP SETA Skills Plan (2014) identifies the following scarce skills in the data returns engendered by universities in South Africa. Key scarce and critical skills to be addressed by the above mechanisms are:

Scarce skills

1. Academic roles

    1. University Lecturers (231101)

    2. Professors and Senior Lecturers (231101)

    3. Computer Science Lecturers (231101)

    4. Mathematics Lecturers (231101)

    5. Engineering Lecturers (231101)

    6. Health Lecturers (231101)

    7. Accountancy Lecturers (231101)

    8. University Tutors (231102)

2. Support roles

    1. Office Administrators (334102)

    2. Artisan: Plumbers (642601)

    3. Training Material Developers (221101)

    4. Finance Managers (121101)

3. Critical Skills

    1. Leadership and management;

2. Communication skills (written and verbal); and

3. Research skills. (ETDP SETA Skills Plan, 146–47)

Having described areas identified as critical and scarce in the sector, with a view to properly addressing these needs in coming decades, the following sections provide a description of curriculum reform and qualifications framework development intended to allow for a better quality of learning experience and also enhanced standards for curriculum in the new South Africa.

3.6 FRAMEWORKS AND CURRICULUM REFORM IN HIGHER EDUCATION

The transformation project engaged with the need for systems reform both at the level of schooling and of higher education. Thus, in 1995, in order to anticipate the reforms enacted in schooling, the NQF was introduced. Mncube and Madiya (2013) provide a survey of the development of this period, and, drawing from commentators such as Wolhuter (2010), affirm the macro-socio-political framing of these systemic changes. Thus, one super-Department of Education (under the first Minister Sibusiso Bhengu, 1994–1999; then Kader Asmal, 1999–2004; and Naledi Pandor, 2004–2009) housed both basic and higher education coordination functions. The introduction of the NQF was a critical intervention in the design and execution of post-secondary schooling qualifications. The system was conceptualised as a unitary system in which provision was made for the development of new qualifications. Teacher education qualifications were re-designed in deliberate recognition of the history of damaging and differential access to teacher education qualifications as offered by a plethora of departments of education through a multitude of teacher training colleges of very variable quality, in the apartheid era.. The purpose of the NQF was thus to provide universities (many of which were newly-merged institutions), private higher education providers and post-secondary colleges with guidance in terms of the qualifications that could be offered, and at which levels, with the object of enabling multiple entry and exit points for life-long learning, and articulation between trades and academic qualifications.

The NQF was divided into three levels: Level 1 was known as the GET band (General Education and Training, and thus most schooling, namely Grades 1–9); Levels 2–4 were known as the FET band (Further Education and Training, and the remaining years of schooling, Grades 10–12); and finally, Levels 5–10 were intended for higher education and training (National

Diplomas, Advanced Certificates, bachelor's degrees, postgraduate degrees and diplomas, Master's degrees (Level 9), and doctorates (Level 10). Mncube and Madiya note that the transformation goals of higher education were aimed, as with schooling, to create a non-sexist, non-racist South Africa in which mobility for those previously disadvantaged by the apartheid regime was made possible through affirmative action, where negative discrimination could not be tolerated and where self-individuation and cultural expression were encouraged (2013, 170). These goals were also described in the 'White Paper on Education' issued by the Department of Education (1995). The type of citizen anticipated by these initiatives, the various legislative acts such as the NQF and white papers, were framed by progressive education: a critical, creative, articulate, independent-thinking, loyal citizen, respectful of difference, intolerant of discrimination, socially conscious and with an understanding of the common good, the eradication of poverty and the protection of the national resources. Naidoo (2014) has argued that successive transformations of education curriculum in the schooling sector have seen these aspirations to create a critical citizenry replaced by a narrower, economically competitive focus with a view to profit and gain within a global and neo-liberal policy framing, which can typically be traced back to the macro-economic policies advocated by the Mbeki and then Zuma administrations (*GEAR* and *ASGISA/JIPSA*). As with the schooling curriculum reforms, the intentions of the NQF were to streamline higher education and enable learners to access higher learning with the purpose not only of gaining academic type qualifications, but also trades and adult education skills with a view to the creation of self-employment and lifelong learning (Department of Education 2001, 13). This planning assumed that teacher education and schooling were already attuned to the needs of the economy and global environment. The assumption was not only untested but dangerous, given the isolation associated with the apartheid period.

What remains typical of documentation relating to higher education in the period leading up to 2005, and also thereafter, is the articulation of high expectations concerning the role that higher education would play in terms of creating not only a productive economy (more a feature of discourse in government documentation after 2005 than before), but a peaceful, productive and democratic state. Altogether absent in this phase was an overview of the state of knowledge production in South Africa that could be used to better inform research funding agendas so that research generation in this critical period of development could be better attuned to the needs of the State. This type of research has also been identified by the Council on Higher Education in terms of the knowledge necessary to ensure that students are prepared for success when making career choices – that should already begin with the selection of subjects taken as part of their schooling:

> Enhancement – broadly used ... to mean provision that improves or enriches learning (as opposed to inserting more conventional content) and that goes beyond what is offered in current programmes – is required in a range of forms: from provision that is necessary to support core learning (such as the explicit development of academic literacies), to broadening the curriculum to include learning that is professionally and socially important in the contemporary world (such as additional languages) and that lays foundations for critical citizenship. Again, in the great majority of existing programmes, there is wholly insufficient curriculum space to enable such provision to be incorporated without compromising the integrity of the 'irreducible core' of knowledge in the curriculum. (Ndebele et al., 19)

So far this chapter has focused on issues in schooling and teacher education, on the basis that understanding the poor performance of the sector depends on understanding the impact of under-performance in schooling (and by implication the under-performance of teachers). Given the priority for developing better-quality schooling, the following sections provide an analysis of the state of research into education in South Africa, which reveals not only the systemic needs of schooling and higher education, but also the flaws within higher education itself.

3.7 THROUGHPUT AND SUCCESS IN HIGHER EDUCATION

A recurring theme in commentary on the release of the National Senior Certificate (NSC) examination results is that the results themselves speak only to those youth who make it to Grade 12. Spaull notes that 'Of 100 pupils that start school, only 50 will make it to Grade 12, 40 will pass, and only 12 will qualify for university. Those 18–24-year-olds who do not acquire some form of post-secondary education are at a distinct economic disadvantage and not only struggle to find full-time employment, but also have one of the highest probabilities of being unemployed for sustained periods of time, if not permanently' (Spaull 2013, 10). From this context it is evident that not only is learner performance a persistent challenge for the schooling sector, but also for teacher training and development. The matter of learner performance is one that closely connects higher education performance to the performance of schools, since school leavers become students at higher education institutions, and the quality of schooling has a direct impact on the performance of school leavers in higher institutions of learning. Simply accessing higher education does not guarantee success either in terms of throughput rates or completion rates for qualifications – a point to which we will return later in this chapter.

Ministers of Education since 1995 have identified access to higher education as a matter that they regard as central to the transformation project. Access not only has to do with whether school-leavers qualify for entry to higher education; it is considered a key challenge because it is perceived to increase the employment possibilities anticipated as an outcome of successful completion of higher education or post-secondary studies. As an end in itself, participation in higher education is often regarded as a prerequisite for the creation of a modern and critical citizen. In more utilitarian terms, good throughput rates, retention rates and success in higher education are all seen as critical for the growth of the economy. In South Africa, there has been a shift in the discourse concerning the role of higher education from its aspirational democratic beginnings (1995–2005), to focus more on ideas of economics, globalisation and competition associated with neo-liberalism (2005–2014, *GEAR* and *ASGISA*).

There is no doubt that high levels of economic growth are a means of alleviating poverty and inequality. Yet South Africa has one of the most unequal distributions of income in the world: the Gini coefficient (which measures inequality in societies), where 0 is absolute equality and 1 is absolute inequality, has risen from 0.596 in 1995 to 0.635 in 2002 (United Nations Report 2004), In addition, the poverty gap, indicating the depth of poverty, has also increased, with the number of people living in extreme poverty, as defined by the United Nations Development Programme, having risen from 9.5% (3.7 million) to 10.5% (4.7 million) between 1995 and 2002 (United Nations Report 2004). In this context alone, pressures on the higher education system have increased and the system itself has come under further scrutiny and concomitant pressure.

Given the large numbers of students who pass the matriculation examination (337 000 in 2012; Cloete 2013, 32), and who qualify for university entrance but cannot find a place there (universities can only accommodate 128 000 new students per annum, only 34% of those who qualify), the challenge with regard to the employment and development of out of school youth is pressing. The government has been successful in enabling students from disadvantaged backgrounds to access higher education through the provision of education bursaries (especially for teacher education, known as the Funza Lushaka Bursary), and a national loan scheme (known as NFSAS). Through provisions, the government in 2014 alone provided r9 billion for students' support in higher education (Ndwheni 2014). Access to higher education has not, however, translated into success, and so higher education institutions (universities, as well as further education and training colleges) have in the last 20-year period invested substantially in bridging and extended curriculum programmes designed to make up the 'deficits' in schooling by enabling more young people to succeed at university level. Bridging programmes, alternative admission programmes and extended curricula are features of higher education institutions in South Africa as the sector struggles to widen access, and also to improve the chances of students' success in the system. These commendable initiatives are nevertheless symptomatic of a school system in which the failures are also the cause of higher education's poor performance. This, in turn, draws attention, inevitably, to the quality of teachers (both those within the system, and those being generated by HEIs).

It is equally clear from the success rates of higher education institutions that graduation does not guarantee absorption into the economy. Problems relating to success (retention, throughput and graduation) in higher education have an impact also on the economy's potential to grow, and commentators such as Cloete and Butler-Adams have noted that '[b]ecause of the state of the economy, these young people can also not find employment, resulting in the fact that approximately 41 percent of the people between the ages of 18 and 24 are currently unemployed' (Cloete & Butler-Adams 2012). Economic growth depends on the availability of skilled graduates suited to market needs, but it is also the expectation that skilled graduates will shape market needs and create further employment opportunities as the economy grows. Education in higher education contexts thus needs to enable responsiveness to the market and to global competition. This confirms again the need for schooling that is of high-quality and provides a solid knowledge base that enables student success to universities and FET colleges.

The CHE Proposal for Undergraduate Curriculum Reform (Ndebele et al. 2013) noted that South Africa's graduate output has major shortcomings in terms of numbers, equity and success rates:

- Despite there being a small intake that has good academic potential, performance in higher education is marked by high levels of failure and dropout. For example:

- Only about one in four students in contact institutions (that is, excluding UNISA) graduate in regulation time (for example, three years for a three-year degree).

- Only 35% of the total intake, and 48% of contact students, graduate within five years.

- When allowance is made for students taking longer than five years to graduate or returning to the system after dropping out, it is estimated that some 55% of the intake will never graduate.

- Access, success and completion rates continue to be racially skewed, with white completion rates being on average 50% higher than African rates.

- The net result of the disparities in access and success is that under 5% of African and coloured youth are succeeding in any form of higher education.

Ndebele et al. (2013, 15) are not hopeful about the prospects for a quick change in the areas highlighted above and argue that: 'These performance patterns are not compatible with South Africa's need to develop the intellectual talent in all its communities. Moreover, there are no grounds for hoping that the patterns are a temporary aberration. They have not changed significantly since the intake cohort of the year 2000.'

While the CHE proposal argues for a need to extend the duration of undergraduate degrees, the suggestion that such an extension can accommodate or address the 'articulation gap' is problematic since most South African children who exit schooling in Grade 12 do not go to university. Their 'gaps' remain unaddressed and are a silent testimony to a schooling system that has failed to prepare students adequately for either work or study or both.

The ambitious national targets set for higher education in South Africa were described earlier in this chapter. Ndebele et al. (2013) argue that there is a range of obstacles to achievement of these in relation to the current effectiveness (capacity and efficiency) of higher education institutions as a whole.

- Low student success and throughput rates, leading to low absolute numbers of graduates.

- Uneven and often unsatisfactory graduate quality, not only in disciplinary or technical expertise but in graduate attributes that are widely seen as necessary for the contemporary world. As the National Development Plan puts it: 'For the increase in the number of graduates to be meaningful, the quality of education needs to improve … The data on the quality of university education is disturbing' (NPC 2012, 317).

- Equity of outcomes. The distribution of graduates continues to be highly skewed along racial lines. The interlocking conditions of low output and lack of equity have a major effect on all forms of development. (Ndebele et al 2013, 33)

Ndebele et al. (2013, 43) state that just over one-quarter of entrants into South Africa's universities are likely to complete their qualifications in time, with a staggering 40% of first-time entrants likely either to drop out or take longer to complete their studies:

- Performance is very poor for all groups across the three qualification types. Even in the four-year professional degrees, which are highly selective in terms of admissions requirements, the rate is only 36%.

- Within the generally poor performance patterns, there nevertheless continue to be substantial racial disparities. Very small proportions of African, coloured and Indian students graduate in regulation time.

- By the end of the regulation time in all three qualification types, more students have been lost to failure and dropout than have graduated – more than twice as many in the case of African and diploma students.

- In all groups, the completion rates are consistently better in the professional Bachelor's degrees in general than in the other qualification types, and overall, performance is poorest in the diplomas. (Ndebele et al 2013, 43)

This bleak picture allows the reader to conclude that whilst planning to massify, the system was a key feature of higher education transformation in the first 20 years; insufficient planning was done to help universities to accommodate such growth in terms of the capacity of human capital, and this was both inadequate and insufficiently thought through. It is simple to assign the costs of an inefficient sector to the schooling sector that prepared students for widened access, but this is in effect only half the narrative. One means of addressing the need for widened access in relation to tapping into existing capacity in South Africa is in relation to the role of private higher education provision as described in sections to follow.

3.8 PRIVATE HIGHER EDUCATION AND TRAINING IN SOUTH AFRICA: UNRECOGNISED PARTNERS IN EDUCATION

There is a long history of private schooling as well as private higher education in South Africa, beginning with missionary colleges and schools which offered high-quality education to an African and black elite until they were prevented from doing so by successive Nationalist governments after 1948. Private higher education is diverse and differentiated as part of the sector and includes institutions such as private universities (St Augustine's and Monash South Africa, for example), colleges (SOLTEK – an industrial and trades college, VEGA – an advertising and marketing college and Advtech – an education consortium owning schools and colleges), and institutes offering programmes in the higher education band across a range of learning fields, as well as small one-person organisations that work primarily in workplace and corporate settings. In 2013 it was estimated that over 113 000 students were enrolled in private higher education institutions (PHEIs) in South Africa (ETDP SETA Skills Plan 2014, 54).

PHEIs are required to register with, and be accredited by, the Department of Higher Education and Training (DHET 2013b, 1), and are responsible for post-school education and vocational training. The DHET registration requirement is only applicable to private institutions that offer learning programmes which result in the award of qualifications at Levels 5–8 of the NQF. Certificate, diploma and degrees, as well as workplace learning (apprenticeship and learnerships), are offered by PHEIs in South Africa.

The types of offerings provided by PHEIs differ from institution to institution due to the fact that providers work across the three NQF sub-frameworks. The ETDP SETA Skills Plan (2014) notes that: 'The more established institutions tend to offer what is known as curriculum-based qualifications while the smaller, single-purpose organisations often offer occupational qualifications including legacy unit-standards based qualifications' (ETDP SETA Skills Plan, 142).

According to the ETDP SETA Skills Plan (2013), the most popular fields of learning (DAC 2010) with regard to the more established Private HET institutions, are:

Culture and Arts

Design Studies; Visual Arts; Performing Arts; Cultural Studies; Music; Sport; Film, Television and Video

Business, Commerce, and Management Studies

Finance, Economics and Accounting; Generic Management; Human Resources; Marketing; Procurement; Office Administration; Public Administration; Project Management; Public Relations

Human and Social Studies

Environmental Relations; General Social Science; Industrial and Organizational Governance and Human resource Development; People/Human-centred; Development; Public Policy, Politics and Democratic Citizenship; Religious and Ethical Foundations of Society; Rural and Agrarian Studies; Traditions, History and Legacies; Urban and Regional Studies

Health Sciences and Social Services

Preventive Health; Promotive Health and Developmental Services; Curative Health; Rehabilitative Health/Services

Physical, Mathematical, Computer and Life Sciences

Mathematical Sciences; Physical Sciences; Life Sciences; Information Technology and Computer Sciences; Earth and Space Sciences; Environmental Sciences. (ETDP SETA Skills Plan 2014, 66)

The majority of PHEIs offer mostly full qualifications. None of the organisations surveyed offer only credit-bearing skills programmes.

3.8.1 Aspirations and delivery: private higher education as key stakeholders for widened access

The National Development Plan (NPC 2012) and the Green Paper describe ambitious targets for higher education as a whole and universities in particular: 'University enrolment to rise to 1.5 million by 2030 from approximately 900 000 in 2011' (DHET 2012a, x). The National Development Plan has a similar target for 2030 of 1.62 million enrolments, and suggests that in order to achieve this, 400 000 graduates will need to be generated per year by that date, up from about 150 000 in 2013, with a special focus on increases in Science, Technology, Engineering and Mathematics (STEM) areas (NPC 2012, 317, 319).

In order to achieve widened access it is clear that key role-players in the private higher education sector will need to be considered more carefully in terms of creating more capacity in the system as a whole. The Department of Higher Education and Training's role as merely a registration and data reporting body (as described by the Higher Education Act no. 101 of 1997) will have to change to become a more proactive role-player. At present private HETs registered with DHET are, by definition, also recognised by the Council on Higher Education (CHE) by virtue of their programmes being accredited by the Higher Education Quality Committee (HEQC). The ETDP SETA is a key role-player as it supports private providers as one of its constituencies.

Although there is a large number of PHEIs, student enrolment in comparison to public higher education provision is small. However, PHEIs play a crucial role in extending and supplementing the post-schooling education and training sector available through public HETs. Given that PHEIs are run on a commercial basis, they tend to offer courses of study for which there is a sizeable paying market.

The ETDP SETA surveys needs and capacity both for private and public higher education in South Africa. It has noted that all 21 SETAs operate in the Occupational Qualifications Sub-Framework (OQSF) space, and that the definition of a Private HET provider would include any accredited provider offering NQF qualification Levels 5–10. That said, in South Africa it remains difficult to ascertain the number of such providers because:

> There is no central accreditation register for all these training providers. The SAQA database of qualifications is not always up-to-date as such data is only updated twice a year;

> Some education and training providers are accredited by more than one SETA. That means there could be double counting; and

> The introduction of the QCTO, phasing out and re-registration of certain SETA accredited qualifications as well as development of new occupational qualifications complicates matters, especially the accreditation statuses of training providers. (ETDP SETA Skills Plan 2014, 66)

As of the DHET's register in 2013, there were 87 registered and 31 provisionally registered PHEIs, yielding a total of 118 operational HET organisations in South Africa. The private higher education sector consists of mostly small, medium and micro-enterprises (SMMEs).

These institutions tend to be found in areas where public institutions do not have a presence. In her report to the DHET, Blom (2011, 29) reflected the provincial spread of private post-school institutions across all ETQAs (inclusive of ABET, FET and HET institutions), which supports the view that PHEIs are widely spread and that most of the organisations have a presence in the more populous provinces such as Gauteng, the Western Cape and KwaZulu-Natal. Other provinces have a very limited presence of Private HET institutions, including the Northern Cape, which has no presence of PHEIs (ETDP SETA Skills Plan 2014, 55). The absence of higher education provision in the Northern Cape and Mpumalanga motivated DHET to establish two new public universities in these provinces in 2014.

In the 20-year period, the size of organisation for Private HET institutions appears to have shrunk in terms of the number of institutions:

> In [2011] ... there were 403 private FET colleges registered with the DHET, although only 277 submitted information to the department. In 2011, a total of 277 private FET colleges employed 8 662 staff and served 134 446 students. (ETDP SETA Skills Plan 2014, 17)

> This was a decrease from 9% to 7% respectively, although there has been a significant increase in the number of larger institutions between 2012 and 2013. (ETDP SETA Skills Plan 2014, 56)

Having described the sector in terms of public and private higher education, this chapter concludes with a series of reflections on the capacity of higher education to provide sufficient support for successful learning for students, as well as for the transformation not only of South Africa as society, but also in terms of delivering on the promise of quality education for meaningful work.

3.9 REFLECTIONS

It is clear that more progress, at a more rapid rate, needs to be made in relation to four key issues in higher education in South Africa. First, the efficiency of the sector is a serious concern. Characterised as sluggish and expensive, data suggest that students (irrespective of race or gender demographics) do not perform well in terms of success rates and dropout rates. While white students as a group still tend to perform better when compared to other groups, Ndebele et al. (2013, 51) has noted that 'white students in contact institutions (mainly historically advantaged universities), fail to graduate within five years'.

Second, if transformation remains the key objective to be realised in ensuring that more people, across the race and gender divides, have better chances of equal success at higher education, then it is of profound concern that the performance of black and coloured students remain the lowest when analysed in the 20-year period of democracy. The success of these groups has to become a feature of planning at the level of schooling as well as higher education. Claims about the system having been massified are countered in relation to the dismal performance of students within it:

> Only 42% of African contact students graduate within five years, and if UNISA (which provides educational opportunities for large numbers of African students) is included, the number drops to 30%. The performance of coloured students in contact institutions is only one percentage point better overall in each case. Given the participation rates ... the net effect of the performance patterns is that only 5% of African and coloured youth are succeeding in higher education. This represents an unacceptable failure to develop the talent in the groups where realisation of potential is most important. (Ndebele et al 2013, 51)

Third, the capacity of higher education to support further massification, without substantive and recurring investment in the development of academics and intellectuals at institutions, has to be enhanced and itself massified in relation to the needs of the economy within certain fields of study.

Fourth and finally, the role of private higher education provision needs to be properly reconsidered by the State in terms of providing for the subsidisation of students and research generation as one would expect in public higher education provision. Without the acknowledgement of private higher education providers by the government as partners in the solution to South Africa's education needs, there is not likely to be any short-term gains made in relation to further widening of access in the sector. In 2012, the government incorporated the technical and vocational training colleges into the higher education sector to be administered by the DHET. The initiative, long overdue, brought into focus the necessary interrelationship between universities and TVET colleges, since the schooling curriculum was designed on the basis of an idea that school pupils could leave schooling in Grade 10 to join a TVET college and follow a more technical or trade-based education, or could exit the schooling sector after Grade 12 and similarly enrol in either a university or TVET college. The idea of a unified and coherent higher education sector was indeed anticipated with the design of the National Qualifications Framework, and so the chapter to follow provides a description of TVET in South Africa from 1995 as part of the higher education sector.

NOTES

1 Hyslop (1990) undertook research on schools and unemployment in the apartheid period.

2 As State support for public institutions has increased (through powerful bursary schemes – for example, Funza Lushaka to support teacher education, or the National Finance Student Assistance Scheme (NFSAS) – the viability of private institutions has sometimes foundered, particularly because students enrolling at such institutions are barred from accessing such State support (see Chapter 7). The reduction in enrolments in private institutions over time and the competition for students meant that some FETs folded and reduced significantly in numbers.

4 Technical, vocational and further education and training in South Africa

4.1 INTRODUCTION

Technical, vocational training and development is the most complex and diverse phase of education and training, comprising four types of institutions (senior secondary schools, technical and community colleges, enterprise-based training, and a wide array of private providers, including for-profit and not-for-profit organisations such as NGOs). Technical, vocational education and training (TVET) comprises three categories of learners: the pre-employed, the employed and the unemployed (Kraak and Hall 1999, 19).

Higher education, as noted in Chapter 3, underwent a profound period of transformation and restructuring, which began in 1998 and reached conclusion in 2004. This fundamental redesign of the entire sector also affected those institutions responsible for the provision of what was termed 'further education and training' (FET; referred to from 2014 onwards as 'technical, vocational education and training', or TVET). The Green Paper on FET, entitled 'Preparing for the Twenty-First Century through Education, Training and Work', was released on 15 April 1998. The white paper 'A Programme for the Transformation of FET' followed soon after, in August 1998. In a remarkably speedy process, the FET Act was passed through parliament and promulgated in November 1998 (20). The lack of a sense of system was a major criticism of the FET sector in the education white paper titled 'A Programme for the Transformation of FET: Preparing for the Twenty-First Century through Education, Training and Work'. The Skills Development Act was passed in December 1998 (21).

The TVET (or FET as it was known) band in South Africa is unique and complex. This is because the senior secondary phase of formal schooling has been incorporated within the further education and training band (Kraak & Hall 1999, 19; Gamble 2003) through NQF levels 3–4. Currently, senior secondary education is too general, providing few opportunities for specialisation relevant to the labour market (as noted also by Young 2006, 60). A further development in the socio-political transformation affecting South Africa along with many other countries across the globe in the late twentieth century has been a shift in the understanding of the role of the State away from what has been termed 'statist', 'social welfare' or 'entitlement' models (states that are viewed as providers-of-all) to a new state–citizen relationship based, firstly, on greater State accountability and effective performance in the delivery of services paid for by taxpayers, and secondly, on a more conscious effort to make the delivery of TVET (as with other social services) a joint cost-sharing endeavour between the state, business and the people. The culture of 'entitlement' associated with former welfare and statist societies has given way (often after heated political contestation) to a new emphasis on performance and quality indicators that provide evidence of State institutional efficiency and cost-effectiveness. These changes have impacted profoundly on the FET band because it is this sector more than any other educational band that requires the joint efforts of all stakeholders for its success and effectiveness (Kraak & Hall 1999, 49).

Kraak and Press (2008) have noted that TVET colleges were meant to provide the training associated with vocational and technical skills, as well as equip students to be responsive to the needs of the private sector. South Africa's economic isolation from 1970–1990 put the sector at a disadvantage from which it has been extremely difficult to recover. To enhance and stimulate the sector, and also the economy, the State made provision for economic policy that encouraged foreign investment, and the redesign and development of the colleges.

In the first reform phase, between 2005 and 2009, an annual growth rate of the economy was anticipated to be around 4.5%. In the second reform phase, between 2010 and 2014, the government sought an average growth rate of 6% of GDP. The Mbeki government's Accelerated and Shared Growth Initiative for South Africa (*ASGISA*) identified skilled artisans and vocational skills as critical for sustained growth. Today, in a period of slower than projected growth, it is evident that the South African labour market lacks sufficient skilled professionals, managers and artisans, and that those parts of the legacy of apartheid remains a contributory factor. The short supply of well-qualified, competent and experienced artisans is frequently highlighted in the media with comments from government, employers and unions.. The expansion of intermediate artisan and technical skills for the growing economy has been identified as one of the five main areas for targeted intervention by the Joint Initiative on Priority Skills Acquisition (JIPSA), which was launched by the government on 27 March 2006.

In 1998, there were 152 technical colleges that were selectively merged or closed down to produce the current FET landscape. In 2011, there were 400 273 students (full-time and part-time) across the 50 public FET colleges, involving 232 campuses. In these publicly funded institutions there were 465 managers, 8 686 lecturing staff and 6 593 support staff (totalling 15 744 employees). It is well understood that colleges are not producing the quality of artisans that industry requires, which is why so few graduates are absorbed immediately into the labour market (Mukora 2008, 64).

In the period following the restructuring of higher education FET/TVET colleges, there developed a burgeoning of private higher education and training colleges, relatively small in size and offering a very restricted, though necessary, array of programmes, practical and otherwise. As TVET colleges have gradually come to be better equipped and to offer practical programmes with workplace-integrated learning (learnerships or apprenticeships), the burgeoning of private higher education for TVET has gradually reduced. Thus in 2011 there were 527 private FET colleges registered with the DHET, but in 2014 this number had been reduced to 365 providers (EDTP SETA Skills Plan 2014). In the public FET college sub-sector, the average age of lecturing staff has decreased from 42 in 2004 to 37 in 2012, meaning that there is an increase in the number of younger staff joining colleges. This is despite the fact that up until 2014 there were no learning programmes designed specifically to train college lecturers in institutions of higher learning. The same trend can be found in the private FET colleges, even though the age profile of employees is much lower, at 35, especially amongst the clerical, service and sale workers, and also agricultural workers.

This chapter surveys the TVET sector over the 20-year period and is divided into several sections. The first section describes the legacy of apartheid's differential education system with regard to technical, vocational training and development. The second section explores the labour force in South Africa in recent times in relation to the scarcity of particular technical and vocational skills. This provides a context in which to situate the growth that has characterised the sector since 1995, and also provides a basis from which to understand the challenges with which the sector is faced in relation to the needs of the economy as well as society for skilled labour. The third section provides a particular focus on TVET, its roles and functions as anticipated by various legislative acts, as well as economic policies adopted by the Mandela, Mbeki and Zuma administrations. The fourth section describes learner enrolments in the TVET sector over a period since 2007, which then leads onto a discussion of programmes and specialisation areas offered within TVET-related qualifications in the fifth section. Section six begins an exploration of the capacity of the sector in relation to staff demographics (qualification levels, race, age and so on), while the seventh section provides some analysis of private higher education TVET provision (again in terms of scope, staffing capacity and qualifications levels). Section eight describes adult education and learning, whilst section nine describes the ETDP SETA Skills Plan analysis of critical and scarce skills in the TVET sector itself (in relation to the capacity of the sector to deliver quality programmes needed in South Africa). The tenth section describes the supply-demand gap analysis, also drawing heavily on the ETDP SETA Skills Plan (2014) for data and information.

The chapter concludes with a series of observations regarding challenges experienced currently in technical, vocational and training development, as a sector, in South Africa, and suggests some possibilities in relation to the evident need to further diversify the sector.

4.2 TECHNICAL, VOCATIONAL EDUCATION AND TRAINING: THE LEGACY INHERITED IN A NEW SOUTH AFRICA

Kraak, together with a group of researchers, undertook a survey in the 1990s of the further education and training (TVET) colleges in South Africa. He affirmed the racialised history of education development described by Hartshorne (1992) and he noted (Kraak & Hall 1999, 150) that the weaker and less effective colleges providing technical and vocational education were ex-Department of Education and Training institutions (associated with the administration of Bantu education during the apartheid period), and homeland institutions, while the majority of effective colleges tended to be the ex-House of Assembly institutions. Kraak and Hall (1999) undertook a detailed case study of the FET colleges in KwaZulu-Natal at a time when control of these was still split between the various race-based tri-cameral Houses of Parliament and the various homeland governments associated with the apartheid period. This research is worth describing in some detail to provide an indication of the scope and depth of the challenges facing colleges in the period just after 1995.

The findings raise four significant issues relevant to the transformation of technical colleges nationally. Firstly, the teaching and learning environment is sub-optimal. Students receive little academic support and almost no academic development programmes exist for lecturing staff. Many curricula were noted as being out of date (noted also by Gamble, 2003). Students with matric appear to gain little added value by enrolling for technical college 'N' certificates. Secondly, the social relations that characterise technical colleges are tense, with few institutions having successfully come to terms with the rapid deracialisation of student enrolments that has taken place over the past five years. Few of these institutions had strategies to deal with the extent of cultural and linguistic diversity that has now materialised on most campuses in South Africa. These problems are likely to manifest themselves in race as well as language terms (see Gamble 2003) unless they are urgently addressed. Thirdly, the labour market surrounding these institutions appears to be totally dysfunctional, with few students obtaining employment after technical college training.

Hall (1995, 136) noted that the vast majority of lecturers at these colleges possessed only junior diplomas rather than Bachelor's or postgraduate degrees. This is not surprising since universities conventionally did not concern themselves with the training of academics for the college (FET or vocational training sector). Gamble (2003, 24) notes that TVET lecturers, because they were not trained for education at universities or colleges, and were drawn mostly from industry backgrounds, struggled to make the link between theory and practice for students.

In 1998, 59% of the teaching staff at TVET colleges in KZN were male. This slight gender imbalance should be interpreted with caution as it is due to the fact that departments in the Engineering subfield are staffed almost entirely by males (94% males) while the opposite is true in Business Studies (82% females), Utility Industries (77% females) and Social Services (87% females). The gender imbalance in these fields is more exaggerated. Females fill 42% of all junior posts (lecturer and senior lecturer), but fill only 28% of senior posts with a tiny group in management (Hall 1995, 130–31). In 1995, most academics on the teaching staff of the colleges in KZN were white (see Table 4.1). Of the white academics there was a 60% (English) 40% (Afrikaans) split, whilst the overwhelming majority of black academics in 1995 spoke isiZulu.

Table 4.1: Racial composition of teaching staff and students

	Black	Coloured	Indian	White
Teaching posts in all colleges	185	57	177	353
% of total	24%	7%	23%	46%
% of total student population	79.4%	1.6%	9.2%	9.8%
Equity ratio, i.e. % teachers / % students	0.3	4.3	2.5	4.7

Source: Kraak & Hall (1995)

In 1997, there were approximately 14 020 FTEs in the 25 technical colleges in KZN with most students (93%) in full-time study. This is an approximate figure because data from four colleges was too inaccurate to be relied upon (Hall 1995, 143). The vast majority of students enrolled in KZN in 1995 were black (89.7%). The majority of students in 1995 were in the age range of 17–26 – in other words, these were typical generally of the higher education student range for initial qualifications.

Formally, FET is defined as that band which provides learning programmes between Levels 2–4 on the National Qualifications Framework (NQF). The FET certificate is awarded on completion of the requirements of NQF Level 4. This flexible approach assumes the establishment of partnerships between and among schools, FET colleges, industry-based training programmes, providers of social and developmental training programmes, and providers of training programmes for small, medium and micro enterprises (Kraak 1999, 67).

Scholars such as Kraak and Mukora have noted that there is a sense of concern about the quality and relevance of FET programmes.

In terms of programme fragmentation, FET schools have few links to the world of work and opportunities for practice. The General Education and Training Phase (GET) in schools was only academic (i.e. there was no articulation between school FET and GET tracks). Black students were especially adversely affected because early school leavers or those who did not succeed, had few opportunities to access adult education colleges or schools. There were also negative perceptions of technical and vocational education as somehow sub-standard, second class, and menial (Allais 2006, 21). Such perceptions, in relation to low staff morale and poor work ethics, has made the sector difficult to reform.

In August 2007, the joint policy statement was tabled by the Ministers of Education and Labour, pointing out the need for change in the organisational structure of the NQF. This was followed by the new NQF Bill gazetted on 15 February 2008 and the proposed Skills Development Amendment Bill gazetted on 28 February 2008 (see Appendix 1). These developments have put the revised NQF model on the table.

The DoL's 'Green Paper on Skills Development' in 1997 proposed the introduction of a national levy/grant system (which was strongly contested by employers) so as to increase investment in training and employer involvement. The learnership system was seen as an intervention to redress the old apprenticeship system and its problems, and create a high quality dual system of learning. Learnerships would be structured as a combination of unit standard-based structured learning and practical work experience that would lead to a qualification on one of the levels of the NQF and guarantee that the successful candidate was competent for a specified occupation.

The green paper pointed out that traditional apprenticeships would remain an important component of the new learnership system. Learnerships effectively would allow employers to enter into a learnership contract with an apprentice for only one or perhaps two NQF levels. This would ensure that more people could access training, but fewer could have the opportunity to attain the all-round knowledge and skill offered by the old apprenticeship system (Mukora 2008, 48).

Amidst all this, the SETAs were expected to manage the introduction of learnerships, which were promoted at an ideological level as a transformation of the 'old' into the 'new', while also ensuring the continued implementation of the apprenticeship system, which the majority of SETA staff had no knowledge of (Mukora 2008, 50).

This leads to a critical concern which has existed as far back as 1990 – that of the relationship between the departments of education and labour, and the insufficient co-ordination between them. An example of this disconnect was illustrated fairly recently when the DoE took a decision to change the curriculum of FET colleges. The DoE decided that, as from January 2007, the 'N' courses previously offered by FET colleges in three-month blocks would be phased out and replaced with new one-year National Vocational Certificate (NVC) courses, offered at NQF Levels 2, 3 and 4, over three years. The N1 course, for example, was the theoretical component for an apprenticeship programme and was provided for in the MTA (Mukora 2008, 56).

One of the amendments to the Skills Development Act (1998) was the establishment of the Quality Council for Trades and Occupations (QCTO) (an equivalent to the Council on Higher Education, which quality-assures university-based programmes for the occupational programmes offered by TVET colleges and some comprehensive universities). Having provided a context for the redevelopment of TVET as a sector after 1995, it is also important to understand the economic context in which such rethinking was to occur. The following sections describe employment needs and growth prospects in South Africa to which the TVET colleges were meant to respond through scarce skills development and training.

4.3 SOUTH AFRICA'S EMPLOYMENT NEEDS AND ECONOMIC GROWTH IN 2013

Kraak and Hall (1999) argued that in the last years of apartheid there had been a decline in the semi-skilled and unskilled categories of labour from 61.3% to 48.4%. They characterised the labour market as 'highly dysfunctional' in its inability to match school outputs with available and emerging jobs (Abedian & Standish 1992; Kraak 1995; Kraak 1999; Kraak & Press, 2008).

There have been shifts in the labour market since the 1990s when white workers comprised 74% of those apprenticed in manufacturing. Black workers are now the backbone of the manufacturing industry (Abedian & Standish 1992; Kraak 1995; Kraak 1999, 42).

In figures provided by the DoL, total industrial training undertaken by the private sector and public training centres declined from a peak of 736 581 in 1986 to a dismal 205 260 in 1994, a mere 2.9% of the economically active population who received some form of training. Registered apprenticeship contracts declined from 33 752 in 1985 to 22 015 in 1994, and the annual indenturing of apprentices declined from 11 573 to 5002 in the same period. Enterprise-based training declined from a peak of 457 255 in 1984 to a dismal 85 736 in 1994 (DoL 1995). (Kraak 1999, 44).

The education and training sector consequently also had to massify (as indeed did universities see Chapter 3) as demand for more and higher levels of education increased. Thus, pressures to massify are on the one hand related to globalisation and on the other, to the need for redress and for better access to the TVET system. In addition to the above, the concept of lifelong learning appears to encapsulate the radical shift in higher education and the TVET sector, from site-based learning in colleges to multi-modal open access learning based in the workplace and accredited through colleges in proximity to industrial or urban locales. As more young and mostly black people survive the school system and matriculate, fewer jobs are available within a slow-growing economy.

By September 2013, the total labour force was 18 638 000, with 14 029 000 employed and 4 609 000 (24.7%) unemployed. More than 2.2 million people were recorded as 'discouraged work seekers'. Using the Unemployment

Insurance Fund (UIF) database, the number of people claiming for un-employment benefits increased to 168 662 in September 2013 from 159 655 in June 2013. This increase in UIF claims was mainly associated with the end of a large number of employment contracts in a number of industries.

The long-term unemployed (those who have been out of work for more than a year) now account for more than half (65%) of the unemployed. A concern is that this group may become unemployable as their skills stagnate and they become increasingly detached from the informal networks that would lead them to new jobs. A total of 69.3% persons amongst the total 4.6 million unemployed persons were in the age group 15–34 years in September 2013. In the same line, the Department of Labour recorded a total of 600 259 work seekers in the Employment Services database in the financial year 2013/14. Only 16 171 work seekers registered on the Employment Services System for South Africa (ESSA) system were placed over the same period. Despite a decline in unemployment rates between September 2013 and September 2014, the changes year-on-year in the labour absorption rates were minimal at 0.6. This does not create a strong basis to halve unemployment by 2020 as projected in the National Development Path (NDP, 2012).

There are three notable features of South Africa's unemployment crisis. First, the number of uneducated amongst the unemployed (52% of the unemployed did not complete secondary education) is a critical composition of the labour force to be considered. The uneducated group is the most likely group to lose their jobs during periods of employment contraction. Second, the youth (15–34 years), who currently constitute more than 69% of the unemployed, are the dominant and identifiable group amongst long-term unemployed individuals in the country (DoL 2013, 23). The third challenge still facing the country relates to inequalities and unfair discrimination in the workplace, in which black people, women and people with disabilities remain marginalised in relation to meaningful and influential participation in the economy.

The Commission for Employment Equity (2013) reported that:

- The representation of Blacks in top management and senior management levels is 27.4% and 37.6 % respectively whereas they constitute over 88.7% of the Economically Active Population (EAP).

- White people in general still dominate with 72.6% at the top management level, which are nearly six times their representation within the EAP and approximately three times the representation of the cumulative sum of Blacks combined at this level.

- The representation of people with disabilities across all occupational levels was recorded at 1.4%, an increase from 0.8% in 2010. Over the years from 2002 to 2012 this is the increase for all employees (i.e. Public and Private Sectors combined). (DoL 2013, 24)

Women have increased their share amongst the employed from 39.93% in 1996 to 42.55% in 2005 (Mukora 2008, 18). In comparison with total employment, only 16.75% of all craft and related trades workers were women in 2005 (down from 17.97% in 1996). It is only in craft and related trades that women dominate. By far the majority of extraction and building trades workers (94,47%); metal, machinery and related trades workers (96.34%); and precision, handicraft, printing and related trades workers (62.51%) are men (Mukora 2008, 19). Around 60% of all craft and related trades workers were younger than 40 years between 1996 and 2005 (Mukora 2008, 24).

A total of 270 586 apprentices qualified as artisans between 1970 and 2004. It would seem that a large number of artisans might have been lost due to migration abroad. Despite challenges there has been growth in the sector. In 2013 there were 670 455 students, up from 358 393 in 2010, in TVET colleges.

In this context, the need for skilled labour, and a labour force that is capable of self-employment, in a context where employment opportunities in the formal sector are limited, is a key challenge facing higher education in South Africa. In order to contextualise that need further, the sections to follow describe in broad terms the role of TVET in the higher education landscape in South Africa.

Gamble has noted that the quality even of workplace learnerships (and apprenticeships) was not even (Gamble 2003, 23). Practical training and brief periods of real experience in the workplace should be complementary processes creating the fit between education and industry placements remains challenging.

A new curriculum for TVET colleges that will lead to a National Certificate (Vocational) qualification – NC (V) – is a comprehensive and coordinated response to this skills development agenda in which better articulated programmes and qualifications can enable student mobility across programmes and providers or learning sites. The NC (V) is a response to scarce and high-demand skills, and also heeds calls from employers saying they want 'thinking' employees (Mukora 2008, 30).

Kraak (2007) notes that between 2001 and 2005 a total of 134 223 learners were enrolled for learnerships. Research has revealed that most of these learnerships are in non-technical fields and, until recently, have tended to be focused at much lower skills levels than those that would be required for artisanal work. This brings into focus the highly problematic phenomenon of access to and success in TVET as a sector. Envisaged to be the powerhouse of skills education in South Africa, evident problems with capacity and learner uptake have prevented the sector from realising these aspirations, as the following sections show.

4.4 LEARNER ENROLMENTS IN PUBLIC TVET COLLEGES

According to Vinjevold (2007), a total of 211 000 learners were enrolled at FET colleges in engineering studies in 2004 (Table 23). Learners in engineering studies constituted more than half (56.57%) of total enrolment at FET colleges in 2004. Nearly two-thirds (62.09%, or 131 000) of engineering learners were enrolled at Levels N1 to N3. Mukora argues that if all these engineering learners can be channelled into skills programmes in the workplace, then FET colleges could make a massive contribution towards the training of 50 000 artisans by 2010 (Mukora 2008, 34).

The National Development Plan for FET, gazetted in December 2008, contains targets for expansion of enrolments up to 2014, as shown in Table 4.2.

Table 4.2: Target for expansion of enrolments up to 2014

Year	National enrolment
2007	25 000
2008	60 000
2009	120 000
2010	177 000
2011	256 000
2012	371 000
2013	538 000
2014	800 000

Source: The National Development Plan 2008

According to the 2011 Annual Survey there was a total of 400 273 students spread across the 50 FET colleges. Data further shows that Gauteng and KwaZulu-Natal provinces enrolled a higher number of students in public FETs as indicated in Table 4.3. The total number of FET students recorded in 2011 exceeds the planned target of 256 000.

Table 4.3: Number of Student Enrolments

Province	Number and % of student enrolments
Eastern Cape	36 958 (9.2%)
Free State	31 365 (7.8%)
Gauteng	97 548 (24.3%)
KwaZulu-Natal	88 166 (22%)
Limpopo	43 148 (10.8%)
Mpumalanga	17 868 (4.5%)
Northern Cape	8 949 (2.2%)
North-West	22 124 (5.5%)
Western Cape	54 147 (13.5%)
Total	400 273 (100%)

Source: DHET (2013), based on 2011 data

Having described the learner enrolments associated with public TVET provision, the sections to follow describe programme offerings and changes instituted to programmes as a result of legislation.

4.5 TVET PROGRAMME OFFERINGS IN SOUTH AFRICA: THE MARKET AND THE COLLEGE

According to the DoL's *Guide for the Development of Five Year Sector Skills Plans and Annual Updates for 2005 to 2010* (Department of Labour 2005), the term 'scarce skill' refers to those occupations for which there is a demand for qualified and experienced people to fill particular roles or occupations in the labour market. The term 'critical skill' refers to a particular skill within an occupation. The concept 'critical skill' can refer to a) a key, generic or fundamental skill such as cognitive skill (problem-solving and learning to learn), language and literacy skill, mathematical skill, ICT skill and working in teams, as well as b) the occupationally specific 'top-up' skills required for performance within that occupation to fill a 'skills gap' that might have arisen as a result of changing technology, new forms of work organisation or insufficient training before entering the job market (Mukora, 9). In the context of such skills, scarcity is a very worrying problem for unemployment levels in South Africa (in other words, those people who are not only unskilled, but who have not been able to access education with a view to attaining a skill, scarce or other).

Mastery of these so-called 'soft skills' is based on a thorough grounding in the fundamentals of reading, writing, calculating and basic IT. This is why the NC (V) comprises three compulsory subjects: Language (first additional), Mathematics or Mathematical Literacy and Life Skills (which includes IT), alongside the four vocational or specialised subjects. Both the compulsory and vocational subjects are spread across 11 programmes or vocational fields of study, including Management, Marketing, Office Administration, Primary Agriculture, Tourism, Civil Engineering and Building Construction, Electrical Infrastructure Construction, Engineering and Related Design, Finance, Economics and Accounting, Hospitality, Information Technology and Computer Science.

Under the Mbeki government, the 11 programmes fall into the priority areas as defined by *ASGISA*. The qualification, offered at NQF levels 2, 3 and 4, allows for its staggered implementation. This means the NC (V) was to be implemented at NQF level 2 from 2007, followed by NQF level 3 to be implemented in 2008 and NQF level 4 in 2009. Unlike the trimester N courses, the NC (V) courses are one-year long programmes. This means a certificate will be awarded after a successful completion of each NQF level, following a national external examination. This structure allows students the flexibility to complete a certificate on one NQF level, work for a year and pick up their studies again (Mukora 2008 31). The NCV has been 'marketed' by the Department of Education as the solution to the lack of artisan development in South Africa, although no workplace training exists that is currently required within the NCV training curriculum. This makes it difficult to make an assessment of the actual contribution of FET colleges to artisan development.

This difficulty has led to a further blurring and confusion as to what the training routes or pathways to becoming an artisan are. In the old system, apprenticeships acquired their theoretical component through the National Certificates Part 1 and 2 (NATED N1 and N2). The Department of Labour through its Artisan Development Committee has announced four routes that people could take to train as artisans, which were gazetted towards the end of December 2007 for public comment before being legislated. This means that the output from FET colleges alone will not be representative of the number of qualified artisans. The four routes are as follows:

- Apprenticeship route
- Recognition to Prior Learning (RPL) route
- Learnership route
- Internship or Skills Programme route (NCV plus).

(Mukora 2008, 31)

Mukora notes that plans to update training programmes for 22 priority artisanship by the end of 2008 required that the State set aside 600 million rand for bursaries for FET students between 2007 and 2010 (Mukora, 33).

Each of the multi-campus public TVET colleges offers education and training on a variety of learning programmes including NATED N1 to N6, NCV, Occupational Qualifications and other short-course programmes. One of the main roles of public TVET colleges is to provide artisan and vocational training programmes to youths and adults. There are various types of courses offered in fields such as Agriculture, Arts and Culture, Business, Commerce, Management, Education, Training and Development, Engineering, Manufacturing, Technology, Building Construction, Social Services and Security. The colleges are also expected to foster the acquisition of intermediate to high-level skills. In addition, they are also designed to lay the foundation for higher education through the articulation of learning programmes as well as to facilitate the transition from school to the world of work. The FET College Act (no. 16 of 2006) focuses on the acquisition of practical skills, applied vocational and occupational competence in order to equip a graduate for employment in an occupation, trade or higher education.

The colleges also offer the NCV programmes at NQF Levels 2 to 4, which were introduced in 2007. The NCV levels correspond with Grades 10 to 12 in the schooling system. A study was commissioned to review the NCV and Report 191 or NATED N1 to N6 programmes, and a report was submitted to the Minister of Higher Education. These programmes are currently being reviewed in terms of curriculum under the auspices of the Quality Council on Trades and Occupations (QCTO). Programmes aside, the capacity to offer these relates not only to the availability of human resources, but also to the development needs of staffing in the TVET sector who provide training and development, as the following sections describe.

4.6 STAFFING AND CAPACITY OF PUBLIC TVET PROVISION IN SOUTH AFRICA

Gauteng has the highest percentage of staff with 23.9% (2074) of staff spread across 8 colleges. KwaZulu-Natal has the highest presence of FET colleges, serviced with the second highest number of 1 874 staff, but this should be seen in the context of the number of students and offerings available (see Table 4.4). The Western Cape has the third highest number of staff across six colleges as well as the third highest rate of enrolment, with 13.5% (54 147) student enrolments in 2011.

Table 4.4: FET Lecturers per Province

Province	Number	% Lecturers
Eastern Cape	1 109	12.8%
Free State	575	6.6%
Gauteng	2 074	23,9%
KwaZulu-Natal	1 874	21,6%
Limpopo	865	9.9%
Mpumalanga	401	4,6%
Northern Cape	151	1,7%
North-West	426	4,9%
Western Cape	1 231	14,1%
Total	8 686	100%

Source: DHET (2013), based on 2011 data

Table 4.5: FET College staff according to gender

Category	Male	Female
Management	59%	41%
Lecturing	54%	46%
Support	42%	58%

Source: DHET (as reported in the 2011 EDTP SETA Skills Plan SSP Update)

4.6.1 Age of public TVET college staff

The age of lecturers varies, with the majority of lecturers in the 31–40 year age range as informed by the ETDP SETA Questionnaire Survey (2012). The average age of lecturers stands at 40 years, which is close to the information obtained from 2010, which identified the average age of lecturing staff as 39 years (Cosser et al. 2010). The average age of lecturing staff in 2002 was 42 years. Clearly there has been a gradual increase in the number of younger staff members joining the colleges, which means that older staff are either resigning, leaving for other jobs, retiring or being affected by attrition (death).

4.6.2 Race categorisation of public TVET college staff

The breakdown of lecturers by population groups is shown in Table 4.6.

Table 4.6: Lecturer Demographics by Population Group

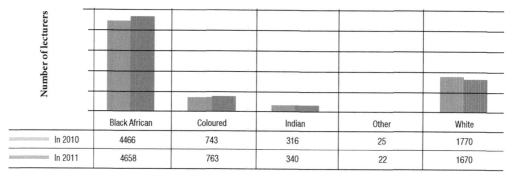

	Black African	Coloured	Indian	Other	White
In 2010	4466	743	316	25	1770
In 2011	4658	763	340	22	1670

Lecturing staff in each population group

Source: DHET (2012)

4.6.3 Qualifications and experience of academic staff at public TVET colleges

A college lecturer is regarded as qualified when s/he has achieved a relevant academic diploma/degree with a teaching qualification. The qualifications of lecturers in FET colleges range from N6 to PhD. The majority of lecturers (37.7%) have an undergraduate diploma, 30.6% have postgraduate diplomas, and lastly, 27.1% are degree holders (Table 4.7). The supply of skills, therefore, comes from universities and other sources as discussed in the next section.

Table 4.7: FET Lecturer Qualifications

Highest (academic) qualification	Percentage
N6	1.9
Undergraduate diplomas	37.7
Degree	27.1
Post-graduate diplomas degree/diploma	30.6
Master's	2.4
PhD	0.3
Total	100%

Source: Mgijima & Morobe, TNA Report (2012, 37)

Having described the human resource capacity of staffing in publicly-funded higher education TVET colleges, the sections to follow provide a similar analysis of the capacity of private higher education for TVET in South Africa. This sector, as noted in the introductory sections of the chapter, has undergone sustained and indeed burgeoning growth since 1995, and thus represents a resource to address skills and critical skills shortages in South Africa.

4.7 PRIVATE HIGHER EDUCATION TVET PROVISION IN SOUTH AFRICA

According to the 2014 DHET national register of private TVET colleges there were 365 entities recorded, but the register does not include private providers who offer part qualifications or short skills programmes as such skills providers are not required by law to do so. In 2014 there was no central database recording all the different types of provisioning. This situation misrepresents and distorts the reality of the numbers within the Private FET sector as many of them offer short courses. Therefore, any attempt to quantify the size and shape of the sector must take into account such disparities. The EDTP SETA, responsible for the survey of such public and private TVET institutions, in its 2014 Skills Plan notes that there is still a serious challenge with regard to understanding the exact size and shape of private TVET institutions, through accurate reporting of student numbers, student retention and drop-out rates and so on.

4.8 PROGRAMMES OFFERED BY PRIVATE TVET HIGHER EDUCATION INSTITUTIONS

Private TVET colleges offer a wide variety of programmes, although provision in the occupational training field predominates, lending credence to the widely-held view that they are responsive to the needs of the workplace. The types of occupational qualifications span from NQF Levels 1 to 6 and include: Agriculture and Nature Conservation; Business, Commerce and Management Studies; Communication Studies and Language; Culture and Arts; Education and Training and Development; Health Science and Social Services; Human and Social Studies; Law, Military Science and Security; Manufacturing, Engineering and Technology; Physical Planning and Construction; Physical Mathematical, Computer and Life Sciences; and Services. In addition, private FET providers also offer the NCV.

4.8.1 Key role-players in private provision of TVET in South Africa

The DHET records registered private TVET colleges. However, databases across DHET, SAQA, Umalusi and the various SETAs remain disparate. While both DHET and Umalusi maintain fairly reliable databases resulting in fairly high correlations between the two, the spread of private FET provision across SETAs is huge, often with training providers being represented and counted by more than one SETA because they offer different programmes that are accredited under different SETAs. The ETDP SETA is responsible for private providers as a constituency.

APPETD (see Chapter 3) is a co-ordinating body and key role-player within the sector and has a number of different types of members which are categorised as follows:

Academy: 89

Institutions: 53

Schools: 59

College: 250

University: 4

General Education and Training: 201

Consultants: 36

The SABPP (South African Board of People Practitioners) is also another role-player in the sector and has signed a memorandum of understanding with the APPETD which is underpinned by four key objectives (APPETD 2012):

• Collaborating to promote skills development by means of high quality learning provision
• Research about challenges, problems and successes in the private providers' landscape
• A drive towards professional registration for staff and students
• Arranging joint events to share knowledge and build capacity.

According to the DHET register of private FET colleges there are a total of 365 private FET institutions registered for the year 2014 compared to 433 registered in 2013 (www.dhet.org.za). The spread of private FET institutions is predominantly in Gauteng, KwaZulu-Natal and the Western Cape.

4.8.2 Labour market profile for private TVET provision

In 2012, the total number of staff recorded was 6 951 (8 662 in 2011), who between them delivered programmes to 113 938 (134 446 in 2011) enrolled students, which is numerically less favourable than the previous year's figures.

4.8.3 Gender of staff in private TVET providers

Most of the 6 951 staff are female with a total of 4 045 (58%). There are more
female managers than male, with a total of 653 (56.7%) compared with 44%
occupied by males (see Table 4.8). There was an even balance for both males
and females of almost 50% for each.

Table 4.8: Number of staff per category and gender, 2012

Staff category & gender	Permanent	Temporary	Total
Lecturing staff	2100	1062	3162
Female	1033	517	1550
Male	1067	545	1612
Management staff	1113	39	1152
Female	628	25	653
Male	485	14	499
Support staff	2410	227	2637
Female	1707	135	1842
Male	703	92	795
Total	5623	1328	6951

Source: DHET, 2013 based on 2012 data

The private sector has a large base of support staff (38%) in comparison with
lecturing staff (45%). Although the reasons for this are not known, it can
be surmised that due to the focus on client care a large number of staff are
employed in non-academic positions to ensure that learners receive quality
service.

4.8.4 Qualifications of private TVET providers in South Africa

Figure 2.6 depicts the wide variety of qualifications that private FET staff
members have completed. Staff in the private FET subsector are qualified,
with the majority (806) having acquired the Level 6 advanced diploma and
634 having achieved a three-year diploma. Few staff hold lower qualifications, all of which indicates the existence of a well-qualified work-force in the
private FET subsector.

In addition to a thriving private higher education TVET sector in South Africa, there also exists a strong tradition of adult and basic education provision, primarily offered through non-governmental organisations with the support of the State, as described in the sections to follow.

4.9 ADULT EDUCATION AND TRAINING IN SOUTH AFRICA

Adult Education and Training (AET) refers to all learning and training programmes for adults (a person who is 16 years and older) on Level 1 or below on the NQF. The Adult Education and Training Act 52 of 2000, which establishes this definition, also allows for the establishment of Public Adult Learning Centres (PALCs) and Private Adult learning Centres (ALCs). The legislative foundation for AET may be expanded upon as follows:

Adult Basic Education and Training (ABET) was introduced into the NQF in 2000 via the Adult Basic Education and Training Act. ABET training consists of four levels, which are equivalent to Grades R to 9 or General Education and Training (GET). ABET is different from GET, however, in that it contains an element of vocationally focused training. Once ABET Level 4 is passed, the learner is granted a qualification of NQF Level 1 and may proceed to FET training or any NQF Level 2 programme.

The Adult Education and Training Act 52 (2000) replaced the Adult Basic Education and Training Act, which was amended to, among others, substitute the expression 'adults basic education and training' for 'adult education and training'. One of the provisions of the act was the 'establishment, governance and funding of public adult learning centres', and the relevant definitions are as follows:

- 'adult' means a person who is sixteen years or older

- 'adult education and training' means all learning and training programmes for adults on level 1 registered on the national qualifications framework contemplated in the National Qualifications Framework Act (Act 67 of 2008)

- 'centre' means a public or private centre.

As per the act, a private centre must be registered with the Head of Department of Higher Education and Training (DHET).

AET allows adults, who have not completed their 'matric', to access post-schooling education opportunities, including college or university-based programmes, as well as enabling such individuals to take on more skilled roles in the workplace. The scope of AET covers a number of different sub-sectors including Business, Industry (including mining), public and private ALCs, Community-based Organisations (CBOs) and NGOs, trade unions, the Department of Correctional Services and universities.

4.10 PROVISION OF AET IN SOUTH AFRICA

According to the EDTP SETA Skills Plan (2014), as of 2013 there are 1671 public ALCs across South Africa, which offer general education to 258 787 learners (DHET 2013). Most Public ALCs operate from schools or community centres and in some cases, mostly in Gauteng, operate from closed schools. While the illustration below provides a visual depiction of the distribution of AET centres per province, as of 2011, the highest concentration remains in KwaZulu-Natal and Limpopo.

4.10.1 Programmes offered through Adult and Basic Education providers in South Africa

The types of programmes offered are primarily ABET qualifications and programmes including the General Education and Training Certificate (GETC) and Senior Certificate programmes. Most learners tend to study part-time. The learning programmes offered tend to cover the following subjects:

- Language, Literacy and Communication
- Mathematical Literacy, Mathematics and Mathematical Sciences
- Natural Science
- Arts and Culture
- Life Orientation
- Technology
- Human and Social Science
- Economic and Management Sciences

In addition, training may also cover:

- Small, Medium and Micro-enterprises (SMMEs)
- Tourism
- Agricultural Science
- Ancillary Health Care
- Aids Education
- Entrepreneurship
- Human Rights Education
- Voter Education

In addition to the ABET Levels 1–4 course offerings at the AET Centres, feed-back from surveys indicated the following school-based academic courses are on offer (Surveys 2014):

- Grade 12 (CAPS)
- CAP Rewriters
- NATED 550 (based on the old curriculum)

Other types of skills training courses also available include: Beadwork; Brick-laying; Cabinet-Making; Carpentry; Catering, Construction; Computer; Dressmaking; Embroidery; Fashion Design; Gardening; Joinery; Needle-work/Sewing; Secretarial; Sewing; and Welding.

Figure 4.1: Provincial spread of NGOs providing adult/continuing education

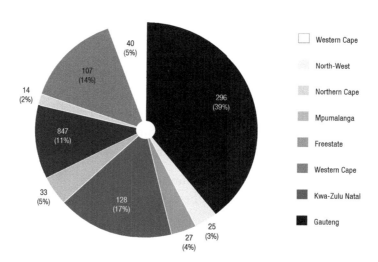

Source: DSD, Department of Social Development, www.dsd.gov.za

4.10.4 Employer profile of AET provision in South Africa

Adult Education and Training (AET) is offered in both the public and private sectors and these tend to be located in the townships and rural areas of South Africa (DHET 2013a). Currently, the public ALCs are the only institutions funded by the State that offer general education to adults. The DHET is now the biggest employer of adult educators through its public ALCs.

Figure 4.2: Provincial spread of AET Centres (n=3279)

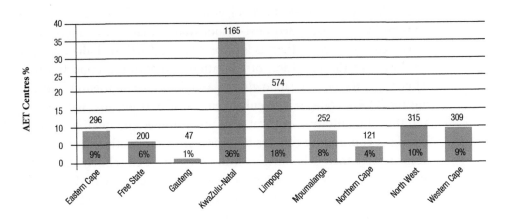

Source: Provincial Coordinators (2014)

Table 4.9 describes the employment rate per race groups in public ALCs. The decrease noted in 2013 may have more to do with the number of returns submitted from ALCs, than an actual reduction of members of staff as noted also in ETDP SETA Skills Plan (2014).

Table 4.9: Employees by race and gender (2011–13) at public ALCs

	2011	2012	2013
African male	3 551	3 392	2 320
African female	12 936	11 105	8 645
Coloured male	342	288	305
Coloured female	455	400	397
Indian male	14	9	8
Indian female	18	25	15
White male	23	28	25
White female	74	60	54
Other male	8	3	26
Other female	9	4	14
Total	17 430	15 314	11 809

Source: DHET (2011), DHET (2012), DHET (2013)

4.11 THE STATE OF EDUCATION AND TRAINING PROVISION IN SOUTH AFRICA

The 'White Paper for Post-School Education and Training' (2013) sets out a vision for a transformed post-school system that will be more equitable, expanded and diverse than it is at present, and will include a key role for employers in the provision of education and training opportunities. The white paper includes the following areas of focus: strengthening and expanding the TVET colleges, the enhancement of partnerships with employers, and the rationalisation of vocational programmes and qualifications; establishing of community colleges to cater mainly for youth and adults who did not complete their schooling or who never attended school; and improving access to post school education and training for people with disabilities.

The ETDP SETA Skills Plan notes the need for increasing the flexibility of Quality Councils to quality assure qualifications on NQF levels from which they were previously excluded (ETDP SETA Skills Plan 2014, 97–98).

Table 4.10: Scarce and critical skills demand in FET Colleges (ETDP SETA SSP 2014)

OFO Code	Occupations	Scarce and critical skills
134 502 134 505 134 503	CEO/Principal Deputy CEO/Principal Campus Manager	**Critical skills** Project management Communication Monitoring and evaluation Conflict management Report writing Policy development Financial management Stress management
134 506	Registrar	Governance and legislation
134 507	Heads of Departments	**Critical skills** Communication Monitoring and evaluation Report writing **Scarce skills** Curriculum design Research skills
212 102 211 101 232 120 235 601 215 101 242 401 242 302 243 101	Professionals Lecturer-Mathematics Lecturer-Science Lecturer-English Lecturer-IT Lecturer-engineering-electrical Training and staff development Marketing and advertising	**Scarce skills** Artisans ICT/IT Engineering Mathematics Pedagogic content knowledge Content knowledge Facilitation Workplace experience **Critical Skills** Research skills Classroom management Coaching and mentoring Assessor, Moderator Facilitator Tutoring

OFO Code	Occupations	Scarce and critical skills
242 301 242 403 242 404	Student Support Services Career counsellor Assessment practitioner Student support officer	Scarce skills Pastoral skills Psychometric testing Counselling Critical skills Data processing Conflict management Career guidance Project management Events management Inter-personal skills
311 501 311 301 652 302 718 201 715 501	Technicians and associated professionals Welding professionals Electronic technicians Fitter and turner Boiler operator Leather processing and operator	Scarce skill IT Critical skill Machine operating
411 101 121 101	Clerical Finance officers	Scarce skill IT Accounting

The TVET college sector is known to have weak institutional capacity: technical colleges are perhaps the most neglected and under-developed institutions in the South African educational landscape. Historically, they have existed on the margins of formal schooling and higher education.

In 2013, the introduction of the policy on Professional Qualifications for Lecturers in Technical and Vocational Education and Training (TVET), aimed at current FET lecturers, provides the impetus to ensure that suitable higher education qualifications are put in place for the training and professional development of lecturers. The policy states that:

> technical and vocational education and training (TVET) plays a pivotal role in developing a knowledgeable and skilled citizenry who are able to contribute effectively to the social and economic development of the country. It is important to ensure that TVET programmes provide real-world skills required by the public and private sectors. Social and economic growth of the country relies heavily on the development and maintenance of a viable, responsive and effective TVET sector. (Government Gazette no. 36554, 7)

4.13 DEMAND AND SUPPLY GAP ANALYSIS FOR TVET IN SOUTH AFRICA

The supply of lecturers into the TVET colleges comes from four sources. Firstly, universities supply graduates who have a degree or diploma, sometimes with a teaching qualification. Secondly, TVET colleges select lecturers from their own students who are excellent performers. The third source is from industry, which supplies experienced individuals but without pedagogical knowledge. Lastly, schools supply colleges with lecturers through the NCV programme. One key initiative has been the introduction of the Policy on Professional Qualifications for TVET (2013), aimed at addressing TVET lecturers' lack of teaching qualifications. One of the first gaps is the number of unqualified and under-qualified lecturers, particularly those with no industry experience or no teaching qualification. There is a need to ensure that lecturers are equipped with an appropriate lecturing qualification and in the future this will need to be aligned to the new policy for TVET lecturers once such qualifications have been registered on the NQF.

The current situation in colleges is that they will only take students based on the number of lecturers they have available in the different fields. While there are large numbers who fail to get entry into colleges, there is little in place to assist in taking care of the shortage of qualified lecturers in colleges. In an effort to satisfy the demand in industries, some colleges have increased their quotas, resulting in an increase in lecturer–student ratios.

An even more serious problem lies with the fundamental subjects, Mathematics, Mathematics Literacy and Life Orientation. Lecturers have had to fill in and teach courses that they have had no training in. One lecturer made the comment: 'Lecturing Life Orientation is a huge frustration because I cannot excel as it is not my speciality. I sometimes feel wasted' (Mgijima & Morobe 2012, 41). A further need is to increase the number of trained TVET lecturers in scarce subject areas, including fundamental subjects like Physical Science, Accounting and Engineering.

There is definitely a very high demand for lecturers in scarce skills area such as Engineering, Mathematics, Physical Science and Accounting. Data from the focused group discussions revealed that one of the major factors contributing to the high failure rate in TVET colleges is 'communication skills' (noted also by Gamble 2003). Thus the demand for communication skills is one priority area for all professionals in the colleges. (ETDP SETA Skills Plan 2014, 132–33).

The analysis of the survey and WSP submissions of 2012–13 shows a dichotomy of academic (training and development) skills in the scarce skills field and business-related skills in the critical skills field. The government's plan to create 300 000 jobs through the Green Economy Accord provides the impetus for new skills in the economy, and the private sector has a role to play. Surprisingly, none of the institutions surveyed nor those who submitted

WSPs for 2011–12 mentioned 'green occupations' (DHET Guidelines OFO, 13) either in the scarce or critical skills category (ETDP SETA Skills Plan, 134–35).

4.14 TVET COLLEGES: A WAY FORWARD

In 2014, the TVET colleges in South Africa were audited. Fourteen of the fifty were given an F for audits according to Bongani Nkosi (07 Nov 2014), while college principals were given a year to fix their severely flawed administrative systems. The audits revealed a number of systemic problems pointing to the absence of capacity for good governance: 'salary overpayments not recovered, no evidence that new positions and tenders were advertised and no supporting documentation for student bursary payments' (Nkosi 2014). Qonde (*Mail & Guardian* 2014) was quoted as saying that the department (DHET) wanted to improve the 'control environment in the colleges, especially financial control environment ... so that we're able to account quite appropriately for monies of the public that go to these institutions'. Despite vast sums of funding being allocated to the colleges (increased from 3.8 billion rand in 2010 to 5.4 billion rand in 2014), and government plans to increase enrolment at the institutions to R1.25 million by 2030. In 2013 only 39% of the colleges' candidates obtained the NCV Level Four certificate, which is equivalent to matric (Grade 12).

Nevertheless, despite these challenges, the TVET band has important contributions to make in the realisation of these economic and social goals. It can contribute in important ways to the development of an export-led and globally competitive manufacturing sector through the education and training of a highly skilled and innovative workforce. But the widely differentiated character of South Africa's economy imposes a range of additional responsibilities Scholars agree that the TVET band is critical to the development of the information economy because it is at the intersection of a wide range of government policies that are critical to the new information economy: macro-economic, industrial, labour market and human resource development policies. Second, TVET is also at the crossroads between GET, HET, work and community and personal life. TVET will become increasingly central to the achievement of lifelong learning by facilitating and encouraging learners along the qualification ladder.

Government has recently begun to explore the possibility of establishing community colleges that are located at a level between universities, on the one hand, and TVET colleges, on the other. TVET colleges operate on Levels 2, 3 and 4 of the NQF, whereas community colleges are expected to operate at least on Level 5 (universities are on Level 5 and higher). Community colleges have been instituted in different parts of the world to provide for the needs of those who have already passed Grade 12 but cannot gain access to universities. Their presence is important in view of massification (the shift from elite participation in higher education to mass participation), the advent of globalisation, competition, differentiation, the free market and the knowledge society.

While higher education attendance in South Africa stands at 17%, which is high in comparison with the rest of sub-Saharan Africa, it is low in comparison with other middle-income countries where this figure is typically from 35% to 40%, and sometimes even higher (RSA 2012a, 38). Of those that form the 17%, the attrition rate is rather high – only about a third of students complete their university courses (RSA 2012a, 41). It is no wonder then that the National Development Plan (2011) states in its prologue that democracy cannot flourish in a sea of poverty, that a sustainable growth and development cycle has to be put into place, and that more people have to be placed in permanent jobs (RSA 2011, 2–3; RSA 2012a, x). Although the plan envisages an increase among students at higher education level, from 17% to 30%, it is clear that universities will not be able to accommodate these greater numbers. This underscores the importance of introducing community colleges, which are known to be much cheaper to establish than universities.

Recently a government initiative to create community colleges has seen 13 former TVET colleges selected to offer programmes at NQF Level 5. Preparations have also been made for offering level 6 qualifications at some of these selected colleges (RSA 2013; RSA 2012b). According to a report by the Centre for Higher Education and Transformation, around 700 000 students are eligible for these forms of training, and it therefore advises that the roles and functions of Further Education and Training Colleges should be extended by allowing them to offer certain university courses as well as courses of their own at university level (Cloete & Butler-Adams 2012, 11–13). The increased diversification of higher education in South Africa, both in terms of institution types and programmes, bodes well for the sector and for youth leaving schools and seeking skilled employment. Capacity development in the sector, however, is critical and so higher education institutions (like universities) need to engage with opportunity in a timely fashion in order to assist colleges with programmes for expansion and effective delivery.

PART TWO:
Transformation for equality of recognition and provision in education

5   Gender and diversity in education transformation

5.1 INTRODUCTION

The South African Constitution (1996) recognises historical and structural inequalities pertaining to groups 'based on perceived or "real" differences' (De Vos 2004, 185). The Bill of Rights frames the protection of particular groups on the basis of discrimination both in the past and present in South Africa as follows:

Chapter 2: Bill of Rights

3. Equality

(1) Everyone is equal before the law and has the right to equal protection and benefit of the law.

(3) The State may not unfairly discriminate directly or indirectly against anyone on one or more grounds, including race, gender, sex, pregnancy, marital status, ethnic or social origin, colour, sexual orientation, age, disability, religion, conscience, belief, culture, language and birth.

Law thus has an important role to play 'in reordering ... power relations in ways which strive to ensure that all individuals are treated as if they have the same moral worth' (De Vos 2004, 185). Rancière argues that '... the rights of (people) and of the citizen are the rights of those who make them a reality. They were won through democratic action and are ... guaranteed through such action' (2006, 74). The 'White Paper on Education and Training' (1995) frames the spirit of reforms in education. 'The realisation of democracy, liberty, equality, justice and peace is a necessary condition for the full pursuit and enjoyment of lifelong learning. It should be a goal of education and training … on the basis that all South Africans without exception share the same inalienable rights … and that all forms of bias (especially racial, ethnic and gender) are dehumanising' (DoE 1995, 22). That said, ideal intentions notwithstanding, policy is unlikely to succeed if little account is taken of the conditions of policy implementation (Enslin & Pendlebury 1998).

The focus on gender in education and as part of necessary change in education is owed also to the feminist (or womanist: see Hassim (2004) on the distinctions between feminism and womanism in the context of the struggle for liberation in South Africa) movement in South Africa and beyond. The famous Women's March on Pretoria in the 1950s illustrates and symbolises the struggle of women for recognition and also the solidarity with men in the struggle for freedom. This appears to be in recognition of the fact that 'gender oppression is everywhere rooted in a material base and is expressed in socio-cultural traditions and attitudes all of which are supported and perpetuated by an ideology which subordinates women in South Africa' (Bentley 2003, 1). Lewis suggests that by the mid-1980s, anti-apartheid organisations such as the United Democratic Front (UDF), and trade unions such as the Congress of South African Trade Unions (COSATU), were acknowledging the distinct dynamic and importance of gender politics and justice (Lewis 2004a). It is thus important to realise that a focus on access, equality and gender included a sense that the rights and opportunities of women in South Africa had to be addressed as part of the transformation project, particularly in sectors such as schooling, higher education, the public service and the economy. It was also recognised that women had played a critical role in the liberation movements and that their resistance (typified in the famous Women's March to Pretoria in 1956) had provided momentum and support for all people oppressed in South Africa under the apartheid regime. Redress, not only in terms of improving the material conditions of women, was thus part of the thinking about what ought to change once the African National Congress came to power in 1994. This has been well documented by a range of scholars, not least by Unterhalter (2003, 2007) and others. Initiatives (for example, the Gender Task Team, 2011) set up by the government have had far-reaching effects on public awareness of women's rights and gender in general. Thus a focus on women in schooling and in higher education is regarded both as necessary and politically appropriate.

Paradoxically, education as a profession is dominated by women and of the four education ministers, the two women, Naledi Pandor and Angie

Motshekga, have enjoyed considerably longer terms of office than the two men, Bhengu and Asmal. That teaching is a profession dominated by women is belied by the notable under-representation of women in leadership and management positions in schools, and in the bureaucracy of the national and provincial education departments. Since 1994 there has been a commitment to secure equity in promotions in education. Despite that initial commitment, by 2007 fewer than 30% of women occupied middle-management positions and even fewer are in top management posts. Pressure from teacher unions is evident in patches, but gender as a political platform within unions tends to be obscured by other leadership issues and scandals. Thus even a prominent female union leader has commented as follows: 'The gains made for women have been bargaining achievements, which produced material benefits such as pay parity, maternity leave, affirmative action for promotion, and so on. However, the organisational life of the union continues to be non-supportive of women' (Mannah 2005, 151). Organisational life, as described here, and culture and ethos, as described later, remain the fundamental barriers to the progress of formerly disadvantaged groups (women, gay people, the poor) in South Africa. In short, society must be made to change, and change can only occur through better teachers and a better higher education system. Disappointment at the lack of progress in the 20 years is evident both amongst scholars and activists concerned with gender and the way it has been approached structurally (that is in terms of appointments, selection and recruitment of women into leadership), and educationally. In education terms two perspectives are worth noting: first the approaches taken towards the teaching of gender awareness or gender issues in schools. These may be described as patchy at best and have often stalled in the face of teachers' own perceptions about gender roles and stereotyping. The second perspective concerns the extent to which pedagogy is deeply encultured with patriarchal and hetero-normative beliefs.

Wolpe (2005) noted ten years after the Gender Equity Task Team (GETT) Report was produced, that there was a marked difference between what had been recommended in the report and what had actually happened by way of implementation:

> The GETT Report recommended the training for teachers in both pre-service and in-service training, in gender understanding. It was recommended that such training include theoretical and experiential understandings, as well as knowledge about violence. The Strategic Plan has settled for far less. The recommendation for the first year, 2004, is that one district official and one teacher per school in all provinces, be trained in equity in the classroom. This is unclear. What does

equity mean? There is no mention of training to deal with broad gender issues and violence. (Wolpe 2005, 127)

In South Africa, concerns about the professional integrity of teachers (not to mention the delivery on policy targets and aims) are a major factor when considering the place and contested nature of gender as both a focus in education, and indeed a national transformation focus. Numerous reports exist of teachers exploiting their positions of authority and failing in their duty of care, and gender prejudice is often a factor (see Appendix 2 for media coverage on the subject). Wilson (2007) argues that 'as this duty of care fades and breaks down within communities, sexual violence against girls is considered "normal". Where the protection and rights are not in place, behaviour in school is likely to reflect the beliefs and norms of the culture, as young girls are exposed to acts of violence they are learning to accept it as an inevitable part of their daily lives' (Wilson 2007, 5). If girls are subject to violence then the same is equally if not more true of people who are not identified as heterosexual. Thus lesbian, gay, bisexual, transgender, transsexual, intersex and queer (LGBTTIQ) children and adults are rendered even more vulnerable to violence in all sectors associated with society, despite constitutional provisions that are designed to protect them from discrimination.

This chapter explores a range of issues arising from the scholarship over a twenty-year period. The first section looks at the motivation behind the inclusion of gender as one of the foci associated with the transformation project in South Africa. The second section provides an overview of data concerning girls' and boys' academic performance in schools within a range of subject areas over a period of time, and then further data concerning dropout and success rates in the context of one province. This data then leads to a reading of issues typically contested in relation to gender in education in South Africa to illustrate the argument that focusing only on quantitative data belies a series of complex issues that pertain to the changes still needed in society itself; changes that can only be effected through better education and by a more confident and competent teacher corps, themselves re-educated for alignment with the values enshrined in the Constitution (1996).

The chapter concludes with reflections on issues of violence, abuse and patriarchy, arguing, in the context of education, that training is not enough if not reinforced by changes in attitudes, perceptions and behaviour on the part of adults in relation to children.

5.2 A FOCUS ON GENDER IN SOUTH AFRICA

Chisholm and September (2005) argue that there is a major gap between gender policies and what happens at the classroom level, and query the extent to which publications raising awareness of the gaps in equality need to be 'mediated and communicated at school level.' Scholars acknowledge the work done in relation to writing policy frameworks with targets regarding representation, but that there is still a 'lack of gender sensitivity amongst departmental officials, coupled with gender rhetoric unmatched by gender-sensitive organisational cultures' (Chisholm & September 2005, 8).

Thus, for example, Subrahmanian (Chisholm & September 2005) refers to evidence of equality 'gains' as a criterion against which to assess the actual development in terms of how many women are in education, employment and leadership, and at which levels 'actions to translate the standard of equality into meaningful redistribution of resources and opportunities, and the transformation of the conditions in which women are being encouraged to make choices. Progress in both arenas has taken place, but I would argue, more in terms of establishing an equality discourse, and considerably less in terms of redistributive actions' (Subrahmanian 2005, 29).

These developments need to be further contextualised within a global perspective in which neo-liberal economic policies focus on driving down the costs of labour, and given that women are already vulnerable in these terms, it is not surprising that they bear the burden of such policies within an already vulnerable context. Neo-liberal economic discourse is increasingly shaping the way in which policy approaches are evolving in other spheres, for example that of social policy and governance systems (Molyneux & Razavi 2002). Education has always been particularly prone to ideological manipulation, given the political nature of the returns arising from it.

Fine (2001) argues that substantively not much has changed in relation to the material conditions of women, and essentially that within this climate, the State has a larger role to play in the protection of vulnerable or minority groups. Although the Post-Washington Consensus acknowledges the importance of history, institutions, processes and social dynamics as relevant to the understanding of development and change, the frameworks and intellectual tools still accord primacy to neo-classical economics and the dominance of the market. The State has been brought back into the picture, but only as a corrective for market failure and on the premise that 'State failure must be no worse than the market failure it is designed to remedy' (Subrahmanian 2005, 33). Mannah (in Chisholm & September 2005), for example, has argued that the Growth, Employment and Redistribution Plan (*GEAR* 1996) and the economic policy espoused by the Mandela and then Mbeki presidencies, entrenched the inequalities of the past, especially in rural African schools. Teachers' unions (notably the South African Democratic Teachers' Union) in this period galvanised against *GEAR*, but since the South African Democratic Teachers Union (SADTU) as a member of the Congress of South African Trade Unions (COSATU), which has been part of a political alliance with the ANC for the last 20 years, the ability to shift *GEAR* was compromised and the impact SADTU might have had at best has been limited. SADTU, as a teachers' union, was directly affected by the cuts in education budgets by the neo-liberal notions of down-sizing (Mannah 2005, 149).

The gains made for women have been bargaining achievements, which produced material benefits such as pay parity, maternity leave, affirmative action for promotion and so on. However, the organisational life of the union continues to be non-supportive of women (Mannah, 151).

That said, the material conditions of women in work (whether teaching or other professions) remain problematic. Though South Africa is celebrated for being seventh in the world in terms of the numbers of women represented in parliament, the *Emerging Voices* report (Nelson Mandela Foundation, Chisholm & Porteus 2011) shows that girls still perform most domestic labour in relation to child-led households, have fewer opportunities than boys in school, tend to drop out more than boys in school (see Mahlomaholo 2011 later in this chapter) and higher education (see Chapter 3), and still tend to earn less than their male counterparts. Wilson (2007) notes that 'School-related violence in developing countries takes place on the context of inequality and specific cultural beliefs and attitudes about gender roles, especially concerning male and female sexuality, a pattern of economic inequality, and in some instances significant political unrest and violent conflict' (Wilson 2007, 4). In 2003 a report released by the Medical Research Council (MRC) noted that 17% of students carried weapons, 41% of students were bullied, 14% belonged to gangs, 15% had been forced to have sex, 15% had been threatened or injured on school property and 19% were injured in fights and 32% felt unsafe at school (MRC 2003; First National South African Youth Behaviour Survey).

Access to stated rights to equity and equality of opportunity is therefore mediated by two limitations: the first concerns the material position of girls/women *vis-à-vis* boys/men, and the second concerns the political will to effect and lead change in a context were competing priorities sometimes hinder either access to, or the expression of, equality for girls/women. Bentley (2003) notes, for example, that arguments made concerning the protection of cultural beliefs in which Customary Law conflicts with Constitutional law are often portrayed as conflicting sets of rights, whereas the claims are 'in fact thinly disguised attempts to entrench the power and privilege of one group over another' (Bentley 2003, 2). Bentley illustrates this reference by referring to the practice in Customary Law of allowing only male descendants to inherit.

The Framework for Women, Girls and Gender Equality in National Strategic Plans on HIV and AIDS in Southern and Eastern Africa (2011) notes that 'Gender Inequality – refers to the socially constructed power relationship between men and women, which proscribes certain behaviours, linked to achieving or sustaining forms of masculinity or femininity, and which also structure access to resources in inequitable ways. These factors typically create situations in which men have greater power and resources than women' (2011).

> Goal 5: NSPs must reduce vulnerability to HIV, and address the structural determinants of HIV transmission for women and girls. Specific interventions and approaches should include:

> Preventing HIV Transmission among Women and Girls: Comprehensive sexuality education for all women, men, girls and boys (both in and out of school) which includes factual information on knowing one's body and a focus on gender equality, human rights, and transforming social norms in order to enable women and girls to decide whether, when, with whom, and how to have sex.

> Goal 10: Key Stakeholders: NSPs must ensure the inclusion in all processes and consideration of the specific needs of the following groups.

Though the Framework makes reference to LGBTTIQ persons explicitly, albeit in a footnote, it is recognised that gender as a category is inclusive of hetero/bisexual women, as well as the range of masculinities and femininities associated with sexuality. Gender is thus endorsed within the Framework as an appropriate focus for education in schools and beyond. The extracts above show the reach anticipated in the Framework with regard to gender in education and gender in relation to communities beyond schools and issues affecting schools (such as HIV/AIDS).

The United Nations' Millennium Development Goal (MDG 3) specifically promotes gender equality and women's empowerment (2005; 2010), as part of the priorities that need to be addressed in Africa. Mahlomaholo (2011, 314) notes that 'the underperformance of girls emanates from research that blames schooling for this phenomenon'. But, as Chisholm (2005) and

Unterhalter (2005) note, there are structural factors, not the least of which include cultural beliefs, perceptions and practices that have an impact on the material circumstances of girls (also noted by Hammond et al. 2007; Mugaga & Akumo 2010). The *Emerging Voices* report notes poverty as the single most important factor in girls' well-being and prospects. Having discussed the framing of aspirations with regard to the eradication of sexism in the workplace and schools, the following sections contextualise discussions concerning gender with reference to girls and schooling.

5.3 CONTEXTS IN WHICH GENDER MATTERS IN SCHOOLS

There is no substantive evidence to suggest that there are differences between girls' and boys' school performance in South Africa. Unterhalter's work on the performance of girls demonstrates this clearly, showing that South African male and female children's performance mirrors international trends. The gross intake rate (GIR) is the number of new entrants into the first grade regardless of age as a percentage of children of official age for entry into primary school. Net intake rate (NIR) is the number of new entrants into primary school of official age for entry as a percentage of all new entrants (Unterhalter 2005, 81).

Unterhalter (83) shows across a range of measures (including gross rates of girls and boys who enter primary and secondary school, those who survive from primary school to secondary school, and gender equity ratios) that there is a consistently higher ratio of girls to boys in the education system. That said, figures associated with the UNESCO report (2003) suggest that girls do not succeed as well as boys within the system.

Table 5.1: Equality of outcomes: Senior Certificate examination results 2001

% female candidates entered	55
% female candidates failed	39
% male candidates failed	32
% female candidates passed	60
% male candidates passed	68
% female candidates passed at higher level	14.5
% male candidates passed at higher level	15.6

Source: DoE 2003, 22–23

Girls achieve at an equal level with boys in many subjects at primary and secondary level. 'While girls do not do as well as boys in maths and physical sciences, their achievements in biology and English are equivalent' (Unterhalter 2005, 84). This is not dissimilar to performance in other countries.

Table 5.2: Equality of outcomes: Senior Certificate results by gender in selected subjects 2001

% female candidates entered passing maths	43
% male candidates entered passing maths	51
% female candidates passing physics	66
% male entered candidates passing physics	71
% female candidates entered passing biology	66
% male entered candidates passing biology	69
% female entered candidates passing EAL	3
% male entered candidates passing EAL	94

Source: Edusource, 2002 (note: EAL = English Additional Language)

The above noted, there are nevertheless disturbing trends when it comes to the rates at which girls and young women exit the education system, whether in schooling or higher education. Explanations for these trends have nothing to do with ability (as shown previously), and everything to do with the positioning of women and girls within South Africa from a cultural and historical perspective. These trends are best illustrated with reference to some research undertaken by academics in South Africa. It goes without saying that this research is informed by feminism and feminist research both internationally and nationally.

5.3.1 Gender in the school curriculum: Life Orientation

Based on the *Beijing Platform for Action*, common aspirations such as focusing on girls' performance in education, promoting the participation of women in government and leadership, and ensuring that curriculum materials are gender responsive, became common features of government policy in developing countries (such as Kenya and SA).

South Africa is a signatory to the MDG, and as such the MDG is committed to eradicating gender inequality as part of the process of improving the lives of all citizens. Access is important as a consideration in relation to access to education, and access in the curriculum. The Gender Policy Framework frames equality in terms of gender as relating mostly to equal opportunities for men and women towards individuation. Research on policy in gender tends to group around three themes:

Gender reform: The removal of obstacles to women and the creation of equal opportunity for women are part of gender reform's commitment to redistribution. Curricula ideally in this theme are non-gender specific or gender blind; there is little account of curricula empowering or constraining women in terms of design and requirements. It has been criticised as political symbolism.

Gender resistance: critical of gender reform and women aspiring to become like men. Draws on radical feminism in which men and women are seen as radically different and the differences have to be accounted for. Curriculum is seen in this theme as a social product in which the subject positions of women and the 'silences' in the curriculum on men have to be accounted for and described.

Gender rebellion: this theme tends to refuse the categories of difference as aspired to within gender resistance, emphasising rather the multifarious forms of gendered identity in which category blurring is a feature or trait. Of all three themes this one is most inclusive in acknowledging the inter-sectionality of gender and sexuality, orientation, transnational, transgender and other identity categories or descriptions. In other words, the complexity of gender is foregrounded in this theme, in which the empowerment of women is not the only cause, there being more than one gender open to consideration.

South Africa's latest two policy shifts in the school curriculum have been the National Curriculum Statement (NCS) and the Curriculum and Assessment Policy Statement (CAPS, 2011). Teaching about gender in both revisions was meant to take place as part of the subject Life Orientation. Simmonds (2014, 643) notes that curriculum-making in both the NCS and in the CAPS is dominated by content relating to gender inequality and the disempowerment of women. The teaching is framed by issues in which the vulnerability of women to abuse is highlighted, as also is their potential failure in observing or policing their own sexuality adequately. Gender in the curriculum is a descriptive characteristic, whereas Judith Butler regards gender as a mode of being, interacting and making sense of the world. Simmonds makes reference to a compulsory (for all secondary school learners) subject in the school curriculum known as Life Orientation, in which gender is meant to feature.

Simmonds argus that girls are portrayed as powerless victims and the agency of boys remains invisible. There is little or no deconstruction of gender binaries, let alone the questioning of gender categories. Furthermore, the role that gender plays in society, and the world of work in particular, is ignored. Thus a refusal to see how or why gender equality is important leads to the invisibility of any account concerning gender and work. This is an example of the curriculum being 'gender blind', but not acknowledging that gender makes a difference to work, and how equality comes to be framed in the workplace. That noted, the 2002 curriculum made reference to gender-race-LGBTTIQ issues across the curriculum. Thus, while the issues have been formally articulated, they are addressed unevenly across the different subjects at primary and secondary level. Furthermore, and as noted elsewhere in the chapter, the transmission of information and its mediation by teachers accounts probably for the deafening silence concerning these issues in day-to-day teaching in South Africa. In the last five years, the DBE has also brought out a much more advanced version of the manual (*DBE Speak Out*, 2010) for dealing with gender issues, which extends the focus found in earlier texts.

In the latest curriculum (CAPS) adaptation, reference to gender is made in relation to values developments around sexual behaviour (and the dangers associated with HIV/AIDS, for example), age-appropriate behaviour (older people, adults, younger people, children), or recreation and leisure activities across cultures. There is in curriculum reform more recognition of the intersectionality of gender in relation to ethnicity, culture, religion and so on, which can allow the teacher to explore areas of ambiguity. Such advances must be seen also in the light of the critique of policy documentation developed by Naidoo (2014), in which she notes the gradual disappearance over time of the discourses associated with education transformation as part of the social and political change anticipated by the Constitution (1996) itself in the early 1990s.

Problematic conceptualisations include the association of sexual activity with unhealthy values, without recognition that religious and cultural beliefs frame sexual mores and associated values (for example, honesty and chastity) differently. Despite the opening up of awareness to enable more sensitive explorations of sexuality and gender, the reality of gender-based violence in schools remains deeply troubling; it suggests that teachers are ill-equipped to broach, let alone lead, discussions in these areas, and that the cultural embeddedness of the schools within communities compromises the position of teachers in relation to the tension between subjects encouraged to be addressed in CAPS, which parents and communities cannot themselves speak about to children with ease or confidence. The point here is that education institutions often carry the full burden of social expectations in terms of change, non-sexism, non-racism, inclusion and gender equality, but are themselves sites for the very contestation of these expectations as articulated by the state, or teachers (and in higher education, by academics). Disappointment is most routinely articulated in relation to the seeming contrast (and even contradictions) between the evident awareness at policy level of the need to address male behaviour in relation to the perceptions of women and men concerning gender equality occurs, and the reality of gender-based violence in schools (and beyond) most often perpetrated by men or boys against girls and women.

For example, the DBE *Teenage Pregnancy* report (2009) reported 59 436 cases of teenage pregnancy, an increase from 8058 in (2004) to 16 320 (2008). Simmonds (2014) notes that NCS to CAPS saw a shift from rights-talk to values-talk (647) with its mentioning of diversity and difference as areas worth exploring. It is clear for Simmonds that policy is responsive to shifts in society, but that teachers and schools need to engage with curriculum-making more inclusively, with a commitment to challenge the boundaries but not at the expense or disempowerment of women. Clearly binary perceptions of gender as held by teachers, let alone children in schools, are problematic. The impact of such perceptions, derived as they are from homes, communities and a wider socio-political milieu, requires a deeper analysis than simply participation rates. With that in mind, the sections to follow explore the impact of factors that affect performance, retention and throughput of girls in schools in one particular province.

It is estimated that the population of the North-West Province is made up of 1 635 500 females and 1 565 400 males (Stats SA 2010). This is more or less in line with the South African national gender distribution of around 52% females and 48% males (Stats SA 2010). Given this observation, it would thus be expected that girls would constitute between 51% and 52% of the participants in this study, but they actually totalled 61% of all the ESLs identified randomly herein (Mahlomaholo 2011, 314).

Mahlomaholo provides illustrative data that links structural factors to performance in schools. Between 1998–2009, about 10 829 youth left school early, before completing their Grade 12, in the North-West Province alone. Of these, 6636 were girls and 4193 were boys. Girls who left school early were mostly unable to secure casual work after school (5606 boys and 3715 girls). Data returned on a survey of boys and girls who left school early indicates that more girls (1444) than boys (1240) had left because they could not 'cope with the demands of learning; thus, ultimately failing their grades' (Mahlomaholo 2011). More girls (275 compared to 157 boys) indicated that they left school because they did not have the energy and the will to walk long distances to school. The *Emerging Voices* report (Nelson Mandela Foundation, Chisholm & Porteus 2011) confirms that many out-of-school youth come from rural areas where the conditions are not conducive to effective learning (not least of which because girls have domestic duties). This is also confirmed in Mahlomaholo's (2011) study, where he found that 'more girls (21) than boys (16) also left school early because they had to look after their siblings who were ill ... [or] ... because of the death and/or the employment engagements of their parents at far-off industrial areas'. Unsurprisingly, then, more girls (1009) are likely to leave school than boys (907) for reasons to do with motivation. Poverty also tended to affect girls (1207) negatively to a greater extent than it affected boys (967) (Mahlomaholo 2011, 317). Unterhalter notes the danger of seeing the challenge only from the perspective of resources: 'The high levels of sexual violence reported in schools are one feature of the ways in which participation in education is not a simple process of enrolment and retention and passing exams as resourcist measures suggest. Sexual discrimination and violence in school intersect with political and cultural forms of subordination, but these relations do not appear in the resourcist measures' (Unterhalter 2005, 85).

It goes without saying that the most vulnerable girls are those from working-class backgrounds in which the roles assigned to girls are menial, low-status and the most open to abuse from older or male siblings (Balfanz & Legter 2004; Fausto-Sterling 2000; Mahlomaholo 2011, 317). An understanding of gender begins with appreciating how boys and girls are socialised before arriving at schools. In a study on the influence of gender on the reception and interpretation of texts by adolescent rural youth in KwaZulu-Natal, Balfour (2000) found that boys appeared to display little awareness of their mutual responsibility for the violence inflicted by men and the silence imposed upon women. Stories in which women were typically maltreated by men tended to evoke empathy only when the discussions between children were mixed male and females. Boys, when interviewed on their own, empathised with the male aggressors and the discussions focused then on the women who had evidently provoked fathers or male peers to inflict punishments. It is evident in much of the research undertaken that a change of perceptions and attitudes is possible when teachers themselves believe in the need for such change and are able to engage readers through literature, history, geography and other social sciences, with a sense of urgency around the need for men to change their attitudes, perceptions and values in relation to women and their abilities to participate fully and equally in society. Through texts and language extension on the one hand, and social critique on the other, learners become aware of how patriarchal norms and values render irresponsibility of men invisible, or their collective power implicit, in the regulating of women's sexuality. What soon becomes evident is that traditional gender roles (man as warrior and decision-maker, woman as agriculturist and carer), even in rural and isolated areas, are in many cases no longer viable, or exist only in corrupt forms (Balfour 2000, 12).

Exploring the performance of gender in schools (Ralfe & Balfour 2008; Buthelezi in De Lange et al. 2010) has shown that the perceptions and attitudes of boys and men, and also women, about what is appropriate and culturally acceptable behaviour, severely restrict the prospects of equality and equal treatment for girls. The performance of boys and then girls, and then young people in schools and universities, needs to be set against this background in South Africa.

Given the evident need for stronger interventions by teachers as well as communities, the following section considers some challenges associated with research and interventions regarding gender in schools.

5.4 RESEARCHING AND INTERVENING IN GENDER REGIMES IN SOUTH AFRICA: SOME EXAMPLES IN AND OUT OF SCHOOLS

In policy terms, women enjoy equal opportunities to men in present-day South Africa. Discrimination on the basis of gender is illegal and there are concerted attempts by the State to ensure that employment opportunities (through the Employment Equity Act of 1998) for women alongside men even in work formerly not considered appropriate to women is not only possible, but also planned. Thus, government departments and employers must report on and present to the Department of Labour (DoL) their Employment Equity plans and forecasts and are, under law, obliged to make provision for the equal representation of women in leadership, skilled as well as unskilled work. For example, the 'White Paper on Affirmative Action in the Public Service' of 1998 stated the following targets:

> 50% of black people should be at management level by 1999;
> 30% of women should be at management level by 1999; and
> 2% of people with disabilities should be at management level by 2005.

A range of statistics reported on from year to year includes the numbers of women in management or senior positions. Despite twenty years of planning at policy level, progress in real terms remains painfully slow. And as has been shown, the primary reason for this has to do with the fact that until social change is effected insert after effected by communities, community leaders, as well as teachers and adults in general, such that girls and women are no longer vulnerable to the material and social conditions that prevent, exclude and hinder their development, policy preparation, reporting and debate necessarily reveal disappointment year on year. Unterhalter notes that the studies on this issue 'tend to note forms of exclusion and discrimination, rather than equal representation. Thus we know that, with some very notable exceptions, women are unequally represented in senior management positions in educational institutions and in senior decision-making bodies in government where resources are allocated' (Unterhalter 2005, 85). Institutions, whether partly autonomous (like universities), or state-controlled (like schools), represent particular opportunities for intervention in the wider society with a view to achieving the creation of an inclusive discourse pertaining to equality for women, persons of different sexual orientations, persons with disabilities. Together with the creation of that discourse there arises an opportunity in institutions to create and give effect to policies that enable and indeed empower previously disadvantaged groups. The expectations thus arising from the State, and finding their focus in public and other institutions, are not misplaced. At the same time, however, institutions are deeply enculturated spaces in which historical patterns concerning power and privilege come to be represented. Thus, while the State might envisage institutions as sites on which transformation may effectively occur, or be initiated, institutions reflect both current trends and developments, historical legacy patterns as well as the aspirations of the State concerning social change with a view to equality and inclusion. It is inevitable that sometimes contrary impulses are reflected and contested within institutional settings. In schools, such contestation sometimes makes reference to tensions between traditional cultural values and those adopted by the institution of the school.

Bentley (2003) has noted in relation to gender and culture, that traditional leaders of rural communities in South Africa argue that 'African culture and traditions are generally more communitarian than those in the West'. For Bentley and others this assertion is largely irrelevant and sometimes even inappropriate when used to justify the treatment of girls as a subordinated and oppressed group, but the argument used to reinforce 'hierarchical norms and practices, at the expense of more vulnerable members of a group, is in some sense justified on this basis' (Bentley 2003, 3). In any analysis, from a legal perspective of collective rather than individual rights, Bentley makes the important point that ideally, 'collective rights are rights that are asserted by collectives, or groups, or communities, but which, in fact, break down to something that can just as well be practised by individuals, and which would retain their viability in the absence of the group. Furthermore, culture and tradition are not necessary conditions for the assertion of such rights, as they are generated by a pre-existing interest or justification for that practice' (Bentley 2003, 4).

The point of the Constitutional dispensation in South Africa is to identify those groups previously subjected to unequal treatment by virtue of their gender, colour or sexual orientation in order to make special provision to rectify the injustices of the past, with a view to the creation of a more equitable and equal future – at least in terms of possibilities for self-development. For Bentley, the question to ask in South Africa is: when is it right to mete out unequal treatment? And the answer to this is that there is still a need for the State to intervene in the interests of groups subject to unequal treatment in order to prevent the continuation of such treatment. Unfortunately this is easier said than done, since meting out unequal treatment to rectify existing inequality, especially when the conditions that produce that inequality are cultural or material, or lie in the fact of poverty, is difficult. Unterhalter notes that there are definite cultural practices that call on males to prove that they are no longer virgins and that they can have girlfriends. In other words, the way in which peer pressure operates is a feature in the development of male sexual violence (Unterhalter 2005, 130).

In this context, the actors producing disadvantage might not only be people or organisations, but could equally be opportunities, communities or geographic localities. The protections enabled by the Constitution can thus only reasonably focus on the protection of particular groups, but the State and society have the responsibility to ensure that conditions that produce inequality are addressed effectively. Education has been seen as a means by which awareness of those conditions is married to the skills and knowledge needed to effect changes in the very terms in which inequality (in its material and other forms) can be changed. Some scholars have undertaken research on how best to raise awareness of the constitutional provisions as part of what it means to be a full citizen in South Africa. Yet, even within the context of initiatives focusing on 'civic education' for example, Finkel and Ernst (2005, 335) note that 'under the right pedagogical and "classroom climate" conditions, civic education can be an effective agent not only for increasing democratic values and skills, but also for facilitating the integration of these orientations into a more general democratic belief system'. This point is also noted by Mahlomaholo, who argues that: 'Good teaching has to be in place in order to identify the possible problems of early school leaving before they occur, together with adequate pre-emptive measures which could involve counselling these girls on a one-to-one basis and in groups' (Mahlomaholo 2011, 319).

Initiatives concerning civic education as sponsored by USAID and other important non-governmental groups are worthy, and often take place in partnership with government. An example of such a national Departmental initiative was the Girls' Empowerment Movement (GEM, 2004–6), and the related Boys' Empowerment Programme (also known as the Boys' Empowerment Movement or BEM), also. Wilson commented on GEM: 'GEM professes that through the establishment of strong partnerships schools/communities can respond to three inter-related threats to education in South Africa – gender inequality, violence in schools and the impact of HIV and AIDS' (Wilson 2007, 7). Methodological weaknesses often accompany intervention initiatives and ultimately undermine them. Thus Wilson, on GEM, reported that there were no assigned activities or practices associated with the GEM programme and so it was left to practitioners to more or less 'do their own thing'. In certain instances the GEM workshops focused on enhancing students' abilities to be creative leaders within the school and beyond through drama, music and sport. The initiative displayed in some surveyed schools could just as easily be regarded as lost opportunities in other schools where the commitment of teachers to the children appears to be less evident: 'On one occasion matric students were taking an exam and the classroom was stormed by teachers. These teachers demanded the exams from the students and tore them up and turned over desks. Students who did not release their exams were beaten and threatened … Yet on the ground in the day to day experiences of girl learners there is very little application of the GEM initiative displayed in most classrooms' (Wilson 2007, 9). These factors support the argument that gender-based violence does not happen simply because children in schools are likely to engage in such acts, but often because the very example provided by teachers is corrupting. A series of factors contribute to the violence that is produced within the schools, but which certainly draws upon what is evident also in community and family life: 'Teachers can be key instruments for change. However, they have their own experiences as gendered beings … This growth can only come through provision of resources and education' (Wilson 2007, 11).

In 2013, the DBE and LEADSA launched the *Stop Rape* (DBE 2013) booklet aimed at providing teachers with a range of lessons and activities to encourage awareness among children of gender-based violence and the unequal power relations that often lead to violence.

Given the concerns expressed nationally and internationally at the prevalence of HIV/AIDS in South Africa, it is inevitable that gender in education has also been concerned largely with HIV/AIDS education. Moletsane, Morrell, Hemson and Pattman (2012) have also shown that the teaching of HIV/AIDS as an issue affecting women particularly in South African schools and higher education institutions has not been informed by any commitment to gender equality and indeed its emphasis on correcting the 'deviance of children' and the promotion of virginity testing served only to reinforce age and gendered inequalities. Moletsane and Morrell in their work in schools confirm that where teachers were more committed to participatory pedagogies, they spoke about how the DramAide intervention had enhanced girls' confidence as reflected in their participation in class, assembly and extra-curricular activities. But in a follow-up ethnographic study in the same school it was found that the rhetoric of gender equality was shallow and short-lived, and that this was attributed to the pervasiveness of sexual harassment and corporal punishment along with a policy of excluding pregnant girls and the domination of men in management (Pattman 2012, 360).

What is clear from studies undertaken by a range of educationists (whether Chisholm at the level of policy analysis, or Finkel and Ernst in the context of civic education in the classroom, or Moletsane et al. (2009) on visual methodologies to address challenges faced by schools and communities in the contexts of poverty and the AIDS pandemic) is that the quality of teaching emerges as the key ingredient to the successful development of learners able not only to understand the knowledge and skills needed to utilise it, but also to understand the imperatives enshrined in the Constitution (1996). Finkel and Ernst, for example, concluded their study by noting that 'frequent exposure to traditional teaching methods may be sufficient for achieving the limited ends of knowledge-based civic lessons, but the successful transmission of political attitudes, values, and participatory dispositions, however, is likely to require additional factors related to credible and likeable instructors, active methodologies, and an open environment for political discussion' (Finkel & Ernst 2005, 341). In itself, simple awareness without, for example, collaborative participation in learning, is unlikely to yield changes in perceptions let alone action in relation to 'civic duty, tolerance, institutional trust, or civic skills, once other variables' (351). This point emerges time and again in scholarly and other accounts concerning education in South Africa: 'active, participatory methods are strongest for generating … skills and positive attitudes towards legal forms of participation, as students come to support the importance of participation and develop the skills to do so by participating in games, role-playing behaviour, and other kinds of simulated political action' (354). If schooling and schools are regarded as sites through which the wider transformation of society can be initiated and even sustained, then higher education bears an even more acute responsibility to provide the intellectual leadership to foster generations of professionals and intellectuals committed to the transformation of South Africa. However, as the following sections to follow suggest, awareness of that responsibility beyond curricula and policy, in teaching and learning is not demonstrated with sufficient consistency in the sector to enable any confident pronouncements with regard to the importance of gender equality, let alone diversity awareness, in a new democracy.

There is no data on the performance or experience of children who identify as LGBTTIQ, which is due to reasons of taboo and unease as regards sexuality education in South Africa.

5.5 SEXUAL ORIENTATION AND IDENTITY ISSUES IN EDUCATION

In relation to persons identified as LGBTTIQ, between 1998–2006 several legal cases removed the criminalisation affecting women as well as other previously marginalised groups such as gay people. For example, the decriminalisation of sodomy in 1998, and the legalisation of same-sex unions in 2006 in South Africa made gay marriage legal and the persecution of gay people a crime. Despite progress, De Vos (2004) argues that 'a mere extension of marriage rights to some same-sex couples will also not lead to a necessary and fundamental re-imagining of the nature of ... intimate relations in our society' (182), on the grounds that '[b]ecause of homophobia, gender inequality and patriarchy in our society, gay men, lesbians and many women in different-sex relationships often do not have the social or economic power to freely "choose" to set the terms of their relationships' (183). De Vos's point applies equally to other areas of society and, in this chapter, is extended to the world of work where this re-imagining is long overdue.

For people unaware of the extermination, torture and marginalisation inflicted on persons who identify, or have been identified as, gay or queer (during and after the apartheid period, but also long before it), the question arises as to why gay people in South Africa require special protection or rights, given that the Constitution (1996) provides for the protection of human rights already. Appiah argues that the need for such measures arises from the fact that the simple right to human dignity is not sufficient protection in a State where a group or individual might still be attacked on the basis of not conforming, amongst others, to a hetero-normative ideal (2005, 109). Where identity cannot be considered as chosen (gay people do not choose their desires), and where the consequences of such identities are severe, rights and protection cannot be assumed.

First, the struggles in South Africa to 'assert' gay identity to enable the individuation for gay people, suggests that acceptance is neither unproblematic, nor cause for (legal or other) restitution (for example, employment equity). The Employment Equity Act (EEA) 55 of 1998 defines 'designated groups' as black people, women and people with disabilities. Thus, whilst explicitly mentioned in the Constitution (1996), no further provision concerning the status of gay people as a group is made. Few seem to have celebrated gay rights as part of 'the world we have won' (Weeks 2007), in the name of non-sexism, non-racism, freedom and equality. And, if gender as a category for the recognition of previously disadvantaged groups is to suffice, then it is clear that in South Africa it is simply a euphemism for referring to biological sex. No application forms for employment make provision for applicants to identify themselves as gay, homosexual, transgendered, lesbian, bisexual or heterosexual. This affirms the relative insignificance, indeed invisibility, broadly speaking, of LGBTTIQ people as a disadvantaged group. This group, despite colour or gender differences, has experienced (and continues to experience) violence and lack of protection in a largely heterosexual and heterosexist state. Given that 'gender' has been selectively reconceptualised as a 'category' in the EEA, the terms 'sexuality' and orientation need to be used to signify the differences in identity that still make for discrimination in South Africa. It could be argued that the invisibility of LGBTTIQ people as part of the transformation of South Africa occurs also because of a lack of education concerning sexuality or 'gender' in schools. For example, a handbook, *Issues on Gender in Schools* (DoE 2002), aims to equip teachers to deal with issues concerning 'gender', but in fact deals narrowly and exclusively with issues concerning women as the subject of a range of discriminatory social practices. In the absence of a genuinely inclusive approach to education, ignorance is aided and reinforced. Sexuality (especially non-hetero-normative sexuality) remains a taboo subject in schools and is seldom addressed by teachers. It is little wonder then that gender features on an equally inconsistent and problematic basis in higher education as described in the following sections.

5.6 GENDER AND HIGHER EDUCATION

The Soudien Report (2012), which surveyed the incidence of victimisation of women and LGBTTIQ persons at universities in South Africa makes passing reference to discrimination against such people on South African campuses only because this minority grouping is rendered largely invisible in the 'big' narrative concerning race transformation in South Africa. Protected by the silence of the Employment Equity Act, employers do not account for sexuality in the same way as race or 'gender', either in terms of employment policies or indeed codes containing universities' values. Why? Perhaps the suffering of LGBTTIQ people is too problematic to consider on a range of other levels? This much is acknowledged even by students in higher education institutions: homophobia was reported as a serious problem at Rhodes University (RU). As a gay student pointed out: 'The views of gays are discounted by house committees. It is easier to ask for more black lecturers than it is to ask for more gay lecturers. (RU meeting with students)' (Soudien et al. 2008, 76). Soudien (2008) confirms that discrimination against gay persons exists and is silenced: 'However, although sexism has been raised in … interactions with institutional constituencies in relation to employment equity, with a few exceptions there has been a deafening silence on sexual harassment in general and in residences … The silence … does not mean that the problem does not exist … it is clear that sexual harassment, of women and gays and lesbians, is rife' (Soudien et al. 2008, 95). It is interesting that the autonomy of higher education institutions means that it remains more difficult to ascertain the extent to which university curricula actively change perceptions regarding gender in higher education.

Teacher education provides a basis from which to track changes at the level of the State, but the extent to which teacher education, or indeed higher education as a whole, prepares young people to contribute to the transformation agenda in South Africa with respect to gender is far from clear or consistent across the sector. An absence of clarity, nationally, about the key issues to which citizens need to be 'alive' contributes to a generalised sense that whatever place gender might occupy in the national consciousness, it is seldom the cause for anything more than complaints concerning the relative absence of women in leadership (and management) and the absolute non-recognition of sexual minority groups that continue to be 'othered' or rendered invisible in consideration of diversity, let alone equality. The need for better awareness is evident in the unease experienced in leadership in South Africa (in and outside schooling or higher education) concerning gender issues in a society that is far from united in terms of its priorities concerning non-sexism, non-racism and discrimination. Chapter 11 of the Constitution makes provision for the recognition of traditional leadership in South Africa. Subsequent legislation pertaining to traditional leadership protects and supports overwhelmingly patriarchal norms, which paradoxically undermine Constitutional prerogatives as regards gender equality. In the context of highly patriarchal community arrangements, traditional and religious belief systems that still jostle for recognition and status, constitutional provisions for non-discrimination need to be strongly and repeatedly articulated.

While universities are meant to promote non-sexism, or non-discrimination of persons identifying as LGBTTIQ, there is no data from universities or other higher education institutions concerning the employment of persons who identify as LGBTTIQ for the reasons discussed above: they are considered invisible in terms of the EEA. Consequently there is also no systemic collection of data on the incidences of hate crimes or victimisation of women or persons who identify themselves as LGBTTIQ students or staff in higher education. The absences, and what they imply, are damning. If schooling makes little or no provision for LGBTTIQ children, then higher education is not any better. The choices for gay people seem binary: contestation and othering, or assimilation and invisibility. If education and employment policies make no provision for gay people as a subordinated, historically disadvantaged group, then it is unsurprising that this group continues to be discriminated against visibly and invisibly by institutions (staff and students alike).

Heteronormativity ascribes, even to sexual identity, normalising discourses that obscure material differences (for example, the assumption that all lesbian experience is the same) between groups. Even when considering the role of women in higher education, the gaps are evident. In 2014, only 4 of the 26 vice-chancellors of South African universities were women, two were white men, whilst the rest were black men. An extensive scholarship exists concerning the conflict that arises even within (heteronormative) higher education institutions between men and women. Morley, for example, questions why gender has escaped attention in the academy, and asks whether cultural scripts for leaders collide with gender performances. Citing Shackleton et al.'s (2006) literature review on women in leadership, Morley argues that there is an essentialised debate (women have better skills, better people intelligence and so on) about women that confirms negative stereotyping. Overall the literature 'blames the gap' (by bemoaning it), and advocates that more women need to be seen figuring in existing structures without questioning the patriarchal power imbued in these structures (Morley 2012). Success, for women, depends on internalising the dominant accountability systems and this can result in leadership being experienced as incarceration in an 'identity cage', with a commensurate loss of authentic identity and autonomy.

In other scholarly disciplines, such as law, it has been argued that using a moral framework to understand race may be less helpful in relation to gender, and may serve to obscure the power relations at work. Instead, as Botha suggests, questions of political disempowerment and material disadvantage should loom large in a court's inquiry concerning cases where gender discrimination features: 'Rather than focusing predominantly on issues of personhood and identity, the Court should concentrate on questions of domination and access to the means of political and economic power' (Botha 2004, 748). The struggles are not straightforward: though defined as a secular matter, the overwhelming majority of religious institutions right from the beginning of the struggle for same-sex marriage in South Africa (and elsewhere) have vehemently opposed it. The Constitution thus mediates value systems (Barnard 2007, 509), but law should act to protect groups against ideological or dogmatic interpretations of cultural institutions (be it marriage or chieftainship).

In South Africa, the focus on race has, for obvious reasons, dominated discussions concerning transformation, equity, and social and economic change. Williams states that 'racial discrimination is powerful precisely because of its frequent invisibility, its felt neutrality … Racism inscribes culture with generalized preferences and routinized notions of propriety … It empowers the mere familiarity and comfort of the status quo by labelling that status quo as "natural"' (Williams 1995, 82). Dealing with gender within the context of race-based prejudice has been more complex because, as Fraser (1996, 218) argues, gender equity is best understood as 'a complex notion comprising a plurality of distinct normative principles'. Part of the difficulty resides with the relative absence of role models for communities in relation to women and LGBTTIQ persons. Notwithstanding the scholarship on women in leadership, or black people in leadership, scholarly discussions of gay identity have tended to focus on the politics of recognition (coming out, being ousted and contesting prejudice) in the social sphere.

There are few accounts, barring perhaps Edwin Cameron's (2005), on leadership and identity in South Africa with reference to being gay, and certainly none in higher education, though that is not to suggest that gay people do not feature in higher education leadership; they do, albeit invisibly. Dealing with gay, transgender, lesbian and transsexual identities is seen as messy in the new hierarchies concerning priorities for transformation, and so gay people, though historically discriminated against, appear to have 'disappeared'.

Women, though a majority grouping in higher education, are similarly invisible in leadership and management. As with schooling, there is a need to challenge the cultures of institutions in which leadership roles are configured to support access for male heterosexual candidates; in fact the institutions are geared to select, groom and enable this group almost exclusively. What emerges is that policy framing without a radical rethinking of education curricula is unlikely to yield the kinds of changes anticipated by the State since 1994; and if the last twenty years are anything to go by, then the actual pace for change is slower than anticipated and certainly more disappointing than had been imagined possible in 1995.

5.7 REFLECTIONS

This chapter has considered a broad range of research on schools from the perspective of enrolment and throughput, to participation and curriculum, and finally on research about gender in higher education in relation to policy framing as well as lived-experience as documented by academics focusing either on women and girls, or gender as pertaining to a wider variety of sexualities and orientations also subject to exclusionary practices and violence. There is a tendency in reporting statistics on girls' performance to reproduce the argument already noted by Simmonds earlier in this chapter. For example, in Southern Africa, UNICEF noted in 2001 that 45% of girls were not enrolled in classes, and of those who were, nearly 40% would drop out before completing Grade 5 (UNICEF 2001; Wilson 2007, 2). Though these rates are not as severe in South Africa, Mahlomaholo and others have shown that the subject positioning of women as labourers with fewer rights to dignity than men, are more vulnerable to socio-economic hardship, as well as violence and restricted opportunities to develop, than men or boys.

Wilson (2007, 3) suggests that the 'recognition of violence against girls as a significant barrier to social and economic development in all parts of the world is linked with the understanding that the societal mistreatment of schoolgirls is reflected in the culture of the nations that marginalize and lessen the value of women and their contribution to the society'. In the developing world the impact of violence on school girls attacks the economic and social well-being of developing counties. What this chapter demonstrates is that despite routine data collection concerning issues affecting girls and women, there is little concerted action to prevent violence in schools and re-educate communities about gender equity. This is as much a policy failure (in which girls alone appear to form the focus) as it is a wider social and educational failure. If teacher training institutions do deal with sexuality, gender and orientation explicitly, it will still be some generations before the impact of that will be felt in schools and higher education institutions. If, as is more likely to be the case, the commitment to gender equality remains ambiguous (both in terms of its practice through policy, implementation and teaching), then South Africans can anticipate that the pace for change will remain slow, and institutions will themselves continue to be sites in which violence continues to feature, and a refusal to combat it remains characteristic. This outlook persists despite the Constitution and 20 years of reform in South Africa, and while patriarchal values and practices continue to enjoy strong social support.

The chapter describes the intersectionality between gender, poverty, life-opportunities and class: the situation of girls remains problematic and the aspirations of the curriculum are met neither by the commitment of teachers nor the openness of communities, where the issues concerning violence are embedded in a variety of values, perceptions and practices in which patriarchy is either unwittingly reinforced (through teachers not addressing issues with boys and girls with a view to changing perceptions, or through addressing gender equality without reference to boys or men, or without reference to other groups of people subject to equally damaging forms of violence or exclusion on the basis of the sexualities or orientations).

There is clearly a need to focus on societal change as anticipated by the Constitution (1996), but which has not received attention from the State, for reasons that have as much to do with a lack of capacity as a lack of awareness. Instead, new wealth as concentrated in the growing middle-class has tended not to change but rather ossify attitudes so that too little self-reflection occurs in relation to the links between aspirational change and material change, as measured, for example, in the standard of living index.

It is true that there are no legal barriers to women's equality in decision-making or participation, but communities and institutions exist by virtue of a culture or ethos that is maintained irrespective of its material frame. While circumstances concerning the relative comfort in which people conduct their lives may change, the fact remains that without an adequate education programme, change in perceptions and behaviour remains unlikely. Education is thus needed for the basic transmission of high-end knowledge, but also to develop sufficiently participatory, collaborative and capable of engaging the learner as a whole person with qualities of insight and compassion, and an ability to engage in action to bring about change. The culture of a community or the ethos of a school or university can render the chances for women or LGBTTIQ people more limited than for others, and when combined with poverty and inaccessibility, they can prove effective barriers to development. Add to this the impact of gender-based violence in and out of education institutions, and it becomes clear that much more effort is required not only in terms of policy provision, but also more importantly in terms of the education of both adults and children (Moultrie & De la Rey 2003). Gender, diversity and education have formed the focus of the chapter, but the very evident need to link debates and research on gender in education, to communities beyond the institutions suggests in itself that the solutions to the problems concerning gender violence may not in fact best reside alone in schools. Instead, there might be a need to strengthen community organisations beyond the school, with a view to providing more safe spaces for women and LGBTTIQ groups, since the likelihood of an unambiguous commitment to gender and change might provide a better basis from which to support social change, of which the school is both part, and only partly representative as an institution.

If achieving gender equity has been considered a cornerstone of the transformation project since 1995, then language, language rights and language education have similarly been considered as a means through which diversity can be encouraged, race integration achieved, and representation of groups guaranteed through a conscious effort to foster, support and enhance multilingualism in schooling as well as higher education in South Africa. Language rights and linguistic diversity are features of South Africa's new democracy, and yet they remain highly contested issues featuring prominently in the media and society in the last 20 years. It is to language, diversity and education that the next chapter addresses itself.

6 Language, education and transformation

6.1 INTRODUCTION

The key issue in education in South Africa has to do with access to quality education. In 2006 it was noted that there were still severe problems concerning the quality of education provided to learners, and also the quality of support (whether by way of infrastructure, resources or competent and qualified teachers). In 2006 it was noted that the efficiency of the system, and the effectiveness of education in South Africa, had deteriorated to such an extent that approximately 80% of all the schools were classified as dysfunctional.[1] In 2005 the results were so poor that only 150 000 Grade 12 learners (representing 12.5% of the initial 1.2 million Grade 1 learners) achieved a matric pass that was of an acceptable standard.[2] Thus access is as much a matter of sourcing education in South Africa as it is about sourcing quality with a view to later success in higher education and secure employment thereafter.

Smit (2007) notes that in this context, the desire for quality education has placed pressures on schools perceived as offering such quality to learners and their parents or families: 'understandably, the schools have responded to the great influx of learners by setting admission policies in accordance with pre-determined class sizes, physical capacity and safety requirements of the facilities and with language policies to uphold good pedagogical practices'. Unsurprisingly, provincial departments have similarly had to initiate measures to enable provision and access to schools that might otherwise have wished to restrict these on the basis that quality in education becomes difficult to ensure where larger groups, or fewer teachers, are entailed (Smit 2014, 5). Since 2005, litigation between schools and the provincial departments concerning access has become a fairly normal occurrence. Smit (2007) and Woolman and Fleisch (2009) describe prominent lawsuits concerning everything to do with allowing access to schooling by pregnant children or allowing access to schools not in the same region as applicants, to other matters such as school dress codes in relation to religious belief. The evident frustrations are often witnessed in the media between provincial departments and school governing bodies, and are symptomatic of assumptions contained in the Constitution (1996) in terms of the rights to education in the language of choice for the learner, or the rights to education as contained in the South African Schools Act, for example. Courts have become forums in which the legislative provisions of the Constitution are 'worked out', often in relation to the acute pressures concerning the need to access quality education in areas where there are either too few schools, or too few schools offering education in the language of preference for learners and their families. Language and the medium of instruction form the content of most lawsuits to date.

This chapter is divided into three sections, the first of which deals with the legislation concerning language use in schools in order to provide the reader with a basis from which to understand subsequent sections, in which the relationship between legislation, its enactment by the State, and the interpretation of such language and schooling, are elucidated. The second section explores the contestation between the State and schools where language rights have formed the basis for differing interpretations of the powers of the State in relation to those of school governing bodies. The third section considers higher education language policy as a means of framing section four of the chapter, in which the development of research and policy to advance indigenous language development is described. The chapter concludes by reflecting on the language policies as adopted in the first few years of the post-apartheid period and their impact on the experiences of learners and students in the schooling and higher education sector.

6.2 CONSTITUTIONAL AND OTHER LEGISLATIVE FRAMEWORKS FOR LANGUAGE AND EDUCATION IN SCHOOLS

The Constitution (1996) as a framing document, from which the South African Schools Act and the Language in Education Policy are derived, makes the following provisions with regard to language specifically:

Provision 6: Languages.

(1) The official languages of the Republic are Sepedi, Sesotho, Setswana, Siswati, Tshivenda, Xitsonga, Afrikaans, English, isiNdebele, isiXhosa and isiZulu.

(2) Recognising the historically diminished use and status of the indigenous languages of our people, the State must take practical and positive measures to elevate the status and advance the use of these languages.

(4) The national government and provincial governments, by legislative and other measures, must regulate and monitor their use of official languages. Without detracting from the provisions of subsection (2), all official languages must enjoy parity of esteem and must be treated equitably.

(5) A Pan South African Language Board established by national legislation must

(a) promote, and create conditions for, the development and use of

(i) all official languages;

(ii) the Khoi, Nama and San languages; and

(iii) sign language; and

(b) promote and ensure respect for

(i) all languages commonly used by communities in South Africa, including

(ii) Arabic, Hebrew, Sanskrit and other languages used for religious purposes German, Greek, Gujarati, Hindi, Portuguese, Tamil, Telegu and Urdu; and in South Africa.

What is notable about the formulation with regard to language policy is that community languages, or heritage languages, may be offered by schools in order to cater for recent migrant or other communities that form part of South Africa's multilingual population.

Chapter 2: Bill of Rights

3. Equality

(1) Everyone is equal before the law and has the right to equal protection and benefit of the law.

(2) Equality includes the full and equal enjoyment of all rights and freedoms. 'To promote the achievement of equality, legislative and other measures designed to

protect or advance persons, or categories of persons, disadvantaged by unfair discrimination may be taken.

(3) The State may not unfairly discriminate directly or indirectly against anyone on one or more grounds, including race, gender, sex, pregnancy, marital status, ethnic or social origin, colour, sexual orientation, age, disability, religion, conscience, belief, culture, language and birth.

*(4) No person may unfairly discriminate directly or indirectly against anyone on one or more grounds in terms of subsection (3). National legislation must be enacted to prevent or prohibit unfair discrimination.

(5) Discrimination on one or more of the grounds listed in subsection (3) is unfair unless it is established that the discrimination is fair.

Section 14 of the South African Schools Act (1996) makes provision for the establishment of four types of schools in South Africa: those that are publicly funded on publicly owned land (in which case the community has the right to elect a school governing body in terms of those provisions made in the Act); those that are privately funded (through fees or endowments) on public land (in this case the school elects its governing body and the State funds the salaries of teachers within existing post-provisioning norms), those that are publicly funded on private land (in which case the land-owner has the right to have major representation on the governing body), and those that are privately funded and on private owned land (in which case fees and endowments alone account for the school's expenditure and the salaries of teachers and support staff). In terms of the Act, schools also have the right to define the language policy for the school on the basis of the languages, or language, used in the community. Obviously, this provision has a major implication for access to education in these schools, a matter to which I return later in this chapter.

In addition to the above, the Language in Education Policy (LiEP 1997) makes further provision for languages in education, with specific reference to schools (Government Notice no. 383, vol. 17997). This document refers specifically to the legislation in which norms and standards for education are described (Norms and Standards Regarding Language Policy: Section 6 (1) SA Schools Act (1996).

1. In terms of the new Constitution of the Republic of South Africa, the government, and thus the Department of Education, recognises that our cultural diversity is a valuable national asset and hence is tasked, amongst other things, to promote multilingualism, the development of the official languages, and respect

for all languages used in the country, including South African Sign Language and the languages referred to in the South African Constitution.

The commitment to multilingualism was first and foremost anticipated as part of the transformation project insofar as it was envisaged that the provisions of the Acts and Constitution would restore dignity to language groups (and thus people) not formerly included in education in South Africa beyond Grade 3. This commitment took cognisance of the legacy of apartheid in relation to linguistic and race divisions in which discrimination on a range of levels, many of which have been documented by scholars cited earlier in this book, was practised on people of colour in South Africa. The new policy was designed to support the transformation project with a view to 'building a non-racial nation in South Africa and communication across the barriers of colour, language and region, while at the same time creating an environment in which respect for languages other than one's own would be encouraged' (LiEP 1997). At its basis was the recognition that South Africa is a multilingual nation.

The LiEP makes reference to research 'demonstrating that, under appropriate conditions, most learners benefit cognitively and emotionally from the type of structured bilingual education found in dual-medium (also known as two-way immersion) programmes. Whichever route is followed, the underlying principle is that home languages should be promoted and that additional languages ought to be acquired in order to facilitate common communication'.

According to LiEP, 'The right to choose the language of learning and teaching is vested in the individual. This right has, however, to be exercised within the overall framework of the obligation on the education system to promote multilingualism'.

4. Aims:

The main aims of the Ministry of Education's policy for language in education are:

(1) to promote full participation in society and the economy through equitable and meaningful access to education;

(2) to pursue the language policy most supportive of general conceptual growth amongst learners, and hence to establish additive multilingualism as an approach to language in education;

(3) to promote and develop all the official languages;

(4) to support the teaching and learning of all other languages required by learners or used by communities in South Africa, including languages used for religious purposes, languages which are important for international trade and communication, and South African Sign Language, as well as Alternative and Augmentative Communication;

(5) to counter disadvantages resulting from different kinds of mismatches between home languages and languages of learning and teaching;

(6) to develop programmes for the redress of previously disadvantaged languages.

Within the context of eleven official languages, how the accommodation of learners' or their parents' preferences would be realised in multilingual settings had to be carefully delineated in legislation so as to avoid impossible situations, and also to allow for new possibilities where, for example, schools may have shifted from one language to another in recognition either of a changed demographic, or a changed set of priorities for the community. High on the list of aims cited above is the development (conceptual, holistic) of the learner. That said, as the legislation is unpacked, as seen in the provisions below, the switch to languages other than the home language becomes possible, and, moreover, the additional language has to be taken as a subject but can also be the language of instruction in Grade 12 (in most cases this would be English or Afrikaans up to 2014).

7. LANGUAGES AS SUBJECTS

The Languages in Education Policy (1997, section 6.7) on Languages as Subjects makes the following provisions:

(1) All learners shall offer at least one approved language as a subject in Grade 1 and Grade 2.

(2) From Grade 3 (Std 1) onwards, all learners shall be offered their language of learning and teaching and at least one additional approved language as subjects.

(3) All language subjects shall receive equitable time and resource allocation.

(4) The following promotion requirements apply to language subjects:

4.

(1) In Grade 1 to Grade 4 (Std 2) promotion is based on performance in one language and Mathematics.

(2) From Grade 5 (Std 3) onwards, one language must be passed.

(3) From Grade 10 to Grade 12 two languages must be passed, one on first language level, and the other on at least second language level. At least one of these languages must be an official language.

(4) Subject to national norms and standards as determined by the Minister of Education, the level of achievement required for promotion shall be determined by the provincial education departments.

In terms of the LiEP, the language of instruction in a school could only be an official language so as to prevent situations where foreign languages are used to exclude local learners, though of course foreign languages could still be school subjects within the curriculum. A further legislative act known as the Norms and Standards regarding Language Policy (SA Schools Act, Section 6 (1), 1996) stated that:

1. Recognising that diversity is a valuable asset, which the State is required to respect, the aim of these norms and standards is the promotion, fulfilment and development of the state's overarching language goals in school education in compliance with the Constitution, namely:

2.

(1) the protection, promotion, fulfilment and extension of the individual's language rights and means of communication in education; and

(2) the facilitation of national and international communication through promotion of bi- or multilingualism through cost-efficient and effective mechanisms,

(3) to redress the neglect of the historically disadvantaged languages in school education.

3.

(3) 'school district' means a geographical unit as determined by the relevant provincial legislation, or prevailing provincial practice.

(4) 'language' means all official languages recognised in the Constitution, and also South African Sign Language, as well as Alternative and Augmentative Communication.

3. The protection of individual rights

4.

(1) The parent exercises the minor learner's language rights on behalf of the minor

learner. Learners who come of age, are hereafter referred to as the learner, which concept will include also the parent in the case of minor learners.

(2) The learner must choose the language of teaching upon application for admission to a particular school.

(3) Where a school uses the language of learning and teaching chosen by the learner, and where there is a place available in the relevant grade, the school must admit the learner.

(4) Where no school in a school district offers the desired language as a medium of learning and teaching, the learner may request the provincial education department to make provision for instruction in the chosen language, and section 5.3.2 must apply. The provincial education department must make copies of the request available to all schools in the relevant school district.

5. The rights and duties of the school

6.

(1) Subject to any law dealing with language in education and the Constitutional rights of learners, in determining the language policy of the school, the governing body must stipulate how the school will promote multilingualism through using more than one language of learning and teaching, and/or by offering additional languages as fully-fledged subjects, and/or applying special immersion or language maintenance programmes, or through other means approved by the head of the provincial education department. (This does not apply to learners who are seriously challenged with regard to language development, intellectual development, as determined by the provincial department of education.)

(2) Where there are less than 40 requests in Grades 1 to 6, or less than 35 requests in Grades 7 to 12 for instruction in a language in a given grade not already offered by a school in a particular school district, the head of the provincial department of education will determine how the needs of those learners will be met, taking into account:

(3)

1. the duty of the State and the right of the learners in terms of the Constitution, including

2. the need to achieve equity,

3. the need to redress the results of past racially discriminatory laws and practices,

4. practicability, and

5. the advice of the governing bodies and principals of the public schools concerned.

This means that Grade 1, 2 and 3 learners are taught in their home language and then switch to the language of instruction (Grades 4 to 9), with one additional language offered as a subject. In practice a rapid transition to English occurs too late. Provincial departments are compelled to keep records of the numbers of children speaking languages in schools, and also to keep a record of the requests lodged by parents to use languages for teaching which cannot be accommodated by schools. Schools are required to consult parents about the language policy of the school since this determines access to the school (see Section 6 (1) of the South African Schools Act, 1996). The Department also provides guidelines to schools in order to ensure that languages can be introduced where the number of requests justifies it. Thus, according to legislation, there ought to be about 40 learners per grade in Grades 1–6, or 35 in Grades 7–12 in order to justify the provision of a language in a school.

The lawsuits concerning the provision of languages within schools are motivated not on the grounds of cynical politics, but often in terms of real pressures exerted on the State to provide education in areas where resources are scarce, or where access to schools is denied to many on the basis of maintaining the language of a few.

Smit argues on the basis of his analysis of these cases that the State has been undeterred by the legal costs and punitive actions that have been incurred when it has (sometimes wrongly) compelled schools to provide access to children who do not conform to the provisions of the LiEP. The contestation is thus not only highly political, but driven at times to lengths where, on the basis of opening access to quality education, the provisions of LiEP are ignored or perverted. Scholars have tended to argue that by compelling schools to change their language policies in order to make English the language of instruction (and thus the second language of both the original and new groups of children in schools), the fundamental claim made in the Constitution (1996) (in terms of not permitting discrimination on the basis of language) is subverted. Furthermore, linguists and language teachers confirm that the introduction of a second language as the language of instruction often complicates the progress made by the learner (lending unwitting credence to the arguments that English, for example, should be introduced even earlier in the curriculum). Smit suggests that this contributes to the poor results of the education system, but such causality has not been established, whereas it is well accepted (and indeed it is the argument put forward in this book) that better performance is linked more closely to better teaching when languages are introduced either as additional languages or languages of instruction in schools.

What is equally clear is that perceptions of the dominance of English are over-stated. English received little support in the apartheid state, and though it became the language of choice after the transition to democracy, the sufficiency of appropriately qualified, let alone competent teachers of the language, has always been more of an issue. In the 1999 South African Institute of Race Relations (SAIRR) survey, isiZulu, isiXhoza and Afrikaans were the three largest language groupings in South Africa and so the choice of English as lingua franca in all State institutions is at best a tenuous one. Simply put, in the decade following the first democratic elections, resources were not placed at the disposal either of schools or universities to develop mother-tongue instruction or to make indigenous languages the languages of learning in the higher education system. The absence of adequate provision for indigenous languages has become more marked over time. Indigenous languages continue to thrive, not because of the efforts of the State or of non-government organisations working with universities (see, for example, the South African Norwegian Tertiary Education Development (SANTED) initiative, referred to in articles by Ndimande-Hlongwa et al. 2010 and Madiba 2010), or the efforts of universities themselves or academics (see, for example, Mathebula 2010 and Du Plessis 2010), but rather because these languages enjoy widespread and popular support, despite the absence of political ownership or material support (see Webb et al. 2012). While languages thrive with only a modicum of institutional support, institutions of higher education have the daunting task of catching up with language development beyond their walls. Heugh (1999) and De Klerk (2002) indicate that most African parents choose English tuition for their children out of necessity and not by reason of available options; an additive bilingual policy is the norm, but because the teachers are not available to teach through the home language, English is still widely regarded as the language of progress and access to higher education, ensuring better chances at upward social mobility.[3]

The position of minority languages is not an innocent one in South Africa. Afrikaans, which in numerical terms is thought of as a minority language, actually has more speakers than English does (though it is regarded as the language of social prestige and learning). Arthur Chaskalson, the founding Justice President of the Constitutional Court in South Africa, suggests that mother-tongue education can be regarded as an attempt to protect the language rights of minority groups. The argument concerning the introduction of single-medium schools (instead of parallel or dual-medium schools) has been seen, by Smit and others, as a means of protecting 'minority' languages against the predations of English, but there is little evidence to suggest that English threatens or diminishes other languages that have long survived and thrived before and after the colonial-apartheid periods thanks to widespread social support from speakers.

6.3 LANGUAGE RIGHTS AND SCHOOL: STATE AND COMMUNITY CONTESTATION

The following sections are a synthesis of Smit's analysis of legal contestation of language rights in South Africa's schools. In 2002–3, the Middelburg Primary School sued the Head of Department of Education in Mpumalanga Province. The department had compelled the schools to admit non-Afrikaans speakers and to change its language provisions. The school argued that the department had ignored the right of the school to establish its language policy. The court concluded that the right to establish a single-medium public school was subordinate to the right of the learner to be educated in his/her home language. The department argued that pressures on access to quality education could not be resisted in the name of the language preferences of a minority educated by obviously well-trained teachers in a school where admission was restricted on the basis of language. That there were only 686 Afrikaans single-medium institutions in 2002, out of approximately 28 000 public schools in South Africa, paled into the political significance of the case itself.[4] Smit argues that: 'The 2% Afrikaans single-medium schools are underrepresented in terms of the national demographic percentages of the language communities in South Africa' (according to the SAIRR 1999 survey statistics, Afrikaans is the majority language of the Northern and Western Cape provinces respectively). This means that the vast majority, approximately 82% of the public schools, are English single-medium schools. Only 17% of the schools in South Africa offer African language instruction (predominantly isiZulu) during the Foundation Phase (i.e. Grades R to 3); thereafter all these schools make the rapid switch to English medium instruction.

In 2004, Seodin Primary School took the Northern Cape Department of Education[5] to court because the department had imposed an order to change the medium of instruction in four schools so that they could function as dual-medium (English and Afrikaans) providers. In this case the motivation of the department (as in other cases) was to deal with over-crowding in existing English-medium schools from predominantly Tswana communities. The school alleged that the department had behaved unjustly and contravened Section 6 (2) of Act 84 of 1996 (Northern Cape) by laying down the language policy for the school and also that 'the decision was politically inspired to unilaterally impose transformation and thus *mala fide*' (Smit 2014). The school lost this case on the basis of a legal technicality and the court found that none of the affected schools had language policies as set out in the Northern Cape Education Act (1998). In this act the policy had to be developed in consultation with the Member of the Executive Council for Education of the province and approved by the MEC. In this case the court agreed with arguments presented by the departments concerning the schools actions to exclude black children on the basis of race as well as language.

The regional context also played an important role in the decision since it was made evident that neighbouring schools were over-subscribed and that there were no other schools within distances reasonable for the children and their families. Furthermore, the numbers of learners requiring admission and instruction in English weighed on the department's decision to enforce a change in language. Afrikaans as a language would not be affected negatively by the introduction of parallel-medium classes in English. Aside from reaching the findings on grounds different from the *Mikro* case, to be described in paragraphs to follow, the issue as to whether the home language would be threatened or undermined by the introduction of another medium was not clear.

In 2005, another court case hit the media headlines in South Africa, this time in the Western Cape where Afrikaans is a majority language. In this case, the governing body of Laerskool Mikro sued the Western Cape Minister of Education.[6] The school was an Afrikaans-medium public school whose governing body had refused to accede to an order of the Western Cape Department of Education to change the school's language policy in order to introduce English as a parallel medium to Afrikaans and therefore enable mostly black children to access the school. In this case the school head-teachers were relieved of their responsibilities and the department appointed administrative officials to manage the school. On the first new school day in 2005, the school admitted 21 non-Afrikaans speakers and appointed teachers to teach them. The Court upheld legislative provisions as per the determination of the South African Schools Act (1996, Section 16 (1) and 6 (2)). The department took the matter to the Supreme Court of Appeal, which rejected this interpretation, arguing instead that section 29 (2) of the SSA (1996) meant that everyone had a right to be educated in an official language of his or her choice, but as Smit suggests, not everyone had 'the right to be so instructed at each and every public educational institution'. The judge referred to the requirement that the best educational needs of the affected learners must be considered. The department's appeal was lost.

The *Mikro* decision confirmed that where it was not practical for the school to offer another language of instruction, then it could not be compelled to do so, and that the right to basic education in the home language could only be justified where it was practicable for the school to offer it. Interestingly the Court also ruled that school governing bodies performed a public function in terms of Section 41 (1) (h) (iv) of the Constitution, and as such were not subject to the control of either the national, provincial or local levels of government.

The Northern Cape courts referred to the *Mikro* case and agreed that the learners did not have a constitutional right to receive their education in English at any of the applicant schools. However, the court reasoned that by virtue of the time delay of five months since the admission of the learners, they had attained a 'vested right' to remain at these schools. Thus the fact of the forced admission of the children into the schools made the court rule not in terms of the provisions in the SSA and LiEP, but in the interests of the learners. Smit concluded that this decision was motivated politically in the interests of the transformation of a single-medium Afrikaans school into a racially integrated English medium school.

Ensuing years have not brought about a resolution to the contestation. In 2009 the Department of Education, this time in Mpumalanga Province, took on Hoërskool (High School) Ermelo. This school is also an Afrikaans-medium school, which was under-enrolled. The department argued that the school's governing body did not have the exclusive right to determine the language policy of the school, especially when it was evident that there was a public need in the region for access to quality education and there were over-subscribed schools in the vicinity. Arguments framed in the discourse of transformation and historical redress were employed by the department. In this case the court held that a narrow reading of Section 29 of the Constitution and Section 6 (2) of the Schools Act (1996) would prevent children from accessing learning in their own languages; hus the right to determine the language policy could be used to deny access and promote race exclusivity, frustrating the transformation goals of section 29 (2) of the Constitution (1996). The implication of this finding was that the school governing body should consider the community adjacent to the school and not just one grouping, taking into consideration overcrowding, historical redress and the changing demographics of the community.

The court confirmed that the head of the Department of Education could relieve the governing body in terms of Section 22 of the SASA (1996), but failed to note the reasonable nature of the school's existing policy. The school finally was compelled to review its language policy after deliberating with the Department of Education. This section demonstrates that the framing of language rights (at the level of the Constitution (1996), and related schools legislation) provides a language community with the means of both preserving and protecting language and culture in the school context. Notwithstanding the provisions to enable school governing bodies, the State nevertheless has, in the light of the pressing need to access education in areas where resources and access are limited, or where it is perceived that language and admissions policies are being used to exclude the legitimate needs of the wider community, sometimes contested the policies put in place in schools. This contestation is ongoing and court decisions differ widely in terms of premises and conclusions, depending on a variety of contextual factors.

6.4 LANGUAGE CHANGE AND IMPACT IN SCHOOLS

The issues concerning language as medium of instruction aside, the picture concerning literacy levels in South Africa is deeply worrying for government and society alike. Reports suggest that by the time many South African pupils reach Grade 4, they are functionally illiterate – mainly because they do not read at all during Grades 1, 2 and 3. Studies of teachers' behaviours (whether for Mathematics, see Carnoy et al. 2012, or for language, see Pretorius & Mampuru 2007) in relation to their subject content knowledge are equally distressing. A key argument made by prominent African (Bamgbose, 2004) and European linguists (Wolf, 2004) is that low levels of performance are tied to the use of English as medium of instruction.

Yet it is Lanham (1995) who examines the implications of such claims more dispassionately, arguing not for the 'purist' pursuit of Standard South African English (SSAE) for all learners, but rather for a more considered understanding of how SSAE might still inform or exist in relation to Black South African English (BSAfE). This is important for my argument since an affirming relationship between one variety and another ensures that they remain mutually recognisable to each other. Lanham (1995, 12) suggests that the standardisation of BSAfE has implications for its international applicability in terms of two concerns mentioned earlier: 'comprehensibility' and 'intelligibility'. In this respect three studies are cited and discussed: Bobda (1991), Strevens (1965), and MacDonald (1990). Without summarising these studies I wish to note that Lanham's findings have been confirmed in findings from IELTS testing with University of Natal students (Balfour 2002). In short, the test results on listening exams show that students experience difficulty regarding the comprehensibility of English as spoken by other different non-native speakers, or by native speakers of the language. Of particular importance is Strevens' finding that non-native speakers of English are less aware of loss or lack of comprehensibility. Lanham (1995) confirms what many South African native and non-native teachers of English will have already experienced: the lack of comprehensibility between speakers of English (native to non-native dialect, or non-native to non-native dialect) requires that meaning must always be mediated by more explanation or accommodation, and that meaning is often lost or retarded by this process (26). These findings suggest that beliefs regarding both BSAfE and SSAE need more scrupulous consideration and that the relationship between the two needs to be more affirming than Wright might suggest.

In South Africa, however, what is understood to be 'English' (let alone SSAE or BSAfE) is problematic because the quality of language instruction is dependent on socio-economic as well as geographical variables. Although controversial, the notion of semi-lingualism cannot be discounted in South Africa because of the damaging legacy of apartheid, and in some cases, missionary education. It is well known that the standardisation of indigenous languages occurred with their transcription by missionaries in the eighteenth and nineteenth centuries. What is often forgotten is that this process was not accompanied by an increase in the rates of literacy for speakers of indigenous South African languages because of colonial, and later, apartheid restrictions on access to education.

What is damning in post-apartheid South Africa is that speakers of indigenous languages possess only a partial awareness of their 'standard' languages, as increasingly do speakers of English, and hence have very little confidence or ability to use its full complexity. The gap between Standard Zulu and popular Zulu is so wide that this is an educational problem and not an ideological one. It is obvious, and documented extensively in Ellis (1994), for example, that deficits in mother-tongue knowledge make it extraordinarily difficult for learners to acquire a target language. If the tools that enable syntactical and grammatical awareness exist only partially in the mother tongue, transference or learning will be retarded in another language. Linguists such as Pienemann (1985) refer to partial learning under these conditions as 'semi-lingualism', leading to the development of an 'interlanguage'.

The implications of the following kinds of research need to be explored if English is to succeed as a lingua franca. It is well-known that proficiency in a target language decreases in proportion to how little it is used, or that near-fluency in a foreign language sometimes entails deteriorating competence in the home language (Ellis 1994). Odlin (1989) has noted, for example, that in contexts where languages are mixed (as must be the case in South Africa), language transfer between the target and the first language (L1) is likely to be negative precisely because the focus is less on target language usage than on 'communication needs'. Ellis (1994, 319) notes that such situations are normative in settings where the target language is an official language of the country, while Kellerman (1977) points out that the distance between the target and native language can act as a barrier to transfer. This point is further problematised by Kachru (1997), who suggests that the very term 'native speaker/ native language' is unhelpful in contexts where learners of a target language learn from other non-native speakers of that language. I would like to suggest, like Zobl (1980) and Ellis (1994), that acquisition is not only dependent on a thorough understanding of the L1, but also on developmental and social factors; a kind of nature–nurture dynamic. For example, Zobl and Ellis suggest that learning a target language can be retarded when a transitional structure that arises early in the interlanguage corresponds with an L1 structure. In contrast, learning might be accelerated when an early transitional structure is not reinforced by a corresponding second language (L2) structure (Ellis 1994, 332). However, the subtlety of this understanding, as well as its implications for the need for effective language pedagogy, is lost in the politics of the debate concerning English and its varieties, and indigenous South African languages.

Education research concerning language and equality tends to focus on explanations for poor achievement arising either from socio-economic factors or political and policy factors. Thus, Prinsloo (2007, 29), for example, argues that: 'Children from poor households and communities, still suffering the gravest effects of the discrimination and oppression of apartheid, are often under-prepared and seriously disadvantaged by their background circumstances when they enter the western-style education system'. She then links this argument to poor performance in schools, suggesting that because poorer children have less access to English, and that transitions made abruptly to English as a medium of instruction after three years of schooling, 'must factor into the equation' (2007, 29). Other scholars, such as Webb (2004), regard the matter as an empowerment issue, following Coomans (2002), who views the right to basic education as an 'empowerment right' (2002, 160), and van der Berg indicates that 'a growing literature shows educational inequality to be a determining factor in earnings distribution' (2001, 5). The evidence for these arguments is not as clear as the arguments themselves and the debates tend to become extreme in formulation: Heugh (2002) points out that it is unlikely that parents would opt for English as the medium of instruction if parents were aware of the 'facts' (that mother tongue education and superior English skills can be developed simultaneously along the lines of additive bilingualism) (Heugh 2002, 180–82). Instead of government pursuit of a policy to enlighten parents and correct these misperceptions, Heugh (2006) argues that language provisions as demonstrated in policy have been systematically undermined in official documents and curriculum change since 1999. The principles at risk include 'equity, non-discrimination, promotion of multilingualism, mother tongue education and meaningful access to optimal cognitive development in education' (2006, 63). That said, there is other evidence to suggest that the under-performance of learners is not so much linked to parents' language choices, school language policies or even constitutional provisions, but rather to low-quality teaching.

Plüddemann (2002), in a study of township primary schools in Cape Town, found that effective bilingual teaching requires materials and resources to enable language awareness, but that well-trained and high-quality teachers were absolutely essential for the success of any intervention. Although an understanding of the principles of additive bilingualism was necessary, Plüddemann feels one should be aware that teachers need practical guidance on the everyday implementation of the system, and more information about appropriate teaching methods with a view to improving literacy practices in the classroom: '[a] major obstacle to developing a culture of reading and writing seems to be teachers' own literacy approaches and their underlying assumptions about print' (2002, 51).

Pretorius (2014) has shown in a study of township schools in Gauteng (and specifically Pretoria), for example, that Foundation Phase teachers are themselves not reading: 'There was virtually no whole-class storybook reading on a daily basis, let alone weekly. There were no book corners, no books for pupils to practise their fledging reading skills, no reading homework given and very few written exercises to reinforce newly acquired reading knowledge.' Numerous other studies have revealed that by the time pupils reach Grade 4, they have acquired massive learning deficiencies and cannot read or solve basic problems in arithmetic. In recent times, the link between poor levels of subject content knowledge and learners' skills levels has become clearer. Pretorius argues that '[o]ne of the strongest contributory factors to the low literacy levels was the fact that much of the teaching and learning that occurred in the Foundation Phase was oral based' (Pretorius in Masondo 2014, 1). The study involved a team of academics and students observing teachers in what are regarded as functional schools, though located in poor urban areas.

Whilst Carnoy et al. (2012) found that teachers of mathematics had too little subject content knowledge to teach the curriculum effectively (resulting in high rates of absenteeism among other things); Pretorius found that Foundation Phase teachers, who are meant to be literacy specialists, were not reading enough to children in classrooms, and were themselves disinclined to read, even if for themselves, relying instead on teacher-directed, mostly oral and aural activities in which children recited sentences or lines with the teacher: 'There was much talk in the classroom, and much oral chorusing of things learnt, but far less reading and writing' (Pretorius in Masondo 2014, 1). In this context, it is also unsurprising that there is very little exposure to reading and writing tools and resources. In order to ascertain whether interventions might have a marked effect on the reading and writing performance of children, Pretorius in several studies has conducted tests of children to ascertain the levels of relative improvement. In terms of singing basic phonics, daily practising of reading words and short extended texts, vocabulary acquisition and development, comprehension, writing activities and storybook reading (activities associated typically with the early years in education), Grade 4 learners performed well in Pretorius's study. Without teaching phonics and vocabulary development, the children were not able to either decode or encode text; in other words, they were simply reciting words and sentences and not understanding them, an 'approach' described by Pretorius as 'disastrous' from a literacy perspective as learners were neither properly taught how to read, nor given opportunities to practise their reading skills in order to be able to read fast and accurately, and engage their reading skills in meaningful ways. Interventions such as those developed by Pretorius have shown an improvement from 19% to as much as 60% in learner performance. Pretorius attributes the low levels of performance to teachers who themselves do not read: 'Research we conducted in Atteridgeville, north of Pretoria, over seven years found that 70% of teachers there don't read. Many of them had fewer than 10 books in their homes,' (Masondo 2014, 1).

Having described the role of languages in schooling, both in terms of the languages to which children have access, as well as the language teaching practices in selected contexts, the sections to follow describe language and higher education development in South Africa. The discussion suggests that while higher education institutions have responded more proactively to the provisions, as described in the LiHEP, with regard to the use of and development of more than one language for teaching and learning in such contexts, that practices in certain institutions still draw heavily on understandings of multilingualism as a problematic issue rather than a potential vehicle for the further transformation of the sector – not only in terms of enabling wider access to, and success in higher education, but also of achieving race and class integration in institutions perceived historically as being elite, exclusive and exclusionary.

6.5 HIGHER EDUCATION, ACCESS AND LANGUAGE DEVELOPMENT

Higher education had the benefit of some years of planning and conceptualisation spearheaded by prominent linguists in South Africa. For example, in *Language Policy and National Unity* (1989), Alexander articulates the vision he was to formally endorse later with the *Langtag Report* (Alexander et al. 1994) regarding the development of a 'language policy' for South Africa. Alexander, who pioneered language policy development in South Africa, wrote: '… the language question cannot be separated from the fundamental problem of social inequality, national oppression, and democratic rights' (1989, 39). In planning and policy development, South Africa's multilingualism was to be highlighted as an important feature of the transformation project.

Alexander's account of the 'argument' regarding English rests on assumptions informing almost every 'progressive' perspective on language varieties found in contemporary linguistics: 'No language is inherently superior or inferior to another' (1989, 52; see also Kachru 1997) in which the use of, or preference for, standard varieties was questioned. In *Sow the Wind* (1985), Alexander spends some time describing the history of how one language/dialect/variety comes to dominate others, yet his vision in 1989, and 1994, of language equality remained somewhat utopian since it posits, *a priori,* a state of affairs where equally useful languages co-exist equitably within the State. Such arguments have been contested by other prominent Southern African linguists, such as Makoni (2002), and revealed as flawed since in refusing to acknowledge the legacy of language politics in South African history and its consequences for the use of English and the wider prevalence of Afrikaans, for example, little distinction is made between languages used *in* the State (locally specific, cultural, religious, ethnic) and languages *of* the State (non-cultural, interethnic, political, intercultural). Nevertheless, debates post-1995 about language have touched inevitably on the perceived hegemony of English and the consequent banishment of 'other' languages (for example, McDermott 1998; Luckett 1993).

The utopian vision with regard to indigenous languages is exemplified by Alexander (1989, 52): 'However, it is equally important for us to understand that the idea that each language bears a particular, unique, 'culture' is equally *out of date*' (1989, 47) (my emphasis) with the emergence of a new national culture arising out of the use of a lingua franca: '... this easier communication [using English as a temporary lingua franca] will in fact be the mid-wife to a new (national) culture' (1989, 55). This emphasis is mirrored in the LiEP and LiHEP policies. For South Africa, according to Alexander (1989), '[w]hat would appear to be a most likely scenario is one where English is universally accepted as *an* official language together with other languages, which would enjoy official status' (54), and later, 'English should be promoted ... in the short term' (63). This 'short term' is what seems particularly problematic in light of South Africa's Language Policy (1997), since it allows for two equally problematic eventualities.

These two eventualities were always evident in writing about English in South Africa, especially in and for the higher education context. Yet few commentators have explored in much detail the significance of the apartheid legacy in the choice of English as a future lingua franca. In *Sow the Wind* (1989), having spent so much time outlining the history of language politics in South Africa, Alexander, as does Wright (1995), fails to consider the implications of the systematic reduction of English, and the systematic advancement of Afrikaans for black South Africans over four generations. Afrikaans was made (brutally for many) to be accessible, whereas access to English was always limited even though it was an official language. Thus 'short-term' development when applied to English as lingua franca, while the other languages are being cultivated, is itself problematic since no lingua franca can ever prove its value if used only 'temporarily'. In the meantime (15 years since 1989), English has increasingly been held responsible for everything from the erosion of Zulu culture (wakaMsimang 1998, 6) to poor matriculation results (Moreosele 1998, 11). In higher education, the use of Afrikaans has gradually come to be replaced by a demand for the use of English; this despite English not being formally chosen as lingua franca, it has become a *de facto* lingua franca without any of the support required for its proper development as the 'common language'. This is a problem of choice and perception. In 1989, Alexander could claim (after Heugh) that English had always enjoyed a positive image in South Africa owing to the fact that it was not the language of the apartheid regime (56). This simplified version of language history in South Africa misrepresents English as somehow being free of taint when, if Soweto's writing in 1976 means anything at all now, it is not the struggle for access to English in 1976, but rather the struggle for 'choice' as represented by English. Inevitably the choice by government of English after 1994 as a lingua franca must represent, to some at least, its prescription, the reason perhaps for alienation from the language. Twelve years after Alexander's (1989) polemic it is clear from media and academic coverage of the issue that the position of English was, and continues to be, much more ambiguous; resented as an inaccessible lingua franca and envied as a 'gateway to progress'.

In a 'debate', where native speakers of English are cautioned not to 'look to England', and speakers of local varieties encouraged not to 'look to native speakers', the 'locals', the 'natives' and the indigenous languages lose, since no constructive engagement with the challenge of language rejuvenation is offered. In this context, English in South Africa seems to be entering a phase described best as its post-colonial twilight; a period of political instability and ambivalence where its 'international allure' and 'local inaccessibility' are both the cause and consequence of an 'imperialism' of South Africa's own creation. The research of Tsung and Clarke (2010) and Duff and Li (2014) suggests that the ambivalence concerning perceptions regarding English or even local lingua franca is not associated only with the post-colonial condition. In Yunnan in China, Duff's research suggested that language shift and the preference for English occur sometimes because of a resistance to a State-imposed language like Mandarin Chinese, and sometimes because English is attractive to young people because of its association with globalisation, social mobility and modernity.

While children emerging from the schooling system seek access to the tertiary education sector, the languages they bring from their communities and regions may not be the same as those used within the universities to which they seek access, and which may be located in regions far from where the child was schooled. Thus, as language policies of schools and universities begin to become implemented, and indigenous languages are developed, there will arise a South African scholarship concerning bilingual education, and a more intensive engagement with issues concerning academic literacy, certainly in English (explored to some extent by Cummins 1999), but also in the indigenous languages used for teaching and learning in South African universities. In this context it is possible to suggest that the pressure to find innovative and accelerated indigenous language learning programmes (modules and short courses), will be intensified. Language pedagogy is thus likely to receive renewed attention in South Africa as the pressure to develop research, and the pressure to access communities of learning, and communities at large, intensify.

What emerges repeatedly in research regarding language choice in South Africa (see Balfour 2008b, for example) is that people negotiate culture, face and identity through more than one language, and balance the need for modernity alongside the value of tradition, together with awareness that multiculturalism is normative in South Africa. This local scholarship focusing on bilingualism is also informed by the experiences of other countries in which multilingualism has become a feature of language planning (see for example, Freeman 1998). What Puhrsch (2007) shows is that within South Africa parents are not blind consumers of hegemonic languages, and learners are not insensitive to the dangers of language attrition or subtractive bilingualism (Lambert 1974). In South Africa, parents come to choose schools and skills that are most likely to either maintain the middle-class status of their children, or propel them into that middle class from the employed working class. Most often English is associated with education that enables that kind of mobility. What emerges in a review of research concerning language development, the alleged hegemony of English, the protection and enhancement of indigenous languages (see, for example, the special issue of the *English Academy Review* (2003), or the 2004 issue of *Alternation*, or Webb and du Plessis 2006) are preoccupations and frustrations about the absence or lack of adequate provision in languages other than English, and the need for the public and organs of public and private sectors to be sensitised to the benefits of multilingualism. Such findings suggest that the development of multilingualism has been retarded by the legacy of apartheid, where quality in education was available only through English or Afrikaans, and that there is a great demand for innovation in indigenous languages development.

6.5.1 Policy contexts and the challenges of higher education institutionalised multilingual practices

Research by Balfour (1999) and Joshua (2007) in South Africa demonstrates, at the level of primary and secondary education, that the provisions made by various acts of legislation for the promotion and development of indigenous languages have not been adequately implemented, owned by communities, or understood by parents, school governing bodies and management teams as well as educators. In part, researchers have described how schools perceive such implantation to be associated with the provision of human and material resources in other languages by the State. In part, such research, as undertaken by Joshua (2007), for example, also shows that parents and management teams in schools continue to promote English as a hegemonic language precisely because they perceive that it will provide their children with a 'competitive edge' in their studies and work. The research undertaken by Balfour and Ralfe (2006) also complicates this landscape further by arguing that transformation initiatives such as *Curriculum 2005* (1997),

Outcomes-based Education, and the *National Curriculum Statement* (2011), cannot be adequately supported at schools because other factors (English as gatekeeper, gender violence, poverty and HIV/AIDS discrimination) are still sufficiently powerful to undermine and even negate the transformational value of policy initiatives.

In South Africa a further complexity has to do with the legislation concerning language rights and indigenous language development itself. I have described this particular set of complexities elsewhere (Balfour 2007), but for the purposes of contextualisation of my argument in this chapter, I would like to summarise them here. The Constitution (1996) allows individuals the right to express themselves in any language that they choose, and also to learn in the language of their choice, while the National Education Policy Act (27, 1996) lends further credence to this by stating that every child has the right to education in her/his mother tongue. The South African Schools Act (84, 1996) allows for school governing bodies to determine the medium of instruction for a particular school. Perhaps the single most significant piece of legislation, the Language in Education Policy (LiEP 1997), is also the most vexatious since, for example, although the Constitution (1996) guarantees the right of the learner to be taught in her/his home language, the LiEP enables governing bodies to determine the language of instruction in a school. Even the 2004 *Ministerial Report on the Use of Indigenous Languages as Mediums of Instruction in Higher Education Institutions* acknowledges that 'unfortunately the policy does not provide detail or give guidance as to how this will be achieved or by whom' (2004, 21). Despite attempts at definition, language policy documentation for schools and HEIs does sometimes appear to give rise to conflicts of interest that have not been resolved through subsequent pieces of legislation such as the Languages in Higher Education Act (2002), in which the provisions of LiEP are extended to higher education. In the next sections of this chapter a description is provided of how these and previously stated complexities find expression within institutional contexts and universities' attempts to develop indigenous languages.

Historically, the University of the Free State (UFS) was an English-medium university (1904–48) which evolved into a predominantly Afrikaans-medium university (1948–93). After 1994, the university, along with several other Afrikaans-medium institutions, adopted English as a medium of instruction alongside Afrikaans (the other universities were the University of Stellenbosch and North-West University). It goes without saying that the introduction of English, although favoured by the State on the grounds that it opened access to students whose home or second language was not Afrikaans, was not favoured by the universities concerned, and a lively and sometimes fractious debate occurred concerning English hegemony and the protection of minor languages such as Afrikaans (du Plessis 2006). After 1994 it became important to view the (re)introduction of English in these institutions as part of the State's initiative not only to broaden access to higher education, but also to foster indigenous languages in terms of the Languages in Higher Education Policy (2002). Du Plessis (2006), in his description of the Free State example, draws on Jernudd and Neustupny's (1987) description of language management in terms of its processes (policy development, cultivation and planning), and outcomes (enhancement, use as cultural capital and protection) as the means by which the State attends specifically to the languages used within it. It is by no means a South African phenomenon, with examples readily available in French/English-medium universities in Canada (notably McGill in Montreal) and Gaelic/English universities in Wales (notably Swansea and Cardiff; see Balfour 2007, for some discussion of the Cardiff example).

Although the use of two languages, such as found in the University of the Free State (UFS) or North-West University (located in North-West Province), may on one level seem to promote bilingualism (indeed the UFS describes itself as a multilingual university), the institutional arrangements made for the use of the languages may sometimes serve to keep them distinct in the lives and minds of the students and academics. For example, dual-medium instruction has been practised at the UFS for some time, where English is used for classes that are repeated at another time in Afrikaans. While this arrangement caters for the language groups within the university, it does not result in coordinated bilingualism for the students. Effectively this remains monolingual education within the same institutional context. This is not to suggest that such instruction is ineffective, but if the goal of the language policy is to promote multilingualism, then the purpose of offering one subject in two languages is to conserve the monolingual use of each language. This practice is also costly for academics (double workloads), and the institution that needs to provide materials and resources in two languages. The expectation in South Africa in Afrikaans-medium institutions in particular is that academics will function as coordinate bilinguals, but attend only to the compound bilingualism evident in their students. Another arrangement, now practised at the North-West University, makes use of simultaneous interpreting, whereby the university makes provision for the use of two languages within the institutional context, at the same time and in the same venue used by the students. Typically, materials development in two languages (in translation), and the use of interpreting facilities are key to the success of this initiative.

I will not concern myself here as to whether the impulse towards bilingualism arises from the need for language protectionism or language promotion. Although there is some debate about these descriptions in South Africa, see for example Van der Walt and Brink (2005), policy frameworks construct the need for the use of indigenous languages as arising from the need to protect these languages, as well as to promote their development and use. At the UFS, while English is officially endorsed in the policy together with Afrikaans, the majority of academics and administrators are in fact Afrikaans home-language speakers and the institution has an identity that is strongly Afrikaans. Policy development, with its subsequent implementation, has been centrally driven (through the Council, with some input from stakeholders within the institution). Thus, the implementation of the UFS policy has become a line management function to ensure that dual-medium language use takes place in instruction and administration. The UFS has established a Language Committee whose role is to advise the university on the process of implementation and to report to Senate and Council on progress annually. Although the implementation of the policy is funded centrally, there is also support pledged for the development of a third language (SeSotho).

Typically, students are identified in terms of the need for language support through the university's admission tests. The funding is used to support such testing initiatives, to develop and support translation and interpreting services to students and staff, and to provide students and staff with access to proficiency modules in both languages in order to enable the attainment of at least functional literacy in one or the other language. These functions, as mentioned earlier, have been delegated to various senior line managers within the institution as a means of ensuring accountability and implementation.

While the university considers that it has effectively included an additional language to accommodate the students who have access to English, it is not clear, either in terms of LiHEP (2002) or the *Ministerial Report on the Use of Indigenous Languages as Mediums of Instruction in Higher Education Institutions* (2004), how this policy enables speakers of the majority indigenous language (SeSotho) to access the institution in their own language. And, while the university has responded to the sensitivities of the Afrikaans-speaking language community (by no means white only), it has in fact responded in terms of its historical positioning. The imperative then is not to make learning accessible through SeSotho and it is not clear from the UFS policy documentation what role SeSotho will play. What is unambiguous is that SeSotho is the majority language of the Free State province and, given that primary and secondary schools are being encouraged to use the language as a medium of learning, there will arise in the not too-distant future a cohort of SeSotho language users with access to English as an additional language, and little or no access to Afrikaans. It is unlikely that a policy which makes available two additional languages to this grouping will prove sufficiently flexible, since this cohort of learners will only be able to access the UFS through English. The next section explores another attempt to make provision for access to an indigenous language, this time through a university in the province of KwaZulu-Natal.

6.5.2 What languages for what future? The University of KwaZulu-Natal

In 2006, the University of KwaZulu-Natal (UKZN) passed its Language Policy and Plan through the University Senate. The Policy advocates additive bilingualism in English and isiZulu, and supports multilingualism more broadly with respect to Afrikaans, the Indian heritage languages, and languages of strategic importance in Africa and globally:

> The University of KwaZulu-Natal identifies with the goals of South Africa's multilingual language policy and seeks to be a key player in its successful implementation. There is a need to develop and promote proficiency in the official languages, particularly English and isiZulu. The benefits for students becoming proficient in English, the dominant medium of academic communication and of trade and industry internationally, and the lingua franca in government and institutions in South Africa, are clear. Proficiency in isiZulu will contribute to nation building and will assist the student in effective communication with the majority of the population of KwaZulu-Natal. This policy seeks to make explicit the benefits of being fully bilingual in South Africa. (UKZN Language Policy 2006, 1)

In the terms outlined above, the policy aligns itself explicitly with the intentions of the national Language Policy for Higher Education (2002), and the *Ministerial Report* (2004) mentioned earlier. The policy suggests that the use of isiZulu should be particularly relevant in certain areas of the curriculum for anyone intending to study in the professions or the humanities. As isiZulu is the language of many rural and urban communities, the university recognises its importance as a language through which to conduct and disseminate research. Unlike the Language Policy of the UFS, the UKZN policy does not advocate dual-medium instruction in isiZulu and English, but rather envisages that certain disciplines and modules will make use of isiZulu in relation to the needs of students and academics as they engage in research and learning associated with professions in law, medicine, health, social work, commerce and education.

The Language Plan (UKZN Language Plan 2006) describes mechanisms and targets that will, over two phases and a period of 20 years, be used to realise the further development of isiZulu as a medium of instruction, administration and communication. It allows for academics, administrators and students who do not have isiZulu to gain access to conversational and other communicative courses (such as translation and interpreting services) in order to become conversant with the language. As with the UFS policy, the UKZN plan identifies line managers, particularly heads of departments and administrative units, as having special responsibilities for its implementation. The plan distinguishes between short-term goals (such as making isiZulu feature in a bilingual greeting service at the switchboard, public notices, written correspondence with the public and signage), and longer term goals, as described here.

In Phase 1 (2008–18) and 2 (2019–29), the university encouraged and facilitated discussions with those academic disciplines associated with the professions (Health Sciences, Education, Law, Accountancy) to assist students and staff to develop appropriate writing skills in English and isiZulu in their disciplines. In this regard the university will make provision, in Phase 1 of implementation, for the use of translation services in isiZulu in the access and first year of degree studies on the basis that it will facilitate the development of course materials and terminology in isiZulu for the acquisition of cognitive academic language proficiency in Phase 2 of implementation (UKZN Language Plan 2006, 4).

What was thus envisaged was that isiZulu would become a comprehensive part of the identity of the institution. The UKZN Language Policy and Plan is a key aspect of what transformation must mean to all participants in education in KwaZulu-Natal. This assertion was supported on the following grounds. The policy provides long-overdue recognition of isiZulu as an important regional language and national lingua franca. The university recognised that the majority language of the region could not, and ought not to remain excluded from higher education in every domain other than isiZulu Studies. In a number of statements made by university managers there has been further recognition that in order for the University to meet its mandate as the 'premier university of African scholarship' it needs to take seriously its commitment to the environment in which much of its research is located, and which much of its community engagement and research attempts to serve. Unlike the UFS Language Policy, the UKZN Policy, by seeking not simply to commit to the development isiZulu as a language but to use and actively promote the language in its own teaching and learning at all levels of the curriculum, seeks to counter a damaging hegemonic legacy of English.

In terms of implementation and progress to date, the following may be noted. The university has made provision for the establishment of a University Languages Board (ULB), which has oversight of the implementation of the policy and plan. The Board consists of elected representatives from all schools offering languages, all faculties of the university, and the four colleges in which those faculties are located. In addition to this, the Board has representation from the Unions, the Students' Representative Council, the University Administration and legal offices, as well as the Provincial Pan-South African Language Board structure. Such broad representation is critical given that the implementation of the policy will affect the vast majority of students and employees, and have consequences for the university's relations with the public and communities. Though structural mechanisms have been set in place to enable buy-in from a number of sectors of the university, the implementation of this policy is unlikely to be cheaper than that found in the UFS. Staff might not be required to conduct double lectures, but the university administration will need to invest considerably in the development of materials in two languages, and the provision of translation and interpreting services along the lines described already for the North-West University (for a further detailed discussion of the UKZN initiative, see 2008).

If the UFS Language Policy (2003) is oriented towards the language communities constituting its present student and staff demographic, the UKZN policy anticipates a fairly rapid and comprehensive change to that demographic. This is owed in part to recognition by the university that the Provincial Department of Education of KwaZulu-Natal has undertaken to make isiZulu a compulsory additional language in schools where it is not already offered. IsiZulu will thus replace Afrikaans as the second official language of the province. Thus, from an educational and intercultural perspective too, access to isiZulu must become an asset as the language gains cultural capital as part of the requirements for employment, for example. Both institutional examples (UFS and UKZN) anticipate that students will access these institutions within the decade, many having been taught through the regionally dominant indigenous languages (SeSotho and isiZulu). It remains to be seen whether developments in the primary and secondary education sectors will deliver cohorts of students equally adept in two languages (English and Sesotho in the Free State, and English and isiZulu in KwaZulu-Natal). The next section of this chapter explores exactly what these possibilities are in relation to some references to primary and secondary education policy and recent research of bilingual language acquisition.

6.5.3 Why indigenous languages for learning in higher education in South Africa?

Spolsky (1998, 48) defines compound bilingualism as occurring through the stages of interlanguages where one, or both, languages within the learner are affected by each other. The long-term goal of language pedagogy is to effect coordinated bilingualism where contact between the two languages does not occur and the child is able, as it were, to speak in one language while simultaneously thinking in another. Compound bilingualism, as noted by Widdowson (2001, 8) is not perceived as ideal for the purposes of language learning since it is conventionally associated with phenomena such as interference and fossilisation (Zobl 1988). I want to argue that for as long as that remains a feature of the language experience of children, compound bilingualism will never develop past its interlanguage (Selinker 1972) stages to a point where the learner is able to give full expression to coordinated bilingualism. Whether one considers the language policy developments at the UFS or UKZN, it is clear that higher education institutions are preparing for learners based on the assumption that these will be full coordinate bilinguals. Yet the South African education system has capacity only for the production of compound bilingualism for reasons described below.

Submersion-oriented pedagogy as described by Genesee (1987), for example, which typically occurs in English-medium schools in South Africa where the language of the teachers and learners is not English, leads to subtractive bilingualism in a context where the target language is perceived as more valuable as cultural capital (Lambert 1974). And while the ability to think and dream in a foreign language is the coordinate bilingual ideal, as Antonie Snijers suggests in the film (Puhrsch 2007), competence in that language sometimes overshadows the mother tongue. In the middle-class multilingual classroom, depicted in the film, what seems to function, both in the role that the teacher adopts using two languages and in the roles the learners adopted when interacting with each other in pairs or groups in one language and with other children, in English is what Widdowson (2001) terms a:

> ... permissive pedagogy: one which allows for, even encourages, the learners' engagement of the L1, but again makes no acknowledgement of its existence in the design of the instruction itself. Monolingual teaching is justified in this case on the grounds that input in the L2, so long as it is comprehensible, will automatically activate learning. (Widdowson 2001, 10)

If it were true that learning is simply activated when the learner is exposed to comprehensible input, how do we explain that the input routinely used in the monolingual non-English classroom does not activate either conscious control over the language, or the ability to use it for purposes beyond the communicative context? For Krashen (1988), the quality of L2 input is critical, whereas for Ellis (1994), the role of the L1 is essential since adequate knowledge of the mother tongue enables the scaffolding (Wong-Fillmore 1985/1994) of language learning to be developed. In both positions there is an assumption that knowledge of the L1 and the L2 is critical for the movement of learning from the state of compound bilingualism to that of coordinate bilingualism. Yet what is demonstrated in the excerpts from both the rural monolingual classroom and the urban middle-class multilingual classroom is that learners are not enabled by the teacher to make use of either the L1 or the L2 as a learning opportunity. This point might seem a little disconnected from previous sections in this chapter in which policy provisions in South African universities were discussed, but it does go to the core of whether the anticipated outcomes, or suggested processes, of such policies are likely to be relevant or even attainable. Given that no formal scaffolding upon which the internal cognitive processing of L2 through the L1 is made explicit, learners are in fact left to make those connections on their own, developing a compound bilingualism that, as we know from the variable success of academic development programmes in South Africa (see Mgqwashu 2007 for a full discussion of academic literacy programmes at selected higher education institutions), seldom progresses beyond the interlanguage stage. Simply put, my argument is that code-switching is neither desirable nor useful in the classroom unless it is incorporated into an explicit pedagogy that seeks to develop the adequate use of the L1 as a tool for acquisition and learning of the L2. The remaining question to ask must be concerned with education since both the monolingual and multilingual contexts provide the only opportunity for learners in South Africa to develop both their formal awareness of the L1, and (at least in the monolingual rural environment) their acquisition of the L2.

6.6 REFLECTIONS

This chapter has surveyed schooling and higher education with regard to language development as anticipated by the Constitution (1996) and framed by the LiEP and the LiHEP. Both documents promote the development of coordinate bilingualism at least, and multilingualism at most. The research internationally supports such policy formulation especially in those contexts that may be regarded as manifestly multilingual. In South Africa, the capacity of higher education undergraduate programmes in general, and teacher education programmes in particular, do not yet support the aspirations contained in policy, the consequences being that while society remains predominantly and evidently multilingual, education institutions are still coming to terms with what this implies for the teaching of languages in schools and higher education settings.

Widdowson (2001) suggests that, contrary to teaching the second or foreign language as it is used by native speakers, it is precisely its foreignness that needs to be accentuated and taught in relation to the L1. At the very least what we need to be undertaking within the education system in South Africa is the introduction of L1 and L2 specialist teachers together in the classrooms of Grade 4 (ages 10–11) at least, if not in Grades 1, 2 and 3 (ages 6–9). This suggestion seems contrary to conventional wisdom regarding mother-tongue education in South Africa, which proposes that children should receive instruction in the mother tongue from the earliest ages of schooling and progress towards increasing use of English, or any additional language, at later stages, and preferably through the use of that language as a medium of instruction. Since very few South African teachers are co-ordinate bilinguals, and since competence in the L1 is what most teachers specialise in, it seems reasonable that every Grade 4 classroom in monolingual contexts in South Africa should be provided with two teachers, or at least one teacher of English together with one teacher assistant specialist in isiZulu, for example.

As language choice becomes more a feature of schooling in the early years, the need to consider coordinate bilingual pedagogies in areas that do not support the development of coordinate bilingualism becomes more pressing.

This chapter provides a fairly extensive review of language as contestation (in terms of rights to home language education) in schools. The sections on higher education demonstrate a degree of openness to the support and development of language policy that better enables bilingualism, while in the concluding sections of the chapter, I have argued that the very foundation of our practices both on the micro-level (the classroom), and on the macro-level (policy formulation and implementation) remains for the most part insensitive to research and to socio-demographic contexts. In these circumstances a careful review of language acquisition research, its integration into curriculum policies, and the development of South Africa's teachers remain key challenges to realising the multilingual potential of the population such that every child, irrespective of language or class background is able to participate in the opportunities made possible by democracy in South Africa.

NOTES

1   Taylor, N. (2006). Focus on: Challenges across the education spectrum. *JET Bulletin*,15, 1–9. Cape Town: JET education Services.

2   Gallie, M. (2007). *If you want to solve your discipline problems in schools, dare to 'fix-up' the adults first!* Keynote address delivered at the International Conference on Perspectives on learner conduct held at North-West University, Potchefstroom, on 4 April 2007.

3   During the apartheid era indigenous languages were developed, but only for use in the early primary school years. The transition to English occurred late, and when Afrikaans was made compulsory and the choice for English removed, protest as regards the oppressive use of Afrikaans gained momentum.

4   Scholtz, L. (2006). Die belang van Afrikaanse onderwys vir die oorlewing van die taal. TGW, 46 (4) Des. 2006. 470-481.

5   *Seodin Primary School v Northern Cape Department of Education* Case no. 117/2004 (NC).

6   *Western Cape Minister of Education v The Governing Body of Mikro Primary School* 2005 (3) SA 436 (SCA).

7   Funding education in South Africa: Schools, universities, colleges and students

7.1 INTRODUCTION

Given the history of unequal education spending in the apartheid era, from schools through to universities and colleges, efforts to raise the quality of education available across the broad range of South Africa's schools, colleges and universities have at best to achieve historical redress, and at worst to ensure equitable distribution of resources (see Fiske & Ladd 2004, and Motala 2006). The history of unequal education means that this dilemma remains contestable and vexatious even 20 years after apartheid's demise. To develop the capacity of young men and women to contribute to the prosperity and also diversity (in linguistic and gender terms as noted in earlier chapters) requires that the resourcing of education be considered carefully as a means through which to support the efforts of teachers, students, academics and the broad range of role-players involved in the transformation project in South Africa. Thus the creation of a robust higher education and schooling sector depends not only on adequate capacity, but on the development of special capacity among selected groups (women, black, Indian and coloured people as well as LGBTTIQ persons)[1] hitherto excluded from meaningful participation or representation in South Africa prior to 1994. That effort, while it might focus on the advancement of previously marginalised communities, needs also to be coordinated in such a way that the entire productive population of South Africa is able to contribute to its further development. It is thus appropriate that the last themed Chapter of this book should focus on the funding of education.

With the selective closure of some teachers' education colleges and their incorporation into universities between 2002–4, and the subsequent mergers between universities and some technikons, there arose a need three years after the conclusion of this process for the Council on Higher Education to review the impact of institutional changes and reconfigurations in South Africa. This chapter draws substantively from the official review documents with selective references to other studies of impact and change in the system as conducted or documented by selected researchers. Approaches to funding have taken two forms: the need for a systemic and special focus on previously disadvantaged groups in the education sector (from black, Indian, coloured, poor and or rural schools, for example, to funding formerly neglected and disempowered institutions in the higher education sector, such as those historically black universities, to the broad swathe of technical, vocational education and training colleges). At the same time there has been a need to fund, systematically, a vision for schooling and higher education as sectors contributing to an equitable, just and high-quality education system capable of providing quality teaching and learning, and in the case of higher education, advanced research capacity. A sound funding basis has been needed to allow for high-end advanced skills training and development of qualifications that enable South Africa to contribute towards global knowledge generation, national, social and economic challenges in order to become competitive after years of economic and political isolation. This chapter has two major parts, the first of which deals with the funding of schooling, and the second of which deals with the funding of higher education.

School types are variable in South Africa. Public schools may be funded entirely by the State (no-fee-paying schools, mostly in poorer communities), or funded by a combination of the State and the private sector (low-fee or fee-paying State schools), or funded by the private sector entirely (private for-profit schools operating as franchisers or consortia), or funded as not-for-profit organisations through registered charities such as churches, for example. Before 1994 this sheer variety of school types and funding models aligned, with the exception of mostly non-profit private church schools, fairly neatly with the race hierarchies of the apartheid State. After 1994, and as a result of the abolition of the Group Areas Act and other related 'influx control' regulations, South African urban areas (already suburban rather than townships or locations such as the areas reserved for black communities prior to 1994) have become more racially diverse. Nowadays, the variety of schools and related funding regimes reveal a new kind of apartheid, associated not with race, but rather with class privilege. The responsibility of the State to make provision for education is enshrined in the Constitution (1996), but it is the purchasing power of the employed population that enables a vast differentiation in education spending to occur between State or private schools, colleges or universities.

The second part of the chapter provides an overview of the substantive issues concerning the funding of higher education provision and priorities (research and historical redress, for example). The Council on Higher Education (CHE) Review of Higher Education in South Africa (see Jansen in CHE Review of Higher Education, 8), identifies six major changes in South African higher education since the middle 1990s: the changing institutional landscape, the rise of private higher education, new modes of delivery, the changing value of academic programmes, the rise of managerialism in the academy and the reorganisation of the qualifications system. Some of these features have been addressed in this book (restructuring of higher education, new modes of delivery and the reorganisation of higher education qualifications through frameworks, quality assessment and articulation routes). In this second part of this chapter, the funding of higher education is considered in relation to three items: research funding, infrastructural funding and student funding since 1995.

Because transformation of the higher education sector was key to State planning in terms of the creation of a non-racial, non-sexist new South Africa, the second section describes the South African Post-Secondary Education Information System (SAPSE), because this, in effect, formed the basis for a reconfigured funding formula for higher education designed to reward outputs (research artefacts, students graduated and so on), as well as inputs (students admitted, staff, buildings). The third section briefly describes those new dimensions of the New Funding Framework (NFF) designed for a unitary higher education sector in a new South Africa, and deals with two key initiatives aimed at widening access to higher education, and increasing participation by students: the National Finance Student Assistance Scheme and the Funza Lushaka bursaries for teachers, picking up themes addressed also in Chapter 2. The fourth section describes how redress and budgeting for the transformation of higher education has occurred (or has not as the case might be), while the fifth section describes previous measures introduced for infrastructure development: planning and recording the existing and new needs of South African universities.

7.2 FUNDING ACCESS AND SUCCESS IN SOUTH AFRICAN SCHOOLS

Given that reform in schooling formed an immediate priority for the State following the demise of apartheid, commentators noted the urgency with which a reorganisation of school-based funding regimes needed to occur. According to Motala (2001) and Kennedy (2006), the State identified the following priority areas aimed at enhancing the quality of education within the school setting:

- Foreground teaching and learning. School policies have emphasised democratic governance and adequate resourcing; the policies need to be linked to pedagogical concerns with quality improvement and need to be in place for quality education.

- Vision and framework need to be linked to concrete interventions for quality improvement at school level. School clustering, particularly with new district boundaries, may also provide invaluable opportunities for districts to share information and strategies on quality interventions.

- Building a sense of agency, responsibility, and accountability within the school appears to be a major factor in 'working schools'.

- Utilising whatever resources they have within themselves and within the local community is crucial.

- Enhancing the role of teachers as pedagogical agents who want to undertake quality teaching, through professional development about teaching.

Quality of education is a key factor in terms of education, and education institutions ought to be perceived by communities as being of credible quality (Reschovsky, 2006). Perceptions of quality drive parents to aspire to choices in the best interests of their children. Invariably, funding (what education can be afforded in relation to what education costs) is a critical discussion point in any family household. The State has the responsibility to ensure that the quality of education provided in those schools, even in those communities least able to afford the 'cost' of education, is credible.

In relation to the above, the funding models to be adopted by schools in South Africa must also take into account the variability of families' choices with regard to the education to be received by their children. While the South African Schools Act (SASA 84,1996) allows for four types of schools (private on public land, public on private land, public schools on public land and private schools on privately owned land), the funding models had similarly to be flexible enough to account for class and other variables (language or religious education, for example). Parents might not be able to afford education in many communities, but that the State had an obligation to provide quality education. In the discussion to follow I draw substantively on work by Fiske and Ladd (2004), Heystek (2014), Chutgar and Kanjee (2009) on funding of schools in South Africa.

According to Heystek (2014), parents can only exercise their rights if there is a choice between schools based on distance and specifically on quality of education. Context (socio-economic, geo-political, and spatial; see the work undertaken by Burgess, Greaves, Vignoles and Wilson, 2009) is a factor that influences parents' choices about the suitability of schools (Maile, 2004). As mentioned in the introduction to this chapter, location is an important variable that parents consider when choosing a school. Locality can involve considerations of convenience, the extent to which a school is seen as integrated with a community, or the status attached to a particularly residential area (Denessen, Driessena & Sleegers 2005). Goldring and Hausman (1999) note also that transport and access are variables that affect parental choice, especially for parents belonging to lower social class groups. Reputation is a further variable, since this can be constructed in largely social as well as academic performance terms in relation to the quality of education and care (Burgess et al. 2009; Denessen, et al. 2005; Goldring & Hausman 1999). Taylor (2001) summarises the various factors parents consider in relation to school choice as: (1) reasons of ideology (religious and/or pedagogical), (2) geographical distance of the school from home, (3) the quality of the education (academic reputation, variety of extra-mural activities, quality of care by teachers), and (4) certain non-educational characteristics of the school, such as the characteristics of the school population. In relation to the other factors, quality of education is reported as playing a significant role in the process of choosing a school (Denessen et al. 2005). Parents' personal values regarding their children's education tend to be aligned with their subjective desired goals of education, informed perhaps by social and professional networks (Bosetti 2004).

A persistent fear about school choice, which is also the reality of economic and class-based affordances in South Africa, is that it will lead to more stratified schools, for example along racial or socio-economic lines, because parents have the choice and the means to make the choice. Indeed Fiske and Ladd (2004, x) suggest that progress in relation to achieving equality of treatment needs to be counter-balanced with awareness that equity of opportunity has not been attained yet. In the 1960–1980s, middle-class black South

Africans, who could afford quality education, enrolled their children in private non-profit schools run mostly by churches. Perceived as offering a better quality of education, being relatively free from the toxic race ideology of the apartheid State (church schools aspired to race integration), and the deleterious language policy, church schools were seen as credible alternatives for those who could afford them. The deliberate absence of State subsidisation of teachers' salaries or children in these schools meant that they became, by default, elite institutions even though in foundation and ethos most were meant to provide quality education for the most deprived portions of the population. Households that could make choices thus tended to be of higher socio-economic status than those households that did (or could) not (Goldring & Hausman 1999; Weiher & Tedin 2002). It has been argued that more gifted academically students from households that commanded the greatest educational resources tended to migrate from public schools into different schools along racial or perhaps class lines (Weiher & Tedin 2002).

Some private schools may be regarded as very low-fee schools as found in Indian cities, for example (Tooley 2007, 38). In South Africa, schools in the North-West Province as run by the Bafokeng Nation (a Setswana-speaking indigenous community), for example, operate as low-fee-paying semi-private schools (in other words, these are public schools on private land). Tooley (2007, 39) found that private schools for the poor are present throughout the developing world. These schools are sometimes perceived as low-quality, but still regarded in communities as offering a better education than those found within the State system.

In South Africa, because of the widely perceived importance of public and private sector partnerships in education, there are existing schooling partnerships, for example the Adopt-a-School programme as described by Heystek (2014), where the government has drawn some private expertise and funds into the public schooling sector. 'Adopted schools', however, remain in the control of the centralised public schooling bureaucracy (CDE 2013, 19). There is also a variety of independent schools (or what are popularly referred to as private schools) that receive a government subsidy, and must comply with the regulations even if privately owned. Heystek notes that more flexibility in how schools are established and regulated could enable a better use of education expertise in innovating and managing schools: 'This new type of public school will make school managers both responsible and accountable for their performance' (Heystek 2014, 39).

South Africa has a number of independent school franchises, for example Curro Holdings, Spark Schools, Nova Schools and BASA. These are not new phenomena: missionary schools operated as consortia since the 1800s in South Africa –the Dominican convents and Christian Brothers colleges, for example, have established education traditions stretching over 200 years. The new franchise schools are not usually associated with church groups, and operate for profit. According to Heystek, the Curro schools grew from 12 schools in 2011 to 39 schools in 2014, and are perceived as high-quality, low-fee paying schools. Heystek notes that:

> The Curro model is divided into four formal categories, namely Curro private schools, Meridian private schools, Curro Castle nursery schools, and Select private schools. The Meridian schools are mainstream schools with enhanced curricula to provide remedial tuition for disadvantaged learners, the Castle schools are nursery schools, and the Select schools are well-established private schools which are purchased by Curro Holdings. The Select schools are managed, supported and further developed by Curro Holdings, but they continue with their existing systems and ethos. (Heystek 2014, 40)

The State has always subsidised registered independent (previously private) schools in South Africa, though not always to the extent where these schools could become low-fee schools. The subsidies to these schools are calculated as a fraction of the cost per learner in the public school system. The funding of these schools is provided as part of a constitutional and statutory responsibility to provide school education to all learners. In addition, the right of reputable, registered independent schools to exist is protected by the Constitution, and the payment of subsidies to them is not excluded (RSA 1998). Independent schools perform a service to their learners which would otherwise have to be performed by the provincial education departments. Subsidising independent schools is more cost-effective, as it costs the State considerably less per learner than if their learners were enrolled in public schools. Subsidy allocations to these schools show preference for those that are well managed, provide good education, serve the poor and are not operated for profit (RSA 1998).

Twenty years into democracy, the divisions that existed between elite private high-fee schools and 'good' public low-fee schools are not as discernible as they used to be. Those independent schools considered as low to medium fee-charging (on average r25 000 per annum or less) can receive a subsidy from the government to accommodate poorer learners. These subsidies are calculated on a sliding scale based on the Provincial Average Estimate of Expenditure per Learner (PAEPL) and the percentage of the school fees as a ratio of the provincial PAEPL. The subsidy levels of these schools are related to the fee levels on a five-point progressive scale. Independent schools that charge the lowest fees will qualify for the highest level of subsidy, while those who charge in excess of 2.5 times the provincial average cost per learner in an ordinary public school are considered to serve a highly affluent clientele and would therefore receive no subsidy from public funds. The independent schools, who charge the lowest fees, will receive a subsidy equalling 60% of the provincial average cost per learner in ordinary public schools.

In order to illustrate the differences between the scales of fees charged by public and private schools in South Africa the Table below illustrates the school fees of two independent schools and two public (urban) schools in the Rustenburg area.

Table 7.1: Comparison of school fees in Rustenburg area

Name	School fees per annum
Independent schools	
Curro Private School	r20 400
Lebone Private School	r51 989
Public schools	
Rustenburg High School	r13 420
Bergsig High School	r11 820

Source: Heystek (2014, 43)

In comparison to no-fee schools that cater for the poor, the school fees of these schools are quite high. Schools that cater for the impoverished communities should have school fees that are significantly lower than r10 000 per annum. In India the 'budget' private schools are charging annual fees of r2000 or less, while a low-fee chain school in Kenya only charges r360 per annum. For contract schools to be an attractive option for government, they need to deliver quality education to the poor in such a way that it saves money for the government. Activists for contract schooling argue that new regulations will certainly have to be adopted in order to have a winning formula (CDE 2013, 22). They argue that the current legislation has the possibility for alternative interpretation to address some aspects of a contract school model. CDE (2013, 22) identified the following as key sections of the SASA that can help to pave the way for contract schools:

• Section 14: outlines the rules when public schools operate on private property. The interpretation of this section has led to court cases. A good example is the agreement between the Royal Bafokeng Institute and the North-West Provincial Education Department, where the Royal Bafokeng received the legal right to contribute to the core curriculum, extra-curricular activities and school governance costs.

- Section 21: outlines the functions allocated to the governing bodies. These functions provide some autonomy to schools, but are limited in scope and do not give schools the power to act as the employer of state-appointed teachers.

According to Heystek (2014, 43, 44) contract schooling (low-fee paying State-subsidised independent schools) can cater for the needs of the poor who do not have access to high-quality education. Partnerships such as these can benefit the public sector by relieving the pressure on the State by using private expertise to improve the performance of the public sector (CDE 2013, 26). Having described the variety of schools in South Africa and the attendant changes in education which do reflect a growing emphasis on class as the defining factor in relation to the affordances parents can exercise in relation to schooling the section to follow provides a brief overview of mechanisms developed by the State to ensure a minimum standard for quality education through the establishment of teacher provisioning norms.

7.2.1 Funding the costs of teachers and schools: Quintiles and post-provisioning norms

The right to an education assumes an equitable provisioning policy and model applicable to all schools in South Africa. The desire to achieve an equitable funding system goes to the point made by Fiske and Ladd (2004, 6) in which they acknowledge that equality of treatment cannot be entirely effective in a context of great structural, economic and social inequalities. The amended document on National Norms and Standards for School-Funding, gazetted in 2011, was phased in during 2014. In these terms revisions were made to the five categories or quintiles for classifying schools prior to 2008. Poor schools had a low quintile ranking, while richer schools (owing to higher fees paid by parents living in areas considered reasonably affluent) had a higher ranking.

The efficacy of the quintile system has been widely debated. Raab and Terway (2010), citing development experts, suggest that even when motivated by equality, the provision of cheap education does nothing to reduce inequality and poverty if the standard of tuition on offer is low (Raab & Terway 2010, 1).

Together with post-provisioning in schools, and aided by legislative acts, schools are compelled to reduce the number of educators if student numbers fall, and to employ educators recommended by the department if they rise. For example, the Employment of Educators Act (76 of 1998) enables the department to propose candidates for vacant posts to a school for (consideration by the SGB for) appointment.

The Department of Basic Education's national poverty distribution table shows that the province with the highest number of well-resourced schools is the Western Cape, with 31.7% of the province's schools falling under quintile 5, closely followed by Gauteng with 31.4%. The province with the highest number of poor schools, previously classified as first quintile, is Limpopo, with 28.2% of its schools in this category. Limpopo also has the least number of schools that were formerly classified as quintile 5 (8%). The Eastern Cape has the second highest number of schools in the first quintile (27.3%), and 11.4% of its schools are classified in quintile 5. Gauteng has the least number of first quintile schools, with only 14.1% of schools falling under this ranking. According to Mtshali (2014, 1), 'Of the province's 2200 public schools, 1237 are no-fee. These no-fee schools cater for 64% of Gauteng's State school pupils'.

According to Chutgar and Kanjee (2009, 18), ways in which quintiles have been determined by the department occurs in relation to the score being 'calculated using national census data: weighted household data on income dependency ratio (or unemployment rate), and the level of education of the community (or literacy rate)'. Chutgar and Kanjee suggest that despite best intentions, 'the schools in the middle often look similar and may appear better or worse in unexpected ways. Schools from Q1–Q4 are barely distinguishable in relation to mean proportion of disadvantaged learners in the school. With respect to average proportion of affluent learners, schools in Q1 are actually better off than schools in Q2 . . . the current quintile ranking system does not work effectively'.

Quintiles as described above are related to the subsidy received by the school from the State. Quintile rankings, based on socio-economic and income profiles of the area in which the school is located, do not take account of the resourcing level of the school. Assumptions with regard to similarities of socio-economic status as associated with the area have proven problematic. In many cases, as noted by Chutgar and Kanjee (2009), many schools ranked as quintile 5, for example, actually have low-income children in them, and so the ranking has become highly problematic, since the poverty/affluence level of children in them is not considered.

In the new policy, and in order to deal with the issues described by Chutgar and Kanjee (2009), quintile schools 1 to 3 are no longer required to charge school fees. Instead, from 2011, these schools received an allocation of r1059 for each pupil, with projected increases year on year (for example, in 2012, quintiles 1, 2 and 3 received an increase to r1116 per child. It was made illegal for no-fee schools to levy fees from parents. Estimates are that 60% or South African learners are in no-fee public schools. The subsidy allocated to fee-paying (and by implication wealthier schools) schools that previously fell under quintile 4 received r503, while quintile 5 schools received only r183 for each learner.[2]

Given the history of inequitable distribution of education resources (in terms of spend on children associated with the race hierarchies of apartheid – see Crouch 1995), and the variability of qualifications (and quality) of teachers in schools, the Post-Provisioning Model (PPM) is a Resource Allocation Model (RAM) used by the Department of Basic Education to optimise the distribution of available educator resources to public schools in South Africa.

The Post-Provisioning Norm (PPN) is meant to achieve, according to Ntuli (2012), an equitable and transparent and resource-efficient allocation of teachers to schools. The PPM is a formula-driven model that primarily allocates educators, as human capital, to public schools based on learner enrolment numbers. In simple terms, the number of learners must exist in ratio to the PPN for a school to be regarded as adequately staffed. Ntuli (2012) demonstrates that the model assumes public choice to be static in relation to school choices. Thus, while the norm might be one teacher per 39–42 pupils (depending on the quintile) in 2014, low-fee and fee paying schools have long used fees as a means of funding the salaries of additional teachers. Since individual attention to children is regarded as one of the characteristics of quality education, the lower the teacher–learner ratio the better-off a school is seen to be. In effect this means that although the PPN provides a consistent base for teacher resource allocations, it condemns by default poor schools to higher teacher–learner ratios. In poorer communities, schools are usually not able to raise funds in the same way as more affluent communities, where additional teaching posts are funded through school fees to bring the teacher–learner ratio down.

Ntuli (2012) also found that the use of the PPN is undermined in poor or remote schools which struggle to attract qualified teachers. Thus, in order to meet the PPN requirements, poor and/or rural schools allocate posts to under-qualified or non-qualified staff. The appointment of qualified educators is thus inevitably skewed. Ntuli (2012) argues further that the PPM punishes small schools unduly since the teacher–learner ratio often creates circumstances in which not enough teachers can be 'afforded' by a school to offer all the subjects in a curriculum. Thus, advantaged schools (no longer along the lines of race, but certainly along the lines of class) can not only afford to have fewer children and more teachers in a school, but can also afford to offer a greater variety of curriculum subjects.

Gustafsson and Patel (2006) have undertaken extensive research on teacher pay in South Africa. They argue that while pay is important, so also are contextual factors such as class size, location of the school, worker hours and the ethos impact on considerations in relation to teacher pay. In the 1990s, there was as much as a 25% rise in teacher pay, in recognition of the poor levels of payment of teacher in previous decades. Gustafsson and Patel (2006) showed that, by international standards, teacher pay had been raised to comparably high levels. Furthermore, teachers entering the system after 2005 were likely to experience more benefits than those entering before the 1990s.

Such models have been criticised by teacher unions in South Africa on the basis that they privilege the already privileged and restrict poorer schools from offering better-quality education to children from households where high quality education is a remote possibility. The following sections explore the complexities of funding higher education in which similar continuities between historic class-based privilege and historic disadvantage, based along the lines of race, interface to make for an intricate funding system that must achieve a similar consistency of equity distribution of resources in circumstances where parity of institutions cannot be assumed.

7.3 FUNDING HIGHER EDUCATION IN SOUTH AFRICA AFTER APARTHEID

The CHE Review (2007) concluded that there was a need for ongoing research into the funding of higher education. While education is proportionately the highest spend when compared to countries in Africa and indeed globally, it represents just one percent of the GDP. Scholars (Baatjes 2005, and Vally 2005) have suggested that the caution to commit more to education arises from neo-liberal economic policies (*GEAR* and *ASGISA*). While funding levels at historically white or advantaged institutions have decreased, these institutions have supplemented the loss through alumni fund-raising, donor, or research funding. That said, the higher education funding system has come in for criticism from scholars such as Bozzoli (2015). Bozzoli argues that sharp increases in student numbers without increasing staffing and infrastructure sufficiently, has lead to the throughput crisis (see Chapter 4 and the conclusion of book).

While some of these universities have merged with other historically disadvantaged universities or colleges (for example the merging of the University of Natal with the University of Durban-Westville to form the University of KwaZulu-Natal in 2004, or the merging of the Natal Technikon with the ML Sultan Technikon in 2004 to become Durban University of Technology), and received 'merger' funding. Most formerly advantaged universities have remained as they were though they might have lost a campus or academic unit (for example, the University of Stellenbosch lost its dental school to CPUT and Rhodes University lost its East London Campus to Walter Sisulu University).

To give effect to historical redress, the increase in education spending was directed at formerly disadvantaged (black) institutions to improve their capacity to deliver quality programmes, and to repair years of infrastructural damage and neglect. In many instances, commentators have noted that the redress has been insufficient to address the scale of inequality that still exists between former white and black institutions. The reasons for this are few and self-evident. The first has to do with location: historically disadvantaged universities were mostly built in areas associated with the former Bantustans of the apartheid era. Thus, the universities of the Transkei, Zululand and Bophuthatswana were built in fairly remote regions close to, or in, former homelands. The race hierarchies of the day were evident in the geo-political location of these institutions and given that population control meant that it was near-impossible for white and blacks to settle in areas of choice, the likelihood of historically disadvantaged institutions attracting white let alone black top academics to academic positions was low. In addition to the discourse of social justice with regard to uplifting institutions, restitution and integration, there remains nevertheless a real urgency concerning the need for these institutions to be successful. Some universities (for example, the University of Fort Hare, 1916, and the University of Western Cape, 1959) have long histories of left-wing intellectual and social activism associated with resistance to the apartheid government, and thus were subject to institutional neglect and damage arising from student and academic protests, and clashes with the police and armed forces. Other institutions (for example, the University of the Transkei and the University of Zululand) had histories of collusion with the Afrikaner nationalist associations (for example, the Broederbond) in terms of their staffing and management. With the transition to a properly democratic dispensation there has occurred an exit of experienced administrators and academics at these institutions, which in turn has left serious governance gaps. This, in turn, meant that despite 20 years of additional funding, the capacity to utilise such resources has been weak at best and dysfunctional at worst. In 2013, for example, four universities – the

Central University of Technology, the University of Zululand (KwaZulu-Natal), Walter Sisulu University (Eastern Cape) and Mangosotho University of Technology (Durban KwaZulu-Natal) – were placed under administration by the Minister of Higher Education and Training, an intervention that arose from systemic financial and administrative malpractice. Thus, the CHE Review questioned the following:

> Moreover, how effective has funding been as a steering mechanism to bring about change in higher education, to what extent there has been an alignment between funding and the other two steering instruments chosen for the transformation of higher education: planning and quality assurance? (CHE Review 2007, 3)

There is a growing body of research on the funding of higher education (for example, Wangenge-Ouma & Cloete (2008), and Wangenge-Ouma (2012). Steyn and De Villiers (2007) have provided an analysis of funding frameworks used for higher education in South Africa since the 1950s (beginning with the Holloway Commission and formula, the changes made by the Van Wyk de Vries Commission, and the subsequent adoption and revision of the SAPSE formulas). While they suggest that '[a] subsidy formula ensures that funding takes place in a fair and objective way, without taking subjective considerations into account. It therefore usually depoliticises the allocation of funds to a large extent' (2007, 12), they acknowledge nevertheless that the use of formulas assumes an equal playing field in terms of the capacity of institutions to meet the criteria for the award of funding. This assumption, as shown in previous chapters, is not sustainable in South Africa given the historic variety of universities established, and the historic and differential spending patterns associated with race groups and the Bantustans.

Furthermore, subsidy formulae pertaining to universities made provision for the accrual of income on the basis of research generation (an activity for which further education and training colleges were not mandated). For research funding, for example, universities accrue a subsidy depending on the research outputs (typically books, articles, Master's and doctoral students graduated, and so on) recognised by the Department of Higher Education. While such provision has long been made in funding formulae in South Africa, different formulae applied to further education and training colleges and also to the funding of teacher training colleges prior to 1994. With the reorganisation and restructuring of higher education in 2004 it became necessary to fund the two new categories of higher education institution, the comprehensive university (which offered specialist academic as well as vocational training) and the research university (which offered specialist academic and professional training in which research generativity featured strongly).

7.3.1 The South African Post-Secondary Education Information System (SAPSE)

According to Steyn and De Villiers (2007, 13), the SAPSE subsidy formula for universities was implemented in 1984 and revised for implementation in 1993, and was applied initially only to the historically white and advantaged institutions. Its effectiveness later made it possible to be applied also to universities associated with the Bantustans. The SAPSE formula underwent a number of important changes that prefigured the New Funding Formula adopted by government (which will be covered in more detail later). In 1987, the technikons motivated a number of changes, some of which are listed below because they provided useful snapshots indicating the priorities of the government in relation to teaching and learning, and awareness of quality as well as fitness for purpose (the economy, the market, national needs):

1 The subsidy per ESS in the Natural Sciences was increased relative to the subsidy per ESS in the Human Sciences.

2 The subsidization of new library collections based on growth in the ESS was decreased significantly.

3 The provision for the replacement and renewal of equipment based on the ESS was increased.

4 The provision for the replacement and renewal of library collections based on the ESS was decreased.

5 A new mechanism (based on estimates of the per capita annual income of students' families) to determine the government contribution ratio for each technikon was implemented.

6 The projection formula for the ESS was revised in such a way that as far as the then current expenditure was concerned, only an annual increase in the projected ESS of six per cent for contact tuition and eight per cent for distance tuition would be subsidized. These higher allowable growth rates of technikons in comparison with universities were the result of a deliberate attempt by the government to increase the size of the technikon sector relative to the size of the university sector. The higher growth in the technikon sector than the university sector during the years 1993 to 1998 can be partly ascribed to these 'allowable' differential growth rates.

7 The subsidy formula was enriched to provide for experiential (cooperative) learning in the technikon sector. (Steyn & De Villiers 2007, 23)

This system applied to both technikons and universities and prefigured important changes post-1994, for example in relation to the creation of new comprehensive institutions (universities rather than technikons comprised the former, but with clearer research development mandates) as well as consensus regarding the need for a unitary funding formula for public higher education in South Africa. The SAPSE system remained in place until 2003 when it was replaced by the New Funding Formula (NFF).

The formula allowed for subsidy to be determined by institutional effectiveness. Thus undergraduate students, for example, received subsidy as calculated on the basis of a norm termed the 'full-time equivalent' (FTE) which was calculated on the basis of the minimum time taken to complete a degree (either three or four years depending on direction and profession) and the number of module credits associated with the degree, either 360 or 480 credits if for a three- or four-year qualification respectively. Students who were enrolled on a part-time or distance basis were calculated at half the value of the FTE because their qualification usually took double the time to complete. Therefore, the formula encouraged universities to put effective measures (teaching and learning support) in place to ensure that students completed within the minimum time allocated. Within the SAPSE configuration, weighting was differentiated in two ways. First, students' choices of degrees accrued different subsidy levels. Thus the Natural Sciences, Commerce, Medicine, Engineering were typically privileged in subsidy-accrual terms over the Humanities and the Social Sciences and Theology – with Education being at the lowest subsidy-accruing level. The rationale for this differentiation was derived from the status of the subject areas identified, and also from the costs incurred by universities to offer such subjects. Engineering or commerce degrees were more expensive to offer because of the requirements associated with professional accreditation bodies (in Engineering or Accounting, for example) over those requirements associated with Education or Arts. Implied in this differentiation was that universities would be encouraged to pursue the recruitment of students to high-status and thus also high-subsidy accrual subjects. This system of subsidy categorisation along the lines of subject areas was known as the CESM (Classification of Education Subject Matter) system; it was first developed in 1982, and has become an enduring feature of the subsidy system even after 1994. Within the broad classifications of subject areas provided in universities there developed a further coding system associated with the subjects themselves. Within these areas (see, for example, Educational Assessment, Evaluation and Research), a code was provided (0712 in this case), and within that code a number of subfields were registered, their codes deriving from the broader subject-area code.

0712	Educational Assessment, Evaluation and Research
071201	Educational Evaluation and Research
071202	Educational Statistics and Research Methods
071203	Educational Assessment, Testing and Measurement
071299	Educational Assessment, Evaluation and Research, Other

Source: CESM: Addendum to the classification of Educational Subject Matter, Manual, 2008, 7

Within the example above, it is evident that the CESM category associated with Education is level 7 and within the classification index:

> Subject matter elements are presented in specific hierarchies in order to facilitate data aggregation, recording and reporting. First order designations are intended to be representative of major categories for classifying knowledge. Second order and third order categories are considered to be natural subdivisions of the major subject matter areas. The hierarchy level of a specific area of study should not be seen as a judgement of the relative importance of that area of study in the South African higher education system. The proposed new classification system has the 20 first order subject matter categories listed ... These first order categories are, as with the 1982 classification, broken down into second order categories, and these in turn are broken down into third order categories. No fourth order categories are used in the proposed new system. (2014, 3)

The CESM categories were then placed into groups that were weighted for funding purposes to assist the DHET with calculating the subsidy to be received by universities.

Funding groups 2004/05 to 2006/07: Funding group CESM categories included in funding group

1 07 education, 13 law, 14 librarianship, 20 psychology, 21 social services/ public administration

2 04 business/commerce, 05 communication, 06 computer science, 12 languages, 18 philosophy/religion, 22 social sciences

3 02 architecture/planning, 08 engineering, 10 home economics, 11 industrial arts, 16 mathematical sciences, 19 physical education

4 01 agriculture, 03 fine and performing arts, 09 health sciences, 15 life and physical sciences

Source: Steyn & De Villiers 2007, 34

The CESM categories were revised in 2008 and again in 2014. Each field descriptor is also accompanied by a brief description so as to enable academics developing programmes or qualifications to identify with a degree of accuracy which field describes the modules and field of the qualification being developed, as made evident in the example below:

2007 Sociology
200701 Sociology

An area of study which focuses on the systematic study of human social institutions and social relationships. Includes instruction in industrial sociology, social theory, sociological research methods, social organisation and structure, social stratification and hierarchies, dynamics of social change, family structures, social deviance and control, and applications to the study of specific social groups, social institutions, and social problems. Focuses also on the human impact on the environment and the individual and group behaviours with. (CESM: Classification of Education Subject Matter, 2007, 177)

Below is the comprehensive list of standard 'fields of study' associated with the CESM documentation:

01 Agriculture, Agricultural Operations and Related Sciences
02 Architecture and the Built Environment
03 Visual and Performing Arts
04 Business, Economics and Management Studies
05 Communication, Journalism and Related Studies
06 Computer and Information Sciences
07 Education
08 Engineering
09 Health Professions and Related Clinical Sciences
10 Family Ecology and Consumer Sciences
11 Languages, Linguistics and Literature
12 Law
13 Life Sciences
14 Physical Sciences
15 Mathematics and Statistics
16 Military Sciences
17 Philosophy, Religion and Theology
18 Psychology
19 Public Management and Services
20 Social Sciences

Source: CESM: Classification of Education Subject Matter, 2008, 4

Thus, when institutions sought to register a new qualification (to use the example of Education above), they applied to the Department of Higher Education and Training (DHET), and listed the relevant codes and their derivatives in order to indicate in which broad CESM category the qualification belonged, and with which subjects and fields the codes were associated. This enabled system operators within government to develop what came to be known as the Programme Qualification Mix (PQM) associated with each higher education institution. Part of the regulation of colleges and universities was always to ensure from both DHET and the institution's side that the qualifications offered by the institution were duly registered as such with the DHET, approved by the Council on Higher Education, listed on the webpages of the South Africa Higher Education authority as approved, and part of the institution's approved PQM. Universities would typically remove qualifications from the PQM if qualifications became outdated, there existed no longer the capacity to offer such qualifications, the associated costs of offering the qualifications were too high in relation to income generated from student numbers, or the qualification no longer fitted the institution's overall strategic plan.

A second mode of subsidy differentiation was developed to account for the differences associated with professional undergraduate degrees and postgraduate degrees (some of which may have been associated with certain professions). The idea here was that the weighting accorded to undergraduate qualifications was proportionately lower to that accrued for higher degrees. According to Steyn and De Villiers, 'the first three years of a first Bachelor's degree have a weight of 1, further years of a first Bachelor's degree, as well as the Honours degree, have a weight of 2, the Master's degree a weight of 3, and the Doctoral degree a weight of 4. In the calculation … for distance tuition, one subsidy student counts only 0.67 of the corresponding value for contact tuition' (2007, 17).

The important issue to note about the SAPSE formula insofar as it differed from previous formulae was that:

> As the above-mentioned cost units have been updated annually by means of projections based on nationally determined indicators to provide for cost escalation at universities, the SAPSE formula is self-adjusting from year to year as far as inflation is concerned. It is important to note that, with the implementation of the SAPSE formula for universities in 1984, State subsidization was for the first time not only based on input parameters, but also on institutional output, that is, courses successfully completed by students (degree credits) and research output of personnel. (Steyn & De Villiers 2007, 19)

7.3.2 Funding a unitary higher education sector in a new South Africa

The NFF was published in terms anticipated by the Higher Education Act (101, 1997), in the Government Gazette (1791). In 2004, a New Funding Framework (NFF) for public higher education was applied by the government Ministry of Education. This chapter does not review the work done of the period 1950–80 since the focus of the book is on education reform after 1995. However, it is important to understand the SAPSE subsidy formula for universities that was developed in the early 1980s since this influenced the subsequent development of the NFF. The CESM categories continued to feature within the new framework, but substantive revisions to the coding were undertaken to allow for the recognition of new subject areas (for example, Information and Communication Technologies) associated with the development of internet and also with globalisation.

That said, Steyn and De Villiers (2007, 31) note that the new system was different in two respects from the SAPSE formula. First, the size and shape of the sector would no longer be demand-driven (although it would remain responsible to needs) since the emphasis on planned enrolment would make for stable variables in the planning of participation in higher education, and would thus also enable universities to expand provision within a national and systemic framework whereby subsidy could be organised in relation to the maximum number of students allowed to a university to enrol in terms of its three-year plan, for example. University planning for enrolments would also be scrutinised in terms of the PQM (described earlier in this chapter) and fitness for purpose. In other words, funding would become dependent not only on the university realising its predicted student enrolment, but also within the fields associated with the university PQM, which had, in turn, to be linked to the particular vision and mission of the university (this latter dimension was of course, the mandate of the CHE, and its quality assurance arm, the Higher Education Quality Committee (HEQC).

The funding associated with the NFF is updated annually, but unlike the SAPSE formula, not always in keeping with inflationary adjustments. In 2014, for example, universities received proportionately less subsidy from the government for research outputs, even though year-on-year outputs have increased in general since 1995. Thus, although in monetary terms the total subsidy granted to public institutions might have increased for research, the allocation per unit (given the increase in units) had declined. In real terms this has meant that competition for a shrinking resource pool increases even as outputs increase.[3] This driver explains in part the shift towards a research orientation even in comprehensive universities (in other words, those institutions devoted to technical and vocational training). The NFF made provision for block grants to universities based on teaching input units (the students enrolled within a programme calculated as full-time equivalents).[4]

Furthermore, the race-based classification of higher education institutions was replaced with the onset of the mergers and the incorporation processes, and this in itself brought to the fore the awareness that the subsidy alone could not deal with historical inequalities associated with the neglect of higher education for black people. The fragmentation of the sector would have to be addressed through the allocation of what has become termed 'a grant for disadvantaged or black students'. To qualify for this grant, university student enrolments would need to comprise more than 40% black students (calculated through the FTE formula). A second type of grant made available was determined by the size and shape of the institution so that large universities were to receive less money to expand than smaller universities. Similarly, it was recognised that, with the merger of some universities to create new ones, and the incorporation of teacher training colleges, universities found themselves to be multi-campus institutions with associated administration costs recognised as a separate funding category. Additional funding was also calculated to assist with long-term loan repayments, merger administrative costs, foundation programme provision (with a view to enabling access to the university) and restructuring costs (Steyn & De Villiers 2007, 37).

What was aimed at with the NFF was a unitary funding system that was premised on rigorous long-term plans (rolling three-year enrolment plans characterised by the capping of numbers in certain universities and some fields, and the stimulation of recruitment of students to other fields) in which transformation goals (redress, access and the development of a new generation of academics) were paramount. There were some criticisms of the NFF as noted here in relation to the assumption that larger institutions were cheaper to run. Steyn and De Villiers noted that there was no empirical basis associated with the assumption and given that several newly-merged universities were now (post-2004) multi-campus institutions, the associated costs would increase. In 2014, a number of the universities placed under administration were large multi-campus institutions and their plight supported this concern. In some respects the practical viability of institutional mergers did not tally with the desired impact of transforming the sector, often crippling already fragile capacity in those institutions most in need of focused good governance (Walter Sisulu University being a case in point in 2014 when it was recognised that the multi-campus model with a centralised university administrative structure was simply not viable).

While it was commendable that funding was made available in grant form for the establishment of foundation programmes, Steyn and De Villiers (2007,

40) noted that this funding was really aimed at compensating for deficiencies evident in the schooling sector and thus in real terms reduced the funding available in the higher education sector overall. That said, the CHE Review (2007) did note that the impact of the NFF was in effect an increase in the funding available to historically disadvantaged universities in relation to a decrease in funding for the historically advantaged universities. The logic of making less funding available to successful universities irrespective of their historical basis (for example, as of 2014, UKZN is a university with a large majority of black students) is problematic since race integration across former advantaged institutions has become a normal feature of higher education.

Student recruitment (enrolment planning), degrees awarded per year and research outputs were thus the drivers of the new formula, together with a focus on quality assurance that would enable the State to achieve its goals of providing meaningful high-quality education in tune with the needs of the country, while widening access and participation by historically disadvantaged groups in the sector. Buildings and capital projects associated with the expansion of higher education as a sector were not planned for at national level, but rather at institutional levels.

7.3.3 Redress and budgeting for the transformation of higher education in South Africa

Prior to 1995, a national and central student loan facility did not exist. As part of the State's commitment to transformation, in terms of enabling wider access, and thus wider participation levels among formerly disadvantaged groups, the National Student Financial Aid Scheme was put in place. NSFAS, as it became known, was established early in 1995 through a legislative act, and was administered by the Tertiary Education Fund of SA (TEFSA), which was founded in 1991 as a not-for-profit company to provide loans to HE students (Steyn & De Villiers 2007, 24). In 2000, TEFSA became the National Student Financial Aid Scheme (NSFAS). Since 1995, the State has annually earmarked allocations for NSFAS to each HE institution. Teacher training prior to 1995 had been conducted by the various Departments of Education associated with the racially differentiated apartheid system. Teacher training colleges, as noted in the previous chapter, were divided among the House of Assembly (white), House of Delegates (Indian), and House of Representatives (coloured), representative bodies associated with the tri-cameral system. Bantustan or homeland colleges of education operated under those various territory administrations while teacher training facilities outside these were administered through the Department of Education and Training. The point to note here is that the various departments possessed bursary schemes which enabled access for students who met the criteria from year to year in various subjects in which teachers were needed in schools. The bursaries took the form of service loans and for each year that a student received one, a further year of work for the department would be entailed. Students in receipt of one bursary from one department would be obliged to work in the region (province or homeland) in which the regional department of education was the authority. In a system characterised by fragmentation, the ability of the State to plan adequately in terms of teacher supply and demand was compromised. That said, generous bursaries from the departments made it possible for thousands of teachers to gain qualifications. After 1995, a centralised and national teacher education bursary fund, known as Funza Lushaka, was set up and administered by the DHET. Based on the same principles of the bursaries allocated previously, the centralised control of these awards, in relation to national needs and even in relation to specific provincial needs, has vastly improved DHET's planning capacity, to the extent that in 2014 departmental officials predicted that the teacher supply-and-demand crisis would become a feature of the past by 2019. These mechanisms to enable access and deal with the crisis in teacher education are described later in the chapter.

According to Steyn and De Villiers, 'Amounts of r28m, r60m and r30m, respectively, were allocated in the financial years of 1998/99, 1999/00, and 2000/01 to universities and technikons for redress purposes. While all historically disadvantaged HE institutions benefited from the 1998/99 redress allocation of r28m, the division of the allocations for 1999/00 and 2000/01 was not disclosed in the Department of Education's (DoE) official budget documents'. Where universities also had to incorporate teacher training colleges, the State provided ad hoc funding in order to right-size fee payments made by students, since teacher education students in colleges had paid lower fees than their university counterparts leading up to incorporation.

NFSAS is essentially a student loan scheme that the State established to provide redress funding in order to enable wider access to higher education and thus contribute to one of the transformation aspirations of the new government.

The mission statement is made up of three distinct elements which describe why NSFAS exists, what we do, and the impact on our constituency:

- NSFAS exists to provide financial aid to eligible students at public TVET colleges and public universities.

- NSFAS identifies eligible students, provides loans and bursaries and collects student loan repayments to replenish the funds available for future generations of students.

- NSFAS supports access to, and success in, higher education and training for students from poor and working class families who would otherwise not be able to afford to study. (NFSAS: Mission and Vision, accessed 2015)

The alignment with transformation goals is evident in the 2013 Annual Report:

> In ensuring that students from poor and working class families are afforded the opportunity of obtaining financial aid, NSFAS contributes to the attainment of the rights contained in section 29 of the Constitution by assisting these students to access post-school education and training, thereby redressing the results of past racially discriminatory laws and practices. In ensuring that students from poor and working class families are afforded the opportunity of obtaining financial aid, NSFAS contributes to the attainment of the rights contained in section 29 of the Constitution by assisting these students to access post-school education and training, thereby redressing the results of past racially discriminatory laws and practices. (NFSAS Annual Report 2013, 9)

NFSAS, as a parastatal organisation with a national mandate to fund higher education students, is responsible not only for managing State funds through the loan scheme, but also for the administration and distribution of monies to universities on behalf of student recipients at universities as well as technical, vocational education and training colleges (TVET, formerly known as Further Education and Training Colleges), to qualifying students at public higher education institutions.

NSFAS was established in terms of the NSFAS Act (56 of 1999), as amended. NSFAS provides student financial aid funds to the 23 public universities and 50 TVET colleges. The act also mandates the entity to recover such loans and to raise additional funding for student loans and bursaries.

In 2013, NFSAS increased its student loans expenditure from r5.9 billion to r7.7 billion (an increase of r1.8 billion). Increases in university fees, and cost-of-living expenses, meant that a projected shortfall in the various funding categories did come about (NFSAS Annual Report 2013, 14). The report notes that 'The number of students assisted also increased in line with the increased funding. In 2012, there were 382 943 students who received financial aid against 289 172 supported in 2011. The number of students funded at universities in 2012 rose to 194 504, while the number of students funded at FET colleges was 188 182, making a total of 382 686. The number of students funded is expected to increase steadily in the next few years. For the first time in the 2013 academic year, the number of FET college students funded by NSFAS is expected to exceed the number of university students funded' (2013, 14). That increasing numbers of students are accessing NFSAS has proved to be a challenge for the State, leading ministers of higher education to sometimes berate universities for their fee increases.

The following section provides an account of the need for quality facilities in which higher education studies and scholarship could take place in South Africa.

7.3.4 Infrastructure development: Planning and recording existing and new needs of South African universities

Investment in infrastructural development (academic buildings as well as residential accommodation) has been managed jointly between universities and the State since the 1960s. The principle concerning infrastructural development, as noted by Steyn and De Villiers, has joint funding on a rand-to-rand basis. There were exceptions to this principle, in relation to the new erection of universities for black South Africans as pursued by the State after the 1970s. In this case, the State funds the whole cost of the erection of buildings on a long-term loan basis. This has continued to be the convention in South Africa after 1994, as in the case of two new universities in 2014 (the Sol Plaatje University and the University of Mpumalanga), the construction and acquisition of buildings for which was funded by the State.

Steyn and De Villiers state that the funding of residential accommodation was managed as follows: 'residences, while a corresponding fixed ratio of eighty-five per cent for academic buildings was implemented in 1967 ... these two contribution ratios remained intact, and were also applied to technikons until 1991, when the system of the subsidization of payments of interest and redemption on long term loans of HE institutions by the State was replaced by a system of direct capital allocations for the erection of new buildings, and for land improvements other than buildings' (2007, 26).

Universities have always had to motivate infrastructural spending within a system of national higher education norms, first established by the Minister of National Education in the 1960s. Within this system, the State issued guarantees to ensure the securing of long-term loans by institutions. In the apartheid era, building grants were advised upon by a special body known as the Advisory Council on Universities (ACU), replaced in 1983 by the University and Technikons Advisory Council (AUT) (Steyn & De Villiers, 2007, 26).

A comprehensive system of space and cost norms for new buildings and land improvements other than buildings (parking areas, open-air recreation areas, streets, pavements, landscaping and so on) was developed in 1979 and adjusted in 1985 (Department of National Education, Report SAPSE-101, 1985). Separate space and cost norms applied to universities and technikons and differed also for residential and non-residential institutions. These norms ensured that new buildings erected at HE institutions satisfied minimum space requirements, but at the same time were not so luxurious that they were unaffordable for the institutions and the State. These norms also formed the basis of the annual SAPSE information returns by universities and technikons to the Department of National Education up to 1998 on the utilisation of space. The space and cost norms for new buildings and other land improvements were revised by the DoE in 1996, but were never officially published. In the revision, the norms for universities were scaled down by about 20%, and equality between universities and technikons was established to a large extent. Since the termination of the SAPSE information system in 1998, institutional space utilisation information is no longer required by the DoE.

Unfortunately, while there is a record provided by the State of the backlogs with regard to infrastructural maintenance and building needs from 1987–99, no information on the state of university buildings and needs exists at the national level after this date (Steyn & De Villiers 2007, 27). This is not to suggest, however, that the universities do not address these needs within the parameters of State funding, and the State does indeed make provision for what are termed 'infrastructural support grants', on the basis that universities must co-fund up to half of the costs of the building projects for which funding is required. Thus, between 2004–14, the North-West University, for example, made extensive use of these funds to not only upgrade and extend buildings on its three campuses (Potchefstroom, Mafeking and Vaal Triangle), but also to support the massive expansion of student residential facilities, especially on the Mafeking Campus. To this extent the DHET keeps a record of funding allocated and requires accountability in terms of completion dates for new or maintained developments. The extent to which this approach enables universities to address consistently the existing quality of infrastructural maintenance requirements is doubtful because it is well-known that some universities already have the advantages of better maintenance capacity and better managed systems for dealing with infrastructural maintenance, as these needs arise on campuses.

Figure 7.1 draws together the discussion in previous sections to show the increase in funding to universities since 2007. The real base for this increase is calculated in relation to inflation.

As funding has increased in allocations to universities, the costs of studies have also increased (see Figure 7.2). This trend has occurred despite the availability of NFSAS and other bursary schemes. In general, the rising costs of education are linked to the poor throughput rates of students (since for every year in which a student is enrolled beyond the minimum period for which a qualification may be completed, the subsidy allocation to universities decreases, illustrating the observation that the system is sluggish and expensive.

Figure 7.1: The funding allocated to universities in real and nominal terms from 2007–2012

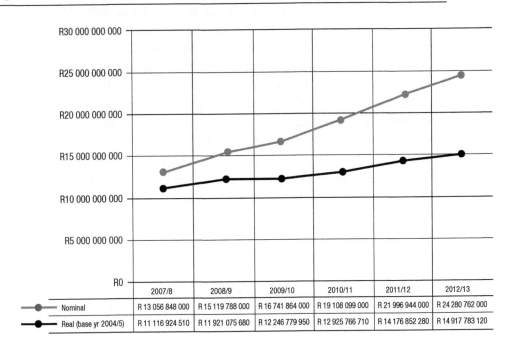

	2007/8	2008/9	2009/10	2010/11	2011/12	2012/13
Nominal	R 13 056 848 000	R 15 119 788 000	R 16 741 864 000	R 19 108 099 000	R 21 996 944 000	R 24 280 762 000
Real (base yr 2004/5)	R 11 116 924 510	R 11 921 075 680	R 12 246 779 950	R 12 925 766 710	R 14 176 852 280	R 14 917 783 120

Figure 7.2: average full cost of study showing percentage real cost of tuition from 2007–2012

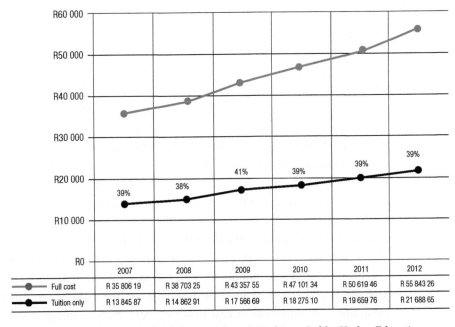

	2007	2008	2009	2010	2011	2012
Full cost	R 35 806 19	R 38 703 25	R 43 357 55	R 47 101 34	R 50 619 46	R 55 843 26
Tuition only	R 13 845 87	R 14 862 91	R 17 566 69	R 18 275 10	R 19 659 76	R 21 688 65

Source: Council on Higher Education (2014) VitalStats: Public Higher Education, 2012

A visitor to South African university or college campuses (let alone to the schools in rural, many township or poor areas) will note with relative ease the differences between education provision (both in terms of infrastructure and in terms of human resources) that reflect the old wounds and fractures associated with apartheid and the new fissures associated with class privilege in South Africa. While accounts of State spending on schooling and higher education are impressive, the systems to ensure that a responsible and equitable dispensation of such funding is done are generally weak. In a country in which 80% of the municipal authorities could not achieve unqualified financial audits in 2014, it is not surprising that schools, colleges and universities experience similar challenges with regard to corruption or graft and wasteful expenditure associated so typically with developing states, whether in Africa, Europe or Asia. These are not 'African' problems, nor can they glibly be ascribed to a lack of experience. Simply put, the development of robust human resources systems to accompany the development of sophisticated financial report systems depends on the capacity of people employed in such work, and also on the quality of leadership within institutions. Schools and universities do not become dysfunctional because of a lack of physical resources, but because of a lack of effective, committed and skilled leadership at all levels of society.

7.4 CONCLUSION

This chapter has described the mechanisms used to address a variety of needs in relation to the equitable funding of schooling on the one hand, and higher education (development, redress and research needs) on the other. In addition to supporting growth and infrastructural development, the State's commitment to assisting children through no-fee and low-fee paying schools is evident and has done much to raise enrolments among children, and effective participation rates among children in schools as well as students in higher education institutions. Through loan provision schemes the State has been able to incentivise talented young people to study in areas where critical skills shortages are experienced, although as of 2015 the demand for scarce skills (engineers, doctors, artisans) still exceeds supply. In teacher education, similar bursary schemes (in the form of pay-back in years of service to the State) have led to substantial gains in terms of teacher supply and demand (Teachers in Schools: Supply and Demand 2013–2025, CDE Report, 2015). The reach and scope of such initiatives have been impressive through it is clear that the reduction in real funding from NFSAS in 2014–2015 has had an impact on the ability of students to pay fees and thus to complete their studies at some universities – the student unrest that is experienced on many South African campuses at the beginning of the academic year is usually linked to lack of adequate funding.

While the chapter has described the development of private schools (in terms of how these are funded), there is an obvious gap cocnerning research about how private higher education institutions (PHEIs) are funded. It cannot be assumed that these institutions are for-profit only. And, whilst the discourse and rhetoric surrounding higher education in South Africa makes frequent reference to the partnerships between the State and PHEIs, there are largely non-existent since even registered PHEIs offering a range of degrees or programmes enjoy no support from the State either in terms of subsidization of research outputs (as is normal for HEIs), let alone subsidisation of students or academics. The absence explains why private higher education sits on the margins of State regulation as well as State strategy in terms of how to address either scarce skills shortages, or widening access to higher education (TVET as well as university).

It would have been easy to include accounts of misuse of public funding by education authorities, or an account of the many race- and gender-related leadership scandals in education in South Africa (the Makgoba Affair at Wits in 1995; the Mamdani Affair at UCT in 1997; the Motimele Affair at UNISA in 2002; the fake Molefe qualifications scandal at Tshwane University of Technology in 2011; the Textbook Scandal of Limpopo Province in 2013; the Velile Scandal at NMMU in 2014; the Grade 12 National Senior Certificate Copying Scandal of 2014: see Appendix 2). There is a list as long as this for every year that has passed since 1995. But to make these aberrations a focus for a more sensational account of the abuse of power or the lack of accountability, when in fact such abuses have been part of a longer pattern of institutionalised abuse of privilege, would suggest that these problems are not new, and remain symptomatic of a society in transition in which the need for excellence in terms of public service delivery (let alone the provision of quality teaching and learning) remains critical. The conclusion of this book will reflect on themes raised and addressed over 20 years of education development in South Africa.

NOTES

1   Throughout this book reference to race categories – black, white, Indian, and coloured – have been made. These are the categories used by the State for reporting purposes in a wide variety of documents. Race categories are per definition not natural, but rather a series of social, political and ethnic constructions, themselves beset with slippages and liminalities. At times the term 'black' is also used to describe black, Indian and coloured people, by the State.

2   Motala (2006) provides an overview of the school's funding system and has commented on the implications for access in terms of class and quality in education.

3   De Villiers & Steyn (2009) have undertaken research on the positive and other effects of the research funding regime in South African higher education. See also Chapter 3 for the impact research funding allocation has made on research productivity in South Africa.

4   FTEs were weighted in terms of being full-time or part-time or distance education students. A further weighting is accorded in terms of whether the students were undergraduate or postgraduate. And, finally, students are also weighted in terms of the CESM category (as relating to their subject choices and degree programmes.

CONCLUSION:
Exiting the mire

PLANNING FOR BETTER QUALITY EDUCATION IN SOUTH AFRICA

This book has provided a review of education in South Africa over the period of the first two decades of democracy. In doing so, an argument has been advanced concerning the emphasis placed on the agency of the State (in terms of political will and resources) in relation to efforts to transform education comprehensively and thoroughly. Dealing with redress and inequality associated with the legacy of apartheid is part of what must be done to create the conditions necessary for a new non-racist, non-sexist and multicultural South Africa. Education institutions (schools, higher education institutions, adult education centres) and national education initiatives (the mass literacy and numeracy campaigns) are perhaps still the only systemic means available to achieve that. The ideals are everywhere evident in policy documentation and have motivated the massive reorganisation of education in the post-apartheid era.

A distinction, as implied previously, does need to be drawn here between the aspirations associated with the ideal of a 'new' South Africa, and the wide-ranging initiatives aimed at dismantling the damaging policies and systems associated with the race hierarchies of the apartheid era. What seems clear 20 years later is that South Africa is still very much a post-apartheid state; in other words, it is still concerned in its politics and education practices with the consequences and legacies of apartheid systems and values (race separation, separate development, race supremacy, ethnocentricity, sexism, homophobia and xenophobia).

The undoing of old systems and values, while facilitated through changes brought about through policy, strategies and frameworks, needs yet to be undertaken at a much deeper level in education praxis. As much is evident when one considers the divisive politics underpinning the legal challenges, whether brought about by State departments, of school governing bodies in relation to language policies that, on the one hand, work to preserve language rights associated with certain groups, and on the other serve to exclude groups from access to quality education and to undermine race integration (a pillar of the transformation project in South Africa). There are dangers in representing the transformation of education simply as a policy or even curriculum project intended to achieve historical redress only. Ndebele et al. (2013, 17) argue that: 'Seeing this problem (student underpreparedness or readiness) as an articulation gap (DoE 1997, 2.34), rather than just as student underpreparedness, opens up possibilities for positive action within higher education, because a gap can be closed from either side', but the social dynamics requiring attention in South African schools and universities or colleges suggest that a commitment to education in its wider sense remains critical, even urgent, if the problems associated with race, gender and language are to be addressed:

> Representivity among graduates, in terms of race, gender and social class, is essential for equity, for developing the talent across the population, for setting a balanced development agenda, and for maintaining the public's respect for and faith in ... education (Ndebele et al. 2013, 32).

The will to accommodate a diversity of groups (whether on the basis of gender, linguistic diversity, ethnic identity or religion) sits in uneasy tension with an imperative to create a new type of society in which differences do indeed become a cause for celebration in an environment of multilingual and multicultural diversity. That shift, from differences that provide the basis for exclusion, to differences that make for a will to come together (and be inclusive), will take a much longer period of time to effect. Thus, what characterises the first 20 years of education reform is not so much the creation of the 'new' South Africa as perhaps the immense effort required (and still needed) to be free from the 'old wounds' (to borrow from a phrase of V. S. Naipaul) associated with the colonial state. In these terms, effort and imagination can, in the first 20 years, be associated with what it has meant to understand what freedom guarantees (in terms of the human right to education at all levels). In the next 20 years, South Africa will explore what those freedoms and rights enable, rather than simply guarantee. It for this reason that transformation remains the most compelling need going forward, since, without visible change and success in this arena, achievement in schooling, let alone the fraught situation in higher education, the replication of race and gender privilege will continue for decades to come.

Of course, this does not imply that transformational development is straightforward and uncomplicated. Enacting the rights that guarantee citizens' freedoms and re-thinking what race integration and diversity might really mean in a 'new' South Africa implies contestation as well as imagination, as both are necessary to develop a consensus regarding what that 'new' might mean. There are questions that require imaginative responses: for example, what does freedom from the various noxious '-isms' and phobias entail in terms of the degrees of acceptance required from people who seek to not only co-exist, but also co-habit peacefully? What kind of education (curriculum) and system (bureaucracy and State agencies) can best enable people to commit actively to and participate across the limitations of race difference, gender difference and class difference, towards the creation of the 'new', rather than simply the 'post'? These questions represent challenges to a new South Africa, especially when considered in relation to the background of the slowdown in the global economy – for example, the Gross Domestic Product (GDP) growth forecast for 2013 was lowered to 2.1% by the National Treasury. The National Treasury also projected that the economy would expand by only 3% (3.5%) in 2014, 3.2% in 2015 and 3.5% in 2016 (National Treasury, 23 October 2013). The point is this: with the population increasing, even marginally, since 2005, economic growth needs to be much higher if unemployment is to be significantly reduced. That, in turn, requires a rethinking of several existing policies that serve consciously or unwittingly to create conditions for exclusion and differentiation.

This chapter has two broad parts. The first part summarises the argument made in each of the preceding chapters of the book. Inevitably the construction of this argument is based on the information presented and thus excludes a range of equally worthy foci that could not be accommodated in the scope and limitations of the book. I am very aware that the account and argument presented here have focused on the role of the State and its various agencies (ministries, departments, universities, colleges, schools). In this sense the exclusion of a focus on the work of a very broad range of non-governmental organisations remains a gap (everything from churches to self-help projects, to research think-tanks such as the policy units sometimes attached to universities, or the research organisations like the Joint Education Trust (JET), Centre for Development and Enterprise (CDE) or religious organisations, private schools and private higher education institutions, community centres and groups). I recognise that a survey of the creative, cutting-edge interventions in policy debates and education practices (for example, the Media in Education Trust's (MiET) work, or Molteno's, the JET or CDE's work across South Africa) might have made a substantive and illuminating additional chapter or even book in itself. This gap suggests not its unimportance, but rather its complexity and rich possibilities in terms of another book in which the focus on the State (and by implication a bias that may well be described as statism) is not primary.

The second part of the chapter focuses on the needs identified by the Education, Development and Training Practices (EDTP) SETA in terms of where planning for the allocation of energy, focus and resources might yet yield further progress, consolidation and development in education in South Africa over the next 20 years. The role of the ETDP SETA is precisely to provide, on the basis of the workplace skills development plans, an indication of where institutions and a range of organisations might yet yield impact. Since this book has been about the impact of change over time, it seems fitting to conclude not merely with my sense of what is needed going forward in education reform in South Africa, but to draw upon the more systematic analysis provided precisely by the organisations mandated to so do, almost always in collaboration with the institutions surveyed. In fact such a review as contemplated in this book must also take into account the role of statutory bodies' advice to the State, in the formulation of commentary on a 'way forward'. Other scholars, such as Breier and Erasmus (2009), have also undertaken extensive work on analysing and understanding skills needs and shortages in South Africa.

The topography of education: A South African landscape

Chapter 1 analysed schooling in South Africa since 1995. A success has been the integration of formerly racially divided departments of education (19 in all) associated with education in apartheid South Africa. Further successes include the fact that primary education is universal, providing increased access to new schools has been achieved, and that the nationwide school feeding programme is a noticeable success. These achievements need to be accompanied by an equally impressive performance of schools or teachers in the system. Thus, while government has claimed improvements year-on-year in pass rates, the system remains plagued by bleak reports (PIRLS, TIMSS, SACMEQ – Southern and East African Consortium for Monitoring Educational Quality) concerning education performance.

Despite departmental initiatives to raise the requirements for teacher education for in-service teachers, the attainment of qualifications for previously unqualified or under-qualified teachers has not made a difference in terms of learner performance. What seems not to have been estimated accurately with the first post-apartheid education curriculum reforms is the capacity of teachers to deliver on the reforms, and the capacity of the education system (in terms of specialists at the levels of subject advisors and curriculum support staff) to support reform.

To address this challenge, the standards and self-regulation of the profession need to be strengthened in terms of the requirements regarding minimum qualifications for teaching. SACE needs to take a stronger role in the profession and engage more meaningfully with teacher education as regards the profession. Self-regulation of a profession is a hallmark of professionalism. In the 20-year period under review, a further success has occurred in terms of the better resourcing and provisioning of schools and teacher pay. This drive should be accompanied by a greater emphasis on quality in teacher education programmes. The codependent nature of schooling and higher education emerges as a strong theme in this book.

The challenges concerning the improvement of learner performance addressed through the redevelopment of in-service teachers cannot be overestimated and thus Chapter 2 focuses on a range of reforms in teacher education in the period of 20 years, beginning with the crisis of confidence and morale in teaching as a profession. Just as the school curriculum has seen four revisions over the 20-year period, so too has teacher development (pre-service as well as in-service) witnessed several changes to the shape of teacher education and the minimum requirements for employment (see the Norms and Standards for Educators, 2000) and more recently the Minimum Requirements for Teacher Education Qualifications (2008), together with the Integrated Strategic Framework for Teacher Education and Qualifications (2011) in South Africa. Assumptions about teacher knowledge have to be interrogated more critically in years to come. While problems of supply and demand of teachers are likely to be resolved in quantity terms by 2020, existing agencies like the Council on Higher Education (CHE) and SACE can have a stronger role to play in the elevation of the profession.

An analysis of the characteristics of higher education as a sector in itself was undertaken in Chapter 3. The rationalisation of institutions that took place in 2004 has not been accompanied by sufficient support for the massicication of access as has occurred in the last 20 years. The capacity of the system to generate and sustain high-quality education for more students begs a more generous approach to funding. The capacity of academics to manage a massified system was similarly over-estimated, and furthermore curriculum development towards the creation of a new South Africa has been patchy at best. While the State has focused on the creation of a complex and adequate system of quality control and related assurance bodies to regulate the sector, the emphasis of such regulation has been on assuring the consistency of size and shape of features associated with qualifications and programmes in terms of the National Qualifications Framework (NQF) and its subsequent revisions. However, articulation problems between technical and vocational qualification and university qualifications, together with role of recognition of prior learning, still need to become lived experience.

That said, a notable success (despite selected institutions being placed under administration over the past 20 years) is that the sector has been structurally transformed (since 2004 there have been more young black people in universities than ever before and they do constitute the majority of the students). Despite progress, there is nevertheless concern expressed about the efficiency of the sector. The participation rate in higher education in South Africa has increased from 15% in 2000 to 18% in 2010. The steady growth since 2005 suggests that the 20% target is likely to be met by 2015/16. However, although significantly higher than the average GER for sub-Saharan Africa, which is 6%, it is well below the average for Latin America (34%) and Central Asia (31%) (UNESCO 2010). In line with such trends, the Green Paper (DHET 2012a) has revised the participation rate target to 23% by 2030, which is still modest. Despite the growth, 'resilience of both historical and systemic factors have combined to put a brake on the momentum of the desire to craft an undergraduate system that delivers on a demanding constitutional mandate to achieve a successful post-apartheid society' (Ndebele et al. 2013, 9).

Chapter 3 also notes the ageing nature of the professoriate, the relative absence of highly-qualified black academics, and the evident problems associated with poor governance and the misuse of public funds at the universities as symptoms of a sector experiencing stress. That said, the State's incentives to stimulate the research capacity of universities in general are a notable success, and this in turn suggests that there is the capacity not only to develop younger, highly-qualified black graduates for higher education but also for the more competitive private sector. Efforts to stimulate research and make academic work more attractive to young graduates can be enhanced.

The expansion of higher education beyond the four major metropolitan centres entails attending to service delivery needs of those regions in addition to the creation of research-generative institutions through developing leadership and management capacity. Such vision and 'drive' are essential especially in relation to the fact that some institutions (4 of the 21 in 2013) were placed under administration (or curatorship) owing to ineffective management.

As a result of the intersectionality of these phenomena (disadvantage, poor working conditions, slow throughput and poor retention rates, leadership problems), it is not surprising that younger qualified people might regard academic work and life as unattractive. Thus concerted effort to revitalise such institutions is needed. In 2014, the State established two new universities in response to these needs, and in 2015 initiated a national academic-staff development programme geared to develop young black academics for the sector. These initiatives are praiseworthy.

Chapter 4 concerns itself with the TVET system of colleges. For the first fifteen years the Further Education and Training colleges (FET) were not part of a unified administrative system with universities, and were instead administered and funded on different terms (even within the apartheid State, the administration of TVET colleges was similarly fragmented along the race lines associated with apartheid), but also in terms of how they were resourced. In 1994, the new government did not inherit a TVET college sector ready for the new opportunities associated with the economic upsurge of the 1990s.

To remedy this situation, the government created skills, education and training authorities to re-establish the complex system of learnerships or apprenticeships linked to TVET colleges, the programmes of which were to be regulated from a quality assurance perspective by the Quality Trades Council (QCTO), along similar lines that the CHE functioned in relation to qualifications offered by universities. Various SETAs (travel and tourism, manufacturing, mining and so on) would then become instrumental in the design of learnerships within industry and employees would be funded for such opportunities through the National Skills Levy. In this system, which in broad strokes makes conceptual sense, two basic requirements inhered. First, there was the requirement that there must be a high level of sectoral responsiveness (that is, employers who were themselves able to describe and provide such data), and second, there was the requirement that the SETAs possess bureaucratic and research capacity so that the national skills plan(s) could be routinely and accurately updated. On both counts, the system has experienced challenges. The research capacity of these organisations has to be strengthened (and there exists already excellent partnerships between universities and some SETAs) so that the quality of mega data analysis from industry is raised.

Part 1 of the book focused on systemic components of education (schooling, teaching, universities, and technical and vocational colleges). Part 2, the second part of the book, has been concerned with how three key issues associated with the transformation project in education in South Africa (language, gender and funding) have been dealt with over the 20-year period in question.

In Chapter 5, the complexities arising from gender inequality, both as a historical fact with deep roots in the colonial and pre-colonial past, and as a present challenge in relation to recognition of diversity as comprising a wider focus than gender (in terms of sexual orientations, for example), are described. The State needs to provide for wider recognition of Constitutional provisions regarding equality if diversity is really to be celebrated as a key feature of transformation. More initiatives are needed to protect and indeed promote historically disadvantaged groups (women, black people, LGBTTIQ people, and so on) as part of being 'South African'.

Interpretations of language policy and rights have sometimes fostered race exclusion and the under-development of indigenous African languages as noted in Chapter 6. Language is a component of South Africa's diversity and transformation project. The debate about the problematic role of English as a semi-recognised lingua franca is considered. Recognition for a lingua franca would have the consequence of rethinking levels of State support for a lingua franca such that it could be accessed adequately by all groups, rather than serve as gate-keeper for what being 'educated' might mean. The chapter concludes by describing the development of indigenous languages for higher education towards an awareness of how multilingualism contributes to interculturalism.

Since issues of access and success in education speak to support and re-sourcing, Chapter 7 describes funding formulae and patterns for the support of schooling and higher education in South Africa, noting the successes achieved by low-fee or no-fee paying schools, the challenges associated with the quintile system, and the post-provisioning norms. Various State funding schemes associated with higher education (Funza Lushaka for teacher education and NFSAS for a huge number of South Africans who might not ordinarily have been able to afford higher education) are described. The ongoing sustainability of such support begs attention in coming years so that challenges associated with massification might be addressed (attracting more academic staff to breathe life into new universities and schools). What remains critical to the successful utilisation of such resources is the capacity to ensure that resources are well-allocated, but also well-invested and utilised. That points to the need for excellence in leadership and development both in public and private institutions, irrespective of race and gender backgrounds (mindful of the protections necessary to ensure the promotion of historically disadvantaged groups).

Having described the book, the next part of this conclusion draws heavily on the Education, Training and Development (ETD) Skills Plan, which is updated annually by the ETDP SETA as part of the advice provided to the Minister of Higher Education and Training.

MAPPING NEEDS AND PRIORITIES AS PART OF THE TRANSFORMATION OF EDUCATION IN SOUTH AFRICA

The second part of this chapter begins with a description of the work of the ETDP SETA and draws from the ETDP SETA's 2014 Skills Plan, which, in turn, is not only derived from data collected from the whole education sector in South Africa (including the non-governmental organisation not surveyed in this book), but also speaks to the recommendations with regard to needs and priorities contained in key policy as well as planning documentation.

The purpose of education is generally to enable meaningful, productive and creative participation in adult life, within the context of community needs and development ideals of the State, the government in South Africa set about creating a series of skills development agencies tasked with working with employers (whether private or public organisations) with a view to identifying workplace skills development needs (from the perspective of employers and also employees through interaction with human resource officers or divisions). Many of the challenges taken up in the ETDP SETA Skills Plan find expression also in the National Development Plan (NDP 2012) with regard to education. For example,

ECD:

Two (2) years of quality pre-school enrolment compulsory to four and five-year olds. This means that there will be a need for ECD practitioners at higher skills levels for these pre-school classes.

Home and community-based ECD services piloted in selected districts. There will be a need to train practitioners for home and community-based ECD services. This is currently a scarce skill and few providers are able to offer qualifications for this type of ECD practitioner.

Investment in the training of ECD practitioners through upgrading their qualifications and developing clear career paths is identified. The ETDP SETA and other stakeholders need to urgently address career-pathing and qualification pathways at the higher levels for ECD, including the development of appropriate diploma and degree options.

Government support for training, resource and other intermediary agencies to support. There is a need for a completely different approach to dealing with the young not in education, employment or training (NEET) learners who require a different set of interventions than those simply transplanted from the formal sector. Most of this target group may never enter the formal economy, therefore interventions have to focus on improving livelihoods and work in the informal economy.

The focus on the provision of early childhood development in South Africa in terms of the NDP (2012) is not accidental. The NDP aspires to provide for the elimination of poverty by 2030 and it is thus unsurprising that the collective of government, and private stakeholders who participated in the development of the NDP, identified education as the key means through which future growth could be sustained. This vision is in keeping with the emphasis placed on education by the founding President, Nelson Mandela, and as such retains the discourse features associated with much of the early education policy and curriculum making. The government in 2014 began to drive the registration of all early childhood care and education centres in an effort to coordinate training needs for ECE teachers and also to ensure that a relatively consistent approach to curriculum and quality of education provision could be achieved (hence the references above to the 'development of appropriate diploma and degree options'). The EPWP Social Sector Plan for 2009/10 – 2013/14 aims at training 80 000 ECD practitioners, including those working in services for 0–4-year olds and Grade R classes at Levels 4 and 5 (ETDP SETA Skills Plan, 102–5). The development of qualifications is a long-term undertaking since the field of early childhood development is a recent one (the Project on Postgraduate Education Research showed that very little research on early childhood had been done in the first decade of democracy as this was still a new field), but already the need had been identified and where qualifications have come to be developed (for example, North-West University launched its Grade R Diploma in 2013), interest from provincial and local authorities has been swift and positive (in terms of funding teachers and practitioners to gain the right qualifications).

The ETDP SETA Skills Plan notes that there has been a growth in ECD services and programmes for 0–4-year olds. Furthermore, as Grade R becomes a feature of all formal education associated with the Foundation Phase in South Africa, there has been a rapid uptake in students entering higher education Grade R qualifications at universities. This has matched the rapid growth of Grade R in schools (from 59% in 2005 to 85% in 2011). Nevertheless, this part of the sector is not without its challenges. Because of the shortage of capacity in relation to teachers offering Grade R, the pattern is for qualified ECD practitioners working with 0–4-year olds to migrate to Grade R (Biersteker 2008) because of the prospect of better salaries and improved education status in the profession. The Department for Social Development (DSD) at national level indicated that the EPWP training for ECD Practitioners, therefore, have become a recruitment system for DBE Grade R. As of 2015, there is still no obligation for ECD practitioners to go back to their ECD sites (centres, nursery schools or crèches) after training, which leaves lower and unskilled workers to manage younger children. It has always been problematic that those practitioners who work with 0–4-year olds often have low levels of formal schooling and are less able to cope with the demands of Level 4 and Level 5.

A provincial study (Dawes, Biersteker & Hendricks 2010) supports reports from the ECD sector that the least-qualified staff works with infants and toddlers and that very few educational activities are offered to this age group. This is a serious concern as increasing numbers of 0–2-year olds are coming into centre programmes. The ETDP Skills Plan notes that 'The development of out-of-centre ECD programmes such as home visiting, parenting education and informal playgroups is an emerging trend in accordance with policy and thus requires a coordinated and comprehensive strategy for reaching poor and vulnerable children who do not attend ECD sites' (ETDP SETA Skills Plan 2014, 111). As noted earlier, the challenge for the government is thus to create the conditions for the improvement of access to quality ECD services for 0–4-year olds, especially for the poorest and most vulnerable children. Towards this end, the government developed the National Integrated Plan for ECD in which it is recognised that such services should be offered at the level of the household (50%), the community (30%), and in formal ECD centres (20%). The ETDP SETA Skills Plan notes that 'this requires skills development interventions for two different categories of ECD practitioners – those working in sites and those working with families and community groups to facilitate achievement of ECD outcomes' (ETDP SETA Skills Plan 2014, 112).

The Department of Social Development has a target of reaching 2.28 million poor children under five years through various ECD services and programmes. Children with disabilities as well as those who are poor, vulnerable and living in rural areas are also priority targets for service provision both in departmental ECD policy and the Children's Act, and in the National Development Plan (2012).

In recognition also of the under-performance of learners (and by implication teachers) in South African schools, the NDP anticipates the need to shift the performance of learners in scarce skills (Literacy, Maths and Science) to levels that are significantly beyond the existing 30% pass mark for these subjects, with a focus on improving performance also in international rankings (TIMSS and PIRLS).

Schooling

The quantifiable targets for schooling for 2030 are:

About 80% of schools and learners achieve 50% and above in Literacy, Mathematics and Science in Grades 3, 6 and 9

Increase the number of students eligible to study Mathematics and Science at university to 450 000 per year

South Africa improves its position in international rankings, and

About 80% of every cohort of learners successfully complete the full twelve years of schooling. (NDP 2012, 275)

Higher education and training similarly received attention in recognition of the links between performance in schools and higher education institutions, as seen in the extract below. In relation to addressing what is termed the 'qualification profile of academics', a strong drive in the efforts to strengthen and develop a new generation of academics was launched in early 2015 that coupled the provision of government-sponsored academic posts in scarce skills areas together with a focus on gender and race, so as to enable universities to address the transformation of race profiles in academic employment.

Public Higher Education and Training

The priorities for higher education are summarised as:

- Widened access, plus greater success (increasing throughput by 75% and graduation rates).
- Matching programmes to the skills development needs of the country.
- How to make graduates more employable, without reducing higher education to simply educating for jobs.

- How to improve the qualification profile of academics, in terms of their disciplines and their teaching-and-learning. How to develop the next generation of academics and researchers.

- The need to drastically increase the number of PhDs by 25% by 2030.

- Improve governance and leadership.

As noted earlier in this book, the accommodation and support of private higher education, in recognition of the widely accepted need for better quality in terms of State and PHEI partnerships, have been noted as gaps in the sector since 1995. An early proliferation of low-quality further education and training colleges (now TVET) in the first decade was regulated effectively with legislation and government monitoring, but was not accompanied by sufficient engagement with this part of the sector with a view to either providing for or understanding the kinds of support required in order for PHEIs to participate meaningfully in higher education as partners. Here is a further opportunity for the State since it is possible to rectify (as anticipated in the NDP, 2012) the need for quality partnerships to create better engagement with government and private higher education. These institutions are a resource rather than a threat to public colleges and universities in the sector, and with better support they can be brought properly into the fold of the State as partners to address widening access and participation (in terms of better throughput and higher retention rates), through the allocation of State subsidy as is normal for public colleges and universities.

> Private Higher Education and Training
>
> The NDP advocates partnerships between government and the private sector to raise the level of R&D, with resources targeted towards building the research infrastructure required by a modern economy. The NDP has implications for improving research capacity within the Private HET sub-sector and adhering to quality standards in education and training.
>
> In addition, there are ambitious targets set for graduate throughput in higher education. (ETDP SETA Skills Plan 2014, 97)

Within the last five years, a raft of legislation has been introduced to respond to gaps that have emerged in the higher education sector, not only in relation to teacher education and universities, but also in relation to technical, vocational education and training. With regard to teacher education, legislation such as the Integrated Strategic Planning Framework for Teacher Education and Development in South Africa (2011–2025) provides for the further development of teachers within South African schools in terms of five established categories:

Category A: School leaders (principals, deputy principals and heads of department) and district and provincial support (particularly subject advisors).

Category B: Practising teachers who require support to develop knowledge and practices that will enable them to implement the National Curriculum Statements (NCS) more successfully.

Category C: Mentor teachers and lead professional teachers (teaching and learning specialists, senior teaching and learning specialists and subject advisors) who should be trained to become mentors for new teachers and lead teachers/facilitators of professional learning communities.

Category D: Unqualified and under-qualified practising teachers.

Category E: Special Needs teachers.

Within the categories above it also recognises the needs of Early Childhood Development and Foundation Phase educators as a particularly important aspect of the Plan, as well as providing for an equitable, adequate and appropriate allocation of funds and other resources to enable all teachers to perfect the art of teaching. The Plan also indicates that teachers of the following subjects must be prioritised for short-course interventions such as Foundation Phase numeracy, home language and English, Intermediate and Senior Phase Mathematics and English, and for the FET Phase: Mathematical Literacy, Accounting and Physical Science.

While early childhood education is noted as an area of focus in the NDP, the government has also responded to needs at the other end of the spectrum with regard to technical and vocational education and training. The Policy and Criteria for the Registration of Qualifications and Part Qualifications on the National Qualifications Framework was compiled and produced by the South African Qualifications Framework (SAQA) as the custodian of the NQF and as part of its mandate, together with the representatives from the three quality councils. The main aim of the policy was to ensure that the NQF, through the three sub-frameworks, would facilitate access to and ensure learner mobility and progression within and across the education and training system through career pathways.

The Policy on Professional Qualifications for Lecturers in Technical and Vocational Education and Training (TVET) (2013) was released in 2013 in order to align articulation routes for TVET qualifications with those already described in the Higher Education Qualifications Sub-Framework (HEQSF, as revised, 2013), (Government Gazette no. 36554, 2013, 3). Adult education has similarly received attention in recognition of the poor articulation provisions provided in the existing frameworks, all of which are meant to enable adult and life-long learning to occur. Thus in 2014, draft legislation on 'Qualifications in Higher Education for Adult Education and Training Educators and Community Education and Training College Lecturers' (DHET 2014) was released for comment. This policy aspires to regularise the connections between higher education institutions (universities) as providers of appropriately designed teaching qualifications for TVET academic staff on the one hand, and Adult Education trainers on the other.

Chapter 4 described the State's attempts to further develop TVET in the aftermath of apartheid's demise and noted the particular challenges concerning the need to breathe renewed life into a historically under-developed and indeed under-funded sector of higher education, which had shrunk and lost capacity as the economy ossified (as a result of the increase of economic and political sanctions in the 1970s and 1980s). Recognising the need, the government in 2013 released the Policy on National Standardised Artisan Learner Workplace and/or Site Approval Criteria and Guideline (2013), with a view to providing a framework for the variety, duration, purpose and location of learnerships or apprenticeships. To regulate assessment and moderation associated with learnership, the National Artisan Moderation Body (NAMB) was appointed by the QCTO as the Assessment Quality Partner (AQP) for all artisan trades including civil, mechanical, manufacturing, electrical and services and support. The EDTP SETA National Skills Plan notes that 'As such, the NAMB developed the policy since it is the Assessment Quality Partner (AQP) appointed by the QCTO to verify that SETA workplace approval systems meet the standards set in the workplace experience curriculum component against the criteria and guidelines provided by the QCTO' (ETDP SETA Skills Plan 2014, 106).

Framing lifelong learning, TVET, university education and adult education is of course the need to provide a mechanism through which prior learning can be described and assessed in terms of its relevance as a means of entry into qualifications within formal education. In recognition of this need, the government in 2013 released the National Policy for the Implementation of the Recognition of Prior Learning (RPL), which was developed in line with the NQF Act of 2008, and which replaced the 2002 policy on RPL and its related criteria and guidelines in 2003. The new policy aims to make RPL more implementable, particularly in recognition of the need to provide for multiple learning pathways and articulation routes associated with the parts of higher education as a sector (within and across the three sub-frameworks). To achieve this, the definitions and scope of the earlier policies and guidelines of RPL had to be expanded and related to practices associated with learning and experience accumulation in all areas of work for which formal qualifications might exist.

As part of the drive to expand access to learning resources, and also to better support learning, the State has identified libraries and resource centres as an area of provision associated with quality education. The 'White Paper on Arts, Culture and Heritage' (1996) makes reference not only to provide resources, but also through the resources to establish a culture of reading in which literary forms come to be prized and cherished by communities (see, for example, Nkondo 2009, 2) (ETDP SETA Skills plan 2014, 100–1).

Research has shown that libraries have been instrumental in the expansion of literacy rates across all ages, as well as being used by the Department of Corrections in the rehabilitation of prisoners (*All Africa* 2013, 2). The ETDP Skills Plan (2014) notes that 'Libraries and archives are also necessary for the proper functioning of democracy through the exchange of ideas and information which can only have positive effects on society as a whole' (107). Equal Education (an education rights watch-dog organisation) (2010) notes that the presence of books or tablets in schools and communities is not enough to establish a culture of reading; it is the presence of a full-time public school librarian or administrator in a well-funded and well-resourced library that raises academic performance in learners between 10% to 25% (Conyngham 2010, 1).

Another key issue affecting the success of education as part of the transformation project in South Africa has to do with education concerning HIV and AIDS as a national pandemic. The National Strategic Plan for STIs HIV and TB for 2012–2016 focuses on key population groups and encourages a multi-sectorial response to HIV. Schooling provides a captive audience and also a stable location in which to educate for 'disseminating information and creating awareness around issues related to HIV' (*National Strategic Plan* 2012, 43). Exciting research evaluating the impact of interventions in schools by the government as well as non-governmental agencies has been undertaken as part of a growing area of education research and development (see, for example, the work undertaken by Mitchell, Stuart, Moletsane, Muthukrishna, Ngcobo, Buthelezi and others). Since the end of the Mbeki Presidency (associated with the embarrassing denialist policies and an almost criminal absence of coordination in terms of treatment provision and roll-out), the two Zuma administrations have succeeded over a period of ten years to ensure that HIV prevalence in children aged 2–14 years has gradually decreased. There is, however, still a need to ensure that teachers are equipped to face challenges. Of particular concern is the impact of the disease on teacher attrition rates and a range of related issues (for example, increased absenteeism and early retirement or mortality). Numerous capacity-building interventions for teachers have taken place focusing on Life Skills as well as providing Learning and Teaching Support Material (LTSM).

Despite the economic upturn from 1995–2005, unemployment has grown in the second decade of democracy in South Africa. South Africa has high rates of unemployment and under-employment. There are approximately 14 million South Africans working or employed, but almost 15 million who are not economically active, including those who are discouraged work-seekers (Statistics SA b 2013). Those currently not working in South Africa are predominantly black, women, the young and the poorly educated. While the unemployment rate has decreased from 25.6% in Quarter 2 to 24.7% in Quarter 3 in 2013, the rate of employment has increased by 308 000 (Statistics SA b 2013, vi). It is not surprising that the highest rates of unemployment are in those areas with the most problematic education provision (such as KwaZulu-Natal, Limpopo and the Eastern Cape), or the most intensive economies (for example, Gauteng). The only province to experience a decline in employment in Quarter 3 of 2013 was the Free State (21 000). Of critical importance to the ETD sector is that 'approximately 3.3 million of the 10.4 million youth aged 15–24 years were not in employment, education or training in Q3: 2013, which indicates the vulnerability of this group' (xiii). The highest rate was among those in the North-West, at 36.6% (xiii). The ETDP SETA Skills Plan (2014) notes that 'this presents serious challenges and opportunities for the ETDP sector to ensure strategies are aimed at contributing to the reduction of unemployment using targeted approaches' (110).

Finally, the ETDP SETA Skills Plan captures some of the work undertaken in relation to the advancement of technology education, awareness and use for teaching and learning. 'There is a greater need to offer e-learning for distance learning through online teaching platforms that enable more students to be reached at any given time as well as offer greater flexibility for the times when students can access teaching material.' (Czerniewicz & Carr 2014, 2). Lecturers require skills to use multimedia to add to their methods of teaching and communicating with students, thereby adding a new facet to learning and helping to manage workloads (Rasooldeen 2014, 1). Such new developments in technology have an impact on the demand and supply side for such skills. The role of digital educational technology and online learning is similarly acknowledged by the CHE as having an 'impact increasingly on teaching and learning in higher education. However, the need for sufficient time-on-task will remain, so changes in the mode of delivery of undergraduate education will not affect the case for systemic change' (Ndebele et al. 2013, 19), though South Africa has yet to engage with open-distance learning in terms of models adopted by European and Indian higher education sectors (in relation, for example, to the use of RPL as a means of enabling wider access).

REFLECTIONS

Ndebele et al. (2013, 9) note, in relation to higher education, that 'people are always at the heart of ... successes or failures. The option to desire success drives educational transformations'.

The CHE has noted that 'recent in-depth curriculum analysis has highlighted that many curricula contain key transitions for which students are differentially prepared. These transitions can be between knowledge domains as well as in various other forms of intellectual demand ... The Engineering degree offers a prime example, with transitions in the knowledge domain from basic to engineering sciences, to complex problems, design and research, for which students are significantly differentially prepared because of their prior educational and socio-economic backgrounds' (Ndebele et al. 18). What this points to is the necessity for transformation to be considered not only in relation to social or political needs, but also in relation to a more nuanced understanding of how education prepares students for success in terms of transitions within schooling and towards transitions in higher education.

It is clear from the chapters dealing with schooling and higher education that low participation rates together with poor completion rates (as described in Chapters 1 and 3, for example) have implications for social and economic development. Thus, while the National Development Plan addresses the need for a larger and much more efficient higher education system, the capacity (of trained and highly skilled academics, and highly literate and competent students) for this to occur cannot simply be assumed of the current capacity base or student profile. Simply put, if anything, the last 20 years of education reform in South Africa has shown that access is not a necessary requirement for success. Thus, while enrolment planning should focus on graduate output, curriculum planning should also focus more coherently on the relationship between success and graduate attributes. Too many South Africans graduate from universities with a limited understanding of their responsibilities towards all citizen groups (this judging from the recurrent problems experienced on formerly white university campuses with incidences of gender abuse, racism and homophobia).

This book has described a range of initiatives undertaken by the State with the support of civil society and many organisations devoted to increasing the effectiveness of the schooling as well as higher education systems (in terms of capacity, performance and responsiveness to the need for quality education for a transformed South Africa). Tendencies to blame one section or another (schooling or higher education) significantly contribute to the longevity of the apartheid education crisis engineered as it was through policy, discrimination and under-development. While focusing on components of the sectors (for example, the need to expand the curriculum from three to four-year degrees in higher education) to address 'contemporary local and global conditions' (Ndebele et al. 2013, 19), the need for quality provision and quality teaching underpins the performance of both higher education and schooling in combination. It is, in fact, the one key issue that needs to be addressed in a concerted and coordinated manner over the next 20 years. At the same time, education for transformation (for social as well as economic change) remains urgent and compelling if the social coherence needed in South Africa is to be addressed, even as the gaps between the rich and educated, and the poor and the under-educated, widen worldwide.

1   Motala and Dieltiens (2010, 2–3) list five risk areas associated with education exclusion in South Africa: out-of-school children, especially in rural areas, who are not able to access education (it is estimated that 2% of SA children never reach school); those children within the system who are either repeaters, or dropouts (estimated at 4%); children who are over-age (it is estimated that 13% of children enrolling are not the right age for their grades); poor quality of learning (testified to in the low literacy and numeracy levels for their age); poor quality of teaching (associated with high levels of absenteeism and low levels of subject content knowledge – see earlier chapters).

REFERENCES

Abedian, I & Standish, B. (1992). The South African economy: A historical overview. In I. Abedian & B. Standish (eds), *Economic growth in South Africa: Selected policy issues*. Cape Town: Oxford University Press.

Alexander, N. (1999). An African renaissance without African languages? Social Dynamics. *A Journal of African Studies,* 25 (1), 1–12.

Alexander, N. (2013). *Language policy and national unity in South Africa/Azania.* Sea Point: Buchu Books.

Allais, S. M. (2003). The National Qualifications Framework in South Africa: A democratic project trapped in a neo-liberal paradigm? *Journal of Education and Work,* 16 (3), 305–23.

Asmal, K. & James, W. (2001). Education and democracy in South Africa today. *Daedalus,* 130 (1), 185–204. www.jstor.org/stable/20027684. Retrieved August 2014.

— (2006). Problems with qualification reform in senior secondary education in South Africa. In M. Young & J. Gamble (eds), *Knowledge, curriculum and qualifications for South African further education.* Cape Town: HSRC Press, 18–45.

— (2014). *Selling out education: National Qualifications Frameworks and the neglect of knowledge.* Rotterdam: Sense Publishers.

Appiah, K. (2005). *The Ethics of Identity.* Princeton: Princeton University Press.

Asmal, K. & James, W. (2001). Education and Democracy in South Africa Today. *Daedalus.* 130 (1), 185–204. http://www.jstor.org/stable/20027684. Retrieved August 2014.

Baatjes, I. G. (2005). Neoliberal fatalism and the corporatisation of higher education in South Africa, education as market fantasy or education as public good? In S. Valley (ed.), *Quarterly Review of Education and Training in South Africa,* 12 (1), 25–33.

Badroodien, A. (2002). Private higher education: A highly contested good? *Perspectives in Education,* 20 (4), 137–43.

Balfour, R. J. (2002). Language curriculum development at tertiary level in South Africa. In C. Addison (ed.), *Alternation,* (Special Issue: Intercultural Communication), 9 (1), 143–53.

— (2003). Between the Lines: Gender and the reception of texts in a rural KwaZulu-Natal school. *Gender and Education,* 15 (2), 183–99.

— (2005). Transforming a language curriculum: Shifting pedagogy for meaningful learning. *Perspectives in Education*, 23 (1), 77–87.

— (2008a). Understanding the pedagogies of exclusion: Towards a language pedagogy of inclusivity for marginalised children in South Africa. In Muthukrishna, A. (ed). *Educating for Social Justice and Inclusion*. New York: Nova Science, 147–62.

— (2008b). Bilinguale bildung und identitat in Sudafrika. In J. Limbach & Katarina von Ruckteschell (eds), *Die Macht Der Sprache*, Langenscheidt KG, Munchen and Berlin & Goethe Institut. e.v. Munchen, 1–14.

— (2010). Mind the gaps: Higher education language policies, the national curriculum and language research. *Language Learning Journal*, 38 (3), 293–305. http://dx.doi.org/10.1080/09571736.2010.511768. Retrieved September 2010.

— (2010). 'The long walk …'. *Language Learning Journal*, 38 (3), 249–51. http://dx.doi.org/10.1080/09571736.2010.511766. Retrieved September 2010.

— (2012). The return to reading: Acquisition, reading, research on narrative and the implications for a multilingual pedagogy for higher education in South Africa. *Alternation*, 19 (2), 190–210.

Balfour, R. J. and Lenta, M. (2009). Research capacity development: A case study at the University of KwaZulu- Natal, 2003–2007. *SAJHE*, 23 (1), 8–20.

Balfour, R. J., Karlsson, J., Moletsane, R. & Pillay, G. (2009). Researching postgraduate on higher education output in South Africa: 1986–2007. *SAJHE*, 23 (1), 43–68.

Balfour, R. J., Moletsane, R. & Karlsson, J. (2011). 'Speaking truth to power': History and research in higher education institutions in South Africa with Balfour, R. J. and Moletsane, R. In R. J. Balfour, R. Moletsane and J. Karlsson (eds), *South African Journal of Higher Education*, Special Issue 25 (2), 195–215.

Barnard, J. (2007). Totalitarianism, (same sex) marriage and democratic politics in post-apartheid South Africa, in *South African Journal of Human Rights*. 23 (3), 500–25.

Beckmann, J. (2008). Aspects of student equity and higher education in South Africa. *SAJHE*, 22 (4), 773–88.

Bamgbose, A. (2004). Sauce for the goose, sauce for the gander: Why an African child should be taught in an African language. In Joachim Pfaffe (ed.), *Making multilingual education a reality for all: Operationalizing good intentions*. Proceedings of the joint Third International Conference of the Association for the Development of African Languages in Education, Science and Technology (ADALEST) and the Fifth Malawian National Language Symposium held at Mangochi, Malawi, 30 August – 3 September 2004, 18–36.

Bentley, K. A. (2003). Whose right it is anyway? Equality, culture and conflicts of rights in South Africa. HRSC Press: Pretoria.

Bertram, C., Wedekind, V. & Muthukrishna, N. (2007). Newly qualified South African teachers: Staying or leaving? *Perspectives in Education*, 25 (2), 77–89.

Beutel, A. M. & Anderson K. G. (2008). Race and the educational expectations of parents and children: The case of South Africa. *The Sociological Quarterly*, 49 (2), 335–61.

Bhana, D. (2013). When schoolgirls become mothers: Reflections from a selected group of teenage girls in Durban. *Perspectives in Education*, 31 (1), 11–19.

Bhana, D., Nzimakwe, T. & Nzimakwe, P. (2011). Gender in the early years: Boys and girls in an African working class primary school. *International Journal of Educational Development*, 31, 443–48.

Bhorat, M., Leibbrandt, M., Maziya, S,, Van der Berg. & Woolard, I. (2001). *Labour markets and inequality in South Africa.* Cape Town: UCT Press.

Billingsley B. S. (2003). Special education teacher retention and attrition: A critical analysis of the literature. Center on Personnel Studies in Special Education, University of Florida.

Bitzer, E. M., Botha, J. & Menkveld, H. (2008). The review of teacher education programmes and transformational quality. *SAJHE*, 22 (6), 1172–84.

Bitzer, E. M. (2010). Some myths on equity and access in higher education. *SAJHE*, 24 (2), 298–312.

Bitzer, E. M. (2004). Scholarship and professional profiling: Possibilities for promoting quality in higher education. *SAJHE*, 18 (1), 19–37.

Bloch, G. (2009). The toxic mix: What's wrong with South Africa's schools and how to fix it. Tafelberg: Cape Town.

Bobda, A. S. (1991). Does Pronunciation Matter? in L.W. Lanham, et al. (eds), *Getting the message in South Africa: Intelligibility, readability, comprehensibility.* Pietermaritzburg: Brevitas.

Blom, R. (2011). The size and shape of private, post-school education and training provision in South Africa. Johannesburg: Centre for Education Policy Development.

Boehm, U. (2000). Education and employment in post-apartheid South Africa: A case study in the Western Cape. September working papers, 4.

Bozzoli, B. (2015). On my mind: Stuck in the past. Opinion. *Financial Mail.* 13 April. http://www.financialmail.co.za/fm/2015/04/09/on-my-mind-stuck-in-the-past. Retrieved September 2015.

Botha, H. (2004). Equality, dignity, and the politics of interpretation. *SA Public Law.* 19. 724–51.

Botsis, H. (2010). White teenage girls and affirmative action in higher education in South Africa. *SAJHE*, 24 (2), 238–43.

Bosetti, L. (2004). Determinants of school choice: Understanding how parents choose elementary schools in Alberta. *Journal of Education Policy*, 19 (4), 387–405.

Branson, N., Garlick, J.,Lam, D. & Leibbrandt, M. (2012). Education and inequality: The South African case. Southern Africa labour and development research unit. Working Paper Series 75.

Breier, M. (2010). From 'financial considerations' to 'poverty': Towards a reconceptualisation of the role of finances in higher education student drop out. *Higher Education*, 60 (6), 657–70. http://www.jstor.org/stable/40930317. Retrieved August 2014.

Brown, B. (2008). Teacher migration impact: A review in the context of quality education provision and teacher training in higher education in Southern Africa. *SAJHE*, 22 (2), 282–301.

Buchler, M. & Ralphs, A. (2000). Rpl challenges higher education and workplace practice: A training and policy conference on the recognition of prior learning: Eskom Training Centre, 3–5 October 2000. JET.

Burgess, S., Greaves, E., Vignoles, A., & Wilson, D. (2009). What Parents Want: School preferences and school choice. www.bristol.ac.uk/cmpo/publications/papers/2009/wp222.pdf.

Bush, T. & Heystek, J. (2003). School governance in the New South Africa. *A Journal of Comparative and International Education*, 33 (2), 127–38.

Cameron, E. (2005). *Witness to AIDS.* New York: Palgrave-Macmillan.

Carl, A. E. 2008. Reconceptualising teacher training at a South African university: A case study. *SAJHE*, 22 (1), 17–40.

Carnoy, M., Chisholm, L. & Chilisa, B. (2012). The low achievement trap: Comparing schooling in Botswana in South Africa. Pretoria: HRSC Press.

Case, A. & Deaton, A. (1999). School inputs and educational outcomes in South Africa. *The Quarterly Journal of Economics*, 114 (3), 1047–84. Oxford: Oxford University Press, http://www.jstor.org/stable/2586891. Retrieved June 2014.

— (1999). School inputs and educational outcomes in South Africa. *The Quarterly Journal of Economics*, 114 (3), 1047–84. http://www.jstor.org/stable/2586891. Retrieved 4 August 2014.

Case, A. & Yogo, M. (1999). Does school quality matter? Returns to education and the characteristics of schools in South Africa. National Bureau of Economic Research working paper 7399. http://www.nber.org/papers/w7399.pdf.

Cele, N. & Menon, K. (2006). Social exclusion, access and the restructuring of higher education in South Africa. *SAJHE*, 20 (3), 400–12.

Cele, N. (2004). 'Equity of access' and 'equity of outcomes' challenged by language policy, politics and practice in South African higher education: The myth of language equality in education. *SAJHE*, 18 (1), 38–56.

Chijioke J. E. (2007). Collaborative partnerships and the transformation of secondary education through ICTs in South Africa, *Educational Media International*, 44 (2), 81–98.

Chisholm, L. (2003). The politics of curriculum review and revision in South Africa. Presented at the 'Oxford' International Conference on Education and Development, 9–11 September 2003, at the session on Culture, Context and the Quality of Education.

— (ed.) (2004). *Changing Class: Education and social change in post-apartheid South Africa*. Cape Town: HSRC Press, 267–291.

— (2009). An overview of research policy and practice in teacher supply and demand 1994–2008. Teacher education in South Africa series. Cape Town: Human Sciences Research Council.

— (2012). On the occasion of the UJ-Kagiso Trust education conversations launch Council Chambers, UJ, presented for Minister Angie Motshekga: Department of Basic Education. http://www.uj.ac.za/EN/Faculties/edu/newsandevents/Documents/Faculty%20of%20Education%20Linda%20Chisholm%20Presenting%20at%20UJ%2011%20April%202012.pdf.

— (2012). Corruption in education: The text book. A Saga symposium hosted by the Public Affairs Research Institute (PARI) and Innovations for Successful Societies. Princeton University, University of the Witwatersrand, August 2012.

Chisholm L., Motala, S., & Vally, S. (eds) (2003). *South African education policy review: 1993–2000*. Cape Town: HSRC Press.

Chisholm, L. & Porteus, K. (2005). *Emerging voices: A report on education in South African Rural communities*. Nelson Mandela Foundation with the HSRC and Education Policy Consortium. Cape Town: HSRC Press.

Chisholm, L. & September, J. (eds) (2005). *Gender equity in South African education 1994–2004*. Perspectives from Research, Government and Unions Conference Proceedings, HSRC Press.

Christie, P. (2006). Changing regimes: Governmentality and education policy in post-apartheid South Africa. *International Journal of Educational Development*, 26, 373–81. www.sciencedirect.com.

— (2010). The complexity of human rights in global times: The case of the right to education. *International Journal of Educational Development*, 30, 3–11.

Chutgar, A. & Kanjee, A. (2009). School Money Funding Flaws. *HSRC Review*, 7 (4), 18–20.

Cloete, N., Maassen, P., Fehnel, R., Moja, T., Gibbon, T., & Perold, H. (eds) (2002). *Transformation in higher education: Global pressures and local realities*. Dordrecht: Springer.

Cloete, N. & Moja, T. (2005). Transformation tensions in higher education: Equity, efficiency, and development. *Social Research*, 72 (3), 693–722. http://www.jstor.org/stable/40971787. Retrieved September 2014.

Cosser, M. (2008). *Studying ambitions: Pathways from Grade 12 and the factors that shape them*. Cape Town: HSRC Press.

Cosser, M. (2011a). The skills cline: higher education and the supply-demand complex in South Africa. www.hsrc.ac.za/en/research-data/ktree-doc/456214/08/2014.

— (2011b). Anyone For teaching? Students, teachers and choices In South Africa. www.hsrc.ac.za/en/research-data/ktree-doc/4562 Retrieved May 2014.

Coomans, F. (2002). In search of the core content of the right to education. In D. Brand & R. Sage (eds), *Exploring the core content of socio-economic rights: South African and international perspectives*. Pretoria: Protea Book House, 159–82.

Council on Higher Education Directorate: Standards Development (2011a). A Framework for Qualification Standards in Higher Education (Consultation Document, November 2011). Summary Of Submissions Received March 2012 and CHE Responses.

— (2011b). A Framework for Qualification Standards in Higher Education (Consultation Document, November 2011). Pretoria: Council on Higher Education.

— (2013). A Framework for Qualification Standards in Higher Education. Second Draft, January 2013.

Council on Higher Education (2004). Policy advice report. Advice to the Minister of Education on Aspects of Distance Education Provision in South African Higher Education 15 March 2004.

— (2007). Review of Higher Education in South Africa: Selected Themes. Pretoria: Council on Higher Education.

— (2010). A New Academic Policy for Programmes and Qualifications in Higher Education.

— (2012). Submission on the Higher Education and Training. Laws Amendment Bill to the Portfolio Committee on Higher Education and Training.

— (2013). The Higher Education Qualifications Sub-Framework.

— (2013). Higher Education Quality Committee. A Framework for Improving Teaching & Learning Project.

— (2014). Vital stats. Public Higher Education 2012. Pretoria: Council on Higher Education.

Cross, M. (2004). Institutionalising Campus Diversity in South African Higher Education: Review of Diversity Scholarship and Diversity Education. *SAJHE*, 47 (4), 387–410. http://www.jstor.org/stable/4151509. Retrieved August 2014.

Cross, M, Ratshi, M. & Sepi, R. (2002). From policy to practice: Curriculum reform in South African education. *Comparative Education*, 38 (2) 171–87.

Crouch, L. (1995). *Schooling funding options and medium-term budgeting for education in South Africa*. Consultant's Report prepared for the Department of Education, South Africa.

— (2005). South Africa equity and quality reforms. *Journal of Education for International Development*, 1 (1). http://www.equip123.net/JEID/articles/1/1-2.pdf. Retrieved 26 July 2014.

Crouch, L. & Lewin, K.M. (2003). Teacher supply and demand in KwaZulu-Natal. In K.M.Lewin, M. Samuel, & Y. Sayed, Y. (eds), *Changing patterns of teacher education in South Africa: Policy practice and prospects*. South Africa: Heinemann Press.

Cummins, J. (1999). The ethics of doublethink: Language rights and the bilingual education debate. *TESOL Journal*. 8 (3), 13–17.

Dahlgren, M., Larsson, S., & Walters, S. (2006). Making the invisible visible. On participation and communication in a global, web-based Master's Programme. *Higher Education*, 52 (1), 69–93.

David, L. (1999). Generating extreme inequality: Schooling, earnings, and intergenerational transmission of human capital in South Africa and Brazil. Research report. Ann Arbor: Michigan University. Population Studies Center. Spons Agency Cape Town University. (South Africa). Andrew W. Mellon Foundation, New York, NY.; National Inst. of Child Health and Human Development (NIH), Bethesda.

De Kadt, E. (2005). English, language shift and identities: A comparison between 'Zulu-dominant' and 'multicultural' students on a South African university campus. *Southern African Linguistics and Applied Language Studies*, 23 (1), 19–37.

De Kadt, J. (2005). Language development in South Africa – past and present. Paper for LSSA Conference, July 6–8 2005. Princeton University.

De Klerk, V. (2002). Language issues in our schools: Whose voice counts? Part 1: The parents speak. *Perspectives in Education*, 20 (1), 1–14.

De Lange, N., Mitchell, C. , Moletsane, R. , Balfour, R., Wedekind, V. , Pillay, D. & Buthelezi, T. (2010). Every voice counts: Towards a new agenda for schools in rural communities in the age of AIDS. *Education as Change*, 14 (1), s45–s55.

De Lange, N., Mitchell, N. & Bhana, D. (2012). Voices of women teachers about gender inequalities and gender-based violence in rural South Africa. *Gender and Education*, 24 (5), 499–514.

Deleon, P. (1994). Reinventing the policy sciences: Three steps back to the future. *Policy Sciences*. 27 (1), 77–95.

Department of Basic Education & LEADSA (2013). *Stop Rape* booklet.

De Villiers, A. P., & Steyn, A. G. W. (2009). Effect of changes in state funding of higher education output in South Africa: 1986–2007. *International Economic Journal*, 20 (2), 129–47.

De Villiers, R. (2007). Migration from developing countries: The case of South African teachers to the United Kingdom. *Perspectives in Education*, 25 (2), 71–76.

Deacon, R., Osman, R. & Buchler, M. (2009). Education scholarship in Higher Education in South Africa, 1995–2006. *SAJHE*, 23 (6), 1072–85.

Denessen, E., Driessena, G., & Sleegers, P. (2005). Segregation by choice? A study of group-specific reasons for school choice. *Journal of Education Policy*, 20 (3), 347–68.

Department of Basic Education (1996). National Education Policy Act (no. 27 of 1996). Approval of The Amendment Policy Pertaining to the National Curriculum Statement Grades R–12.

— (2008). Annual Report 2007–2008.

— (2009). Annual Report 2008–2009.

— (2009). National Examinations and Assessment report on The National Senior Certificate Examination Results Part 2.

— (2009). National Curriculum Statement (NCS) Curriculum And Assessment Policy Statement Further Education and Training Phase Grades 10–12.

— (2009). Trends in education macro indicators report.

— (2010). Report on The National Senior Certificate Examination results 2010.

— (2010). Annual report 2009–2010.

— (2011). Annual report 2010–2011.

— (2011). Annual Performance Plan 2011–2012.

— (2011). Annual Performance Plan 2012–2013.

— (2011). Annual Performance Plan 2014–2015.

— (2011). National Senior Certificate Examination national report on learner performance in selected subjects 2010.

— (2011). National Senior Certificate Examination national diagnostic report on learner performance.

— (2011). Report on the National Senior Certificate Examination 2011 School Performance Analysis.

— (2011). Report on the National Senior Certificate Examination 2011. Technical report.

— (2011). Report on the National Senior Certificate Examination 2011. National diagnostic report on learner performance.

— (2011). Progress in international reading literacy study 2011. South African children's reading literacy achievement. Summary report.

— (2011). Annual National Assessment. A guideline for the interpretation and use of ANA results.

— (2011). National Protocol For Assessment Grades R–12.

— (2011). Report of The workshop on The Draft Research Agenda, Department of Basic Education Conference Centre Sol Plaatje House, Pretoria 14 September 2011.

— (2012). Annual report 2011–2012.

— (2012). National Senior Certificate Examination national diagnostic report on learner performance.

— (2012). National Senior Certificate Examination schools subject report.

— (2012). National Senior Certificate Examination school performance report.

— (2012). Annual National Assessment 2012. Diagnostic report.

— (2012). Annual National Assessment. A guideline for the interpretation and use of ANA results.

— (2013). National Senior Certificate Examination national diagnostic report on learner performance.

— (2013). National Senior Certificate Examination school performance report.

— (2013). National Senior Certificate Examination schools subject report.

— (2013). Report on The National Senior Certificate Examination 2011. Technical report.

— (2013). The incremental introduction of African languages in South African schools. Draft policy.

— (2013). Annual National Assessment 2013. Diagnostic report.

— (2013). Circular S5.

— (2013). Annual report 2012–2013.

— (2008—13). School Realities, 2008–2013.

— (2014). School Realities, 2014.

Department of Education (1997). Education White Paper 3: A programme for the transformation of higher education. Pretoria, 24 July 1997.

— (2012). Approval of the regulations pertaining to the National Curriculum Statement Grades R–12 2012. *Government Gazette*, 570.

— (1999). Education Statistics in South Africa at a glance, 1999.

— (2001). Education Statistics in South Africa at a glance, 2001.

— (2003). Education Statistics in South Africa at a glance, 2003.

— (2005). Education Statistics in South Africa at a glance, 2005.

— (2007). Education Statistics in South Africa at a glance, 2007.

— (2009). Education Statistics in South Africa at a glance, 2009.

— (2010). Education Statistics in South Africa at a glance, 2010.

— (2011). Education Statistics in South Africa at a glance, 2011.

— (2000). National Education Act 1996: Norms and Standards for Educators. Government Notice 45 (20844), February 2000.

— (2002). *Issues on gender in schools: an introduction for teachers.* Pretoria: Government Printing Works.

— (2009). Policy Revised National Curriculum Statement Grades R–9 (Schools) overview.

Department of Higher Education (2011). Joint Communiqué on the implementation of the new policy on teacher education qualifications (September 2011).

Department of Higher Education and Training (1997). 426 Higher Education Act (101/1997): Draft Policy Framework for the Provision of Distance Education in South African Universities.

— (1998). National Qualifications Framework Act 913 (67/2008); General and Further Education and Training Quality Assurance Act (58/2001); Higher Education Act (101/1997) and Skills Development Act (98/1998): Proposed Qualifications Sub-frameworks.

— (2008). Addendum to the classification of Educational Subject Matter (CESM), manual.

— (2012). Presentation to the ISPFTED in South Africa: Clarifying roles and responsibilities. Joint presentation to the Parliamentary committee, 15 May 2012.

— (2012). Draft Policy Framework for the Provision Of Distance Education In South African Universities.

— (2013). White Paper for Post-School Education And Training. Pretoria: Government Printing Works.

— (2013). Policy on Professional Qualifications for TVET. Pretoria: Government Printing Works.

— (2015). ISPFTED in South Africa 2011–2015: Frequently asked questions.

— (2015). ISPFTED in South Africa 2011–2015: full version.

— (2015). Presentation to the ISPFTED in South Africa 2011–2015. Technical report.

Department of Labour. (1998). Employment Equity Act 55 of 1998. Parliament of South Africa. Cape Town: Government Printing Works.

Department of National Education (1985). Report SAPSE-101. Pretoria: Government Printing Works.

De Vos, P. (2004). Desire and the re-imagining of the South African Family. *South African Journal of Human Rights*, 20, 179–206.

Dieltiens, V. (2000). Democracy in education or education for democracy? The limits of participation in South African school governance. Phd dissertation, Johannesburg, June 2000.

Donohue, D. & Bornman, J. (2014). The challenges of realising inclusive education in South Africa. *South African Journal of Education*, 34 (2), 1–14.

Duff, P. & Li, D. (2014). Rethinking heritage languages: Ideologies, identities, practices and priorities in Canada and China. in P. P. Trifonas & T. Aravossitas (eds), *Rethinking heritage language education*. Cambridge: Cambridge University Press, 45–65.

Dunne, M. (2014). Interventions to enhance girls' education and gender equality: Education in South Africa. *International Journal of Educational Development*, 30, 3–11.

Du Preez, P. & Roux, C. (2010). Human rights values or cultural values? Pursuing values to maintain positive discipline in multicultural schools. *South African Journal of Education*, 30 (1), 13–26.

Du Plessis, T. (2006). Tweetalige hoeronderwys vir Suid-Afrika? Taalbeleidsontwikkeling by historiese afrikaans medium universiteite as gevallestudie (*Bilingual higher education for South Africa? The case of language policy development at Afrikaans medium universities*). *Tydskrif vir Geesteswetenskappe*. 46 (2), 100–11.

Du Toit, A. (2009). Institutionalizing free inquiry in Universities during regime transitions: The South African Case. *Social Research*, 76 (2), 627–59.

Education for All (EFA) (2013). Country progress report: South Africa.

ETDP SETA (2014). Education, training and development practices: Education and Training Authority Sector Skills Plan: 2015–2016. Pretoria: Department of Higher Education and Training.

Edward, B., Fiske & Ladd, H. F. (2006). Equity: Education reform in post-apartheid South Africa. Capetown: HSRC Press.

Ekong, D. & Cloete, N. (1997). Curriculum responses to a changing national and global environment in an African context. In N. Cloete, J. Muller, M. Makgoba and D. Ekong (eds), *Knowledge, identity and curriculum transformation in Africa*. Cape Town: Maskew Miller Longman.

Ellis, R. (1994). *The Study of Second Language Acquisition*. Oxford: Oxford University Press.

Engelbrecht, P. (2006). The implementation of inclusive education in South Africa after ten years of democracy. *European Journal of Psychology of Education*, 21 (3), 253–64. www.jstor.org/stable/23421606. Retrieved August 2014.

Enslin, P., Pendlebury, S., & Tjiattas. M., (2003). Knaves, knights and fools in the academy: Bureaucratic control, social justice and academic work. *Journal of Education*, 31, 75–91.

Erasmus, J. & Breier, M. (eds) (2009). *Skills Shortages in South Africa: Case Studies of Key Professions*. Cape Town: HSRC Press.

Esakov, H. J. (2009). Reading race: The curriculum as a site of Transformation. *SAJHE* 23 (1), 69–82.

Evans, S. (2013). SA ranks its maths and science second last in the world. In *Weekly Mail & Guardian*, 17 April 2013.

Fausto-Sterling, A. (2000). The five sexes: Revisited. *The Sciences*, 18–23.

Fedderke, J. W., De Kadt, R. & Luiz-Source, J. M. (2000). Uneducating South Africa: The failure to address the 1910–1993 legacy. *International Review of Education*, 46 (3/4), 257. http://www.jstor.org/stable/3445489. Retrieved August 2014.

Fine, B. (2001). Neither the Washington nor the post-Washington consensus: An introduction. In B. Fine, C. Lapavitsas & J. Pincus (eds), *Development policy in the twenty-first century: Beyond the post-Washington consensus*. London: Routledge.

Finkel, S. E. & Ernst, H. R. (2005). Civic education in post-apartheid South Africa: Alternative paths to the development of political knowledge and democratic values. *Political Psychology*, 26 (3), 333–64.

Fiske, E. B. & Ladd, H. L. (2004). *Education reform in post-apartheid South Africa*. Washington, D.C.: Brookings Institution Press.

Fleisch, B., Taylor, N., Du Toit, R. & Sapire, I. (2010). Can workbooks improve learner performance? Findings of the randomised control trial of the Primary Mathematics Research Project 1. Paper presented at the Wits School of Education Research seminar, Staff Lounge, 24 August 2010.

Framework for Women, Girls, and Gender Equality in National Strategic Plans on HIV and AIDS in Southern and Eastern Africa (2010). http://www.athenanetwork.org/assets/files/Framework%20for%20Women,%20Girls,%20and%20Gender%20Equality%20in%20NSPs.pdf. Retrieved 29 August 2014.

Francis, D. & Le Roux, A. (2011). Teaching for social justice education: the intersection between identity, critical agency, and social justice education. *South African Journal of Education*, 31, 299–311.

Fraser, N. (1996). Gender equity and the welfare state: A post-industrialist thought experiment in S. Benhabib (ed.), *Democracy and difference: Contesting the boundaries of the political*. New Jersey: Princeton University Press.

Freeman, R. D. (1998). *Bilingual education and social change*. Clevedon: Multilingual Matters.

Gamble, J. (2003). *Curriculum responsiveness in FET Colleges*. Cape Town: HSRC Press.

Genesee, F. (1987). *Learning through two languages: Studies of immersion and bilingual education*. Santa Cruz, CA: National Center for Research on Cultural Diversity and Second Language Learning.

Gewer, A. (2013). Improving quality and expanding the FET College system to meet the need for an inclusive growth path. Presentation to Umalusi AVET Provider Forum: JET Education Services, 16 May 2013.

Gloppen, S. (2005). Social rights litigation as transformation: South African perspectives. Institute Development Studies and Human Rights CMI Working Papers. http://www.cmi.no/publications/publication/?1965=social-rights-litigation-as-transformation.

Goldring, E. B., & Hausman, C. S. (1999). Reasons for parental choice of urban schools. *Journal of Education Policy*. 14 (5), 469–90.

Govender, L. (2004). Teacher unions, policy struggles and educational change, 1994 to 2004. In L. Chisholm (ed.), *Changing class: Education and social change in post-apartheid South Africa*. Cape Town: HSRC Press, 267–91.

Government Gazette (2011). National Protocol For Assessment Grades R–12, Government Notices no. 722 and no. 723, Government Gazette no. 34600 of 12 September 2011 and amended as Government Notice no. 1115 and no. 1116, Government Gazette no. 36042 of 28 December 2012.

Grace, G. (1995). *School Leadership: Beyond Education Management, an Essay in Policy Scholarship*. London: Falmer Press.

Gultig, J. (2000). The University in post-apartheid South Africa: New ethos and new divisions. *SAJHE, SATHO,* 14 (1), 37–52.

Gustafsson, J. & Patel, F. (2006). Undoing the apartheid legacy: Pro-poor spending shifts in the South African public school system. *Perspectives in Education,* 24 (2), 65–77.

Hammond C., Linton D., Smink, J. & Drew, S. (2007). Dropout risk factors and exemplary programs: A technical report. Alexandria, VA: Communities in Schools.

Harber, C. & Mncube, V. (2011). Is schooling good for the development of society? The case of South Africa. *South African Journal of Education,* 31, 233–45.

Harris, S., Yves, Z. (2003). Private versus public schools in post-apartheid South African cities: theory and policy implications. *Journal of Development Economics,* 71, 351–94.

Hart, G. (2002). *Disabling globalisation: Places of power in post-apartheid South Africa.* Pietermaritzburg: University of Natal Press.

Hartshorne, K. (1992). *Crisis and challenge: Black Education 1910–1990.* Cape Town: Oxford University Press.

Hassan, S. (2011). The needs and perceptions of academics regarding their professional development in an era of educational Transformation. *SAJHE,* 25 (3), 1011–3487.

Hassim, S. (2004). Nationalism, feminism and autonomy: The ANC in exile and the question of women. *Journal of Southern African Studies,* 30 (3), 433–56.

Heard. (2010). Gender, sexuality and HIV: Report on the HEARD Get Together. Workshop report, September 2010, UKZN.

Henrard, K. (2002). Post-apartheid South Africa's democratic transformation process: Redress of the past, reconciliation and 'unity in diversity'. *The Global Review of Ethno politics,* 1 (3),18–38.

Heugh, K. (1999). Languages, development and reconstructing education in South Africa. *International Journal of Educational Development,* 19, 301–13.

Heugh, K. (2002). Revisiting bilingual education in and for South Africa. Cape Town, PRAESA. Occasional papers.

Heugh, K. (2006). Die prisma vertroebel: taalonderrig geinterpreteer in terme vankurrikulumverandering, *Tydskrif vir Geesteswetenskappe.* 46 (2), 63–76.

Heystek, J. (2004). School governing bodies: The principal's burden or the light of his/her life? *South African Journal of Education,* 24 (4), 308–12.

— (2014). Affordable, quality, private education in a rural community: Assessing potential for a low-fee private school in the Royal Bafokeng Nation. A report prepared by North-West University for the Royal Bafokeng Nation. Phokeng: Royal Bafokeng administration.

Higgs, L. G., Higgs, P. & Wolhuter, C. C. (2004). Re-thinking gender (in)equality within the South African academic profession. *SAJHE,* 18 (1), 273–89.

Hlalele, D. & Alexander, G. (2012). University access, inclusion and social justice. *SAJHE* 26 (3), 487–502.

Hlongwane, Z. (2012). Green paper for post-school education and training. Department of higher education and training. www.saqa.org.za/docs/papers/2012/greenpaper.pdf.

Hodson, P. & Thomas, H. (2003). Quality assurance in higher education: Fit for the new millennium or simply year 2000 compliant? *Higher Education,* 45 (3), 375–87. http://www.jstor.org/stable/3447486. Retrieved May 2014.

Horsthemke, K. (2004). Knowledge, education and the limits of Africanisation. *Journal of Philosophy of Education,* 38 (4), 571–87.

Howard, R. E. & Steven, E. F. (2005). Civic education in post-apartheid South Africa: Alternative paths to the development of political knowledge and democratic values. *University of Virginia Political Psychology*, 26 (3), 333–64.

Howie, S., Staden Van, S., Tshele, M., Dowse, C., & Zimmerman, L. (2011). PIRLS 2011. Progress in international reading literacy study 2011. Summary report on South African children's reading literacy achievement. Pretoria: University of Pretoria CEA.

HRSC Review 1 (1) March 2003. Cape Town: HSRC Press.

— 1 (3) September 2003. Cape Town: HSRC Press.

—10 (1) March 2012. Cape Town: HSRC Press.

— 10 (3) September 2012. Cape Town: HSRC Press.

— 10 (4) November 2012. Cape Town: HSRC Press.

— 11 (1) March 2013. Cape Town: HSRC Press.

— 11 (4) September 2013. Cape Town: HSRC Press.

— 11 (5) November 2013. Cape Town: HSRC Press.

— 12 (2) April/May 2014. Cape Town: HSRC Press.

— 12 (3) June/July 2014. Cape Town: HSRC Press.

— 2 (3) September 2004. Cape Town: HSRC Press.

— 2 (4) November 2004. Cape Town: HSRC Press.

— 3 (10) March 2005. Cape Town: HSRC Press.

— 4 (2) June 2006. Cape Town: HSRC Press.

— 5 (2) June 2007. Cape Town: HSRC Press.

— 7 (4) November 2009. Cape Town: HSRC Press.

— 8 (2) August 2010. Cape Town: HSRC Press.

— 12 (1) February 2014. Cape Town: HSRC Press.

— 11 (3) July 2013. Cape Town: HSRC Press.

— 11 (2) May 2013. Cape Town: HSRC Press.

Hugo, P. (1998). Transformation: The changing context of academia in post-apartheid South Africa. *African Affairs*, 97 (386), 5–27, Oxford University Press on behalf of The Royal African Society. http://www.jstor.org/stable/723472. Retrieved 4 August 2014.

Human Sciences Research Council (HSRC) (2001). Annual report, 2000–2001.

— (2002). Annual report, 2001–2002.

— (2003). Annual report, 2002–2003.

— (2004). Annual report, 2003–2004.

— (2005). Annual report, 2004–2005.

— (2006). Annual report, 2005–2006.

— (2007). Annual report, 2006–2007.

— (2008). Annual report, 2007–2008.

— (2009). Annual report, 2008–2009.

— (2010). Annual report, 2009–2010.

— (2011). Annual report, 2010–2011.

— (2012). Annual report, 2011–2012.

— (2013). Annual report, 2012–2013.

Hutchings, C. (2006). Reaching students: Lessons from the Writing Centre. *Higher Education Research and Development*. 25 (3), 247–61.

Hyslop, J. (1985). Food, authority and politics: Student riots in South African schools 1945–1976. In S. Clingman (ed.), *Regions and Repertoires: Topics in South African Politics and Culture.* Johannesburg: Ravan Press, 84–115.

— (1989). School boards, school committees and educational politics: Aspects of the failure of Bantu education as a hegemonic strategy, 1955–1976. In P. Bonner, I. Hofmeyr, D. James and T. Lodge (eds), *Holding Their Ground: Class, Locality and Culture in 19th and 20th Century South Africa.* Johannesburg: Ravan/Witwatersrand University Press.

— (1990). Schools, unemployment and youth: Origins and significance of student and youth Movements 1976–87. In B. Nasson and J. Samuel (eds), *Education: From Poverty to Liberty.* Cape Town: David Philip.

— (1990). Teacher resistance in African education from the 1940s to the 1980s. In M. Nkomo (ed.), *Pedagogy of Domination: Towards a democratic education in South Africa.* Trenton: Africa World Press.

— (1993). 'A destruction coming in': Bantu education as response to social crisis. In P. Bonner, P. Delius and D. Posel (eds), *Apartheid's Genesis 1935–1972.* Johannesburg: Ravan Press/ Witwatersrand University Press, Johannesburg.

— (1990). Schools, unemployment and youth: Origins and significance of student and youth movements 1976–87. In B. Nasson and J. Samuel (eds), *Education: From poverty to liberty.* Cape Town: David Philip.

— (1999). *The classroom struggle: Policy and resistance in South Africa, 1940–1990.* Pietermaritzburg: University of KwaZulu-Natal Press.

Iphofa, M. (1997). President's education initiative: Final report phase 1. JET, commissioned by National Department of Education.

ITERP (2014). An examination of aspects of initial teacher education curricula at five higher education institutions. The Initial Teacher Education Research Project (ITERP) progress report, August 2014.

Jansen, J. (1998). Curriculum reform in South Africa: A critical analysis of outcomes-based education. *Cambridge Journal of Education,* 28 (3), 321–31.

— (2001). Image-ining teachers: Policy images and teacher identity in South African classrooms. *South African Journal of Education,* 21 (4), 242–46.

Jansen, J. & Taylor, N. (2003). Educational change in South Africa 1994–2003: Case studies in large-scale education reform. *Country Studies Education Reform and Management Publication* series, 2 (1).

Jernudd, B. & Neustupny, J. V. (1987). Language planning: For whom? In L. Laforge, (ed.), *Proceedings of the International Colloquium on Language Planning.* Quebec: Les Presses de l'Université Laval, 69–84.

JET ITERP (2012). The B Ed and PGCE programs at the North-West University (Potchefstroom Campus). Draft case study report, November 2012.

Joint Education Trust (JET) (2003). Annual report.

— (2004). Annual report.

— (2005). Annual report.

— (2006). Annual report.

— (2007). Annual report.

— (2008). Annual report.

— (2009). Annual report.

— (2010). Annual report.

— (2011). Annual report.

— (2012). Annual report.

— (2013). Annual report.

— (2000). Annual Review.

Johnson, B. & Cooper, D. (2014). Some theoretical considerations of 'engaged scholarship' and 'use oriented research' at a new university in South Africa: The Vaal University of Technology. *Southern African Review of Education,* 20 (2), 97–120.

Jones, G. (2013). Mired in the crisis: SA running out of time to tackle education woes. In *Financial Mail.* January 18–23, 2013, 25.

Joseph, J. & Francois, B. (eds) (2014). The state of education: A clear look at what was, what is and what needs to happen next. *Inside out,* (3), 1–32.

Joshua, J. (2007). Language matters in a rural commercial farm community: Exploring language use and implementation of the Language-in-Education Policy. Unpublished PhD dissertation, University of KwaZulu-Natal.

Kachru, B. (1997). World Englishes 2000: Resources for research and teaching. Literary studies East and West. In L. E. Smith & M. L. Forman (eds), *World Englishes 2000.* Honolulu: University of Hawaii Press, 209–51.

Kallaway, P. (2002). Introduction. in P. Kallway (ed.), *The History of Education under Apartheid, 1994–1998.* Pinelands: Pearson Education SA, 39–52.

Kellerman, E. (1977). Giving learners a break: Native language intuitions as a source of predictions about transferability. *Interlanguage Studies Bulletin,* 2, 58–145.

Karlsson, J. (2002). The role of democratic governing bodies in South African schools, *Comparative Education,* 38 (3), 327–36.

Keet, A. & Carrim, N. (2006). Human rights education and curricular reform in South Africa. *JSSE,* 5 (1), 87–101.

Keevy, J. (2006). The regulation of teacher education in South Africa through the development and implementation of the National Qualifications Framework (1995–2005). 'Preparing teachers for a changing context' conference hosted by the Institute of Education, University of London, 3–6 May, 2006.

Keizan, S. & Duncan, N. (2010). From their perspective: Explanations of patterns of racialised social interactions among a group of post-apartheid adolescents. *South African Journal of Psychology,* 40 (4), 465–86.

Kennedy, M. M. (2006). From teacher quality to quality teaching. *Educational Leadership.* March, 14–19.

Kermyt, G. A., Case, A. & Lam, D. (2001). Causes and consequences of schooling outcomes in South Africa: Evidence from survey data. *Social Dynamics: A Journal of African Studies,* 27 (1), 37–59. http://www.tandfonline.com/loi/rsdy20#. VazSnoWAgy4. Retrieved June 2014.

Khosa, G. (2010). The South African national education evaluation system: What will make it work? Occasional paper 1, JET services, August 2010.

Kraak, A. (1995). South Africa's segmented labour markets: Skill formation and occupational mobility under apartheid, 1979–1993. *Work Employment and Society,* 9 (4), 657–87.

Kraak, A. (2008). The education–economy relationship in South Africa, 2001–2005. In A. Kraak & K. Press (eds), *Human resource development review 2008: Education, employment and skills in South Africa.* Cape Town: HSRC Press.

Kraak, A. & Hall, G. (1999). *Transforming further education and training in South Africa A case study of technical colleges, KwaZulu-Natal. Volume One: Qualitative findings and analysis.* Unit for Systemic Studies Group: Education and Training. Pretoria: HSRC Press.

Krashen, S. (1988). *Second language acquisition and second language learning.* Hemel Hempstead: Prentice Hall.

Kristin, H. (2001). Post-apartheid South Africa's democratic transformations: Redress of the past, reconciliation and 'unity in diversity'. *The Global Review of Ethnopolitics*, 1 (3), 18–38.

Kruss, G. & Kraak, A. (eds) (2003). *A contested good? Understanding private higher education in South Africa.* New York: Palgrave.

Kumar, M. S. V. (2012). The new landscape for the innovative transformation of education. *Social Research*, 79 (3), 619–31.

Lam, D., Ardington, C. & Leibbrandt, M. (2011). Schooling as a lottery: Racial differences in school advancement in urban South Africa. *Journal of Development Economics*, 95, 121–36.

Lambert, W. E. (1974). Culture and language as factors in learning and education. In F. Aboud & R. Meade (eds), *Cultural factors in learning and education.* Bellingham, WA: Fifth Western Washington Symposium on Learning.

Lanham, L. W., et al. (eds) (1995). *Getting the message in South Africa: Intelligibility, readability, comprehensibility.* Pietermaritzburg: Brevitas.

Language in Education Policy (1997). www.education.gov.za/link. Retrieved 14 July 1997.

Le Grange, L. (2007). Integrating western and indigenous knowledge systems: The basis for effective science education in South Africa? *International Review of Education*, 53 (5), 577–91.

— (2011). (Re)thinking (trans)formation in South African (higher) education. *Perspectives in Education*, 29 (2), 1–9.

Le Grange, L. & Beets, P. (2005). Geography education in South Africa after a decade of democracy. *Geography*, 90 (3), 267–77. http://www.jstor.org/stable/40574095. Retrieved August 2014.

Le Roux, A. (2014). 'We were not part of apartheid': Rationalisations used by four white pre-service teachers to make sense of race and their own racial identities. *South African Journal of Education*, 34 (2), 1–16. http://www.sajournalofeducation.co.za.

Lemon, A. (1995). Education in post-apartheid South Africa: Some lessons from Zimbabwe. *Comparative Education*, 31 (1), 101–14.

Lewin, K. M., Samuel, M., & Sayed, Y. (eds) (2003). *Changing patterns of teacher education in South Africa: Policy practice and prospects.* South Africa: Heinemann Press.

Luckett, K. M. (1993). 'National Additive Bilingualism': Towards the formulation of a language plan for South African Schools. *Southern African Journal of Applied Language Studies*, 2 (1), 38–60.

Luckett, K. M. (2001). Responding to equity and developmental imperatives: Conceptualizing a structurally and epistemically diverse undergraduate curriculum in post-apartheid South Africa. *Equity and Excellence in Education.* 34 (3), 26–35.

Mabizela, M. C. (2003). The evolution of private provision of higher education in South Africa. In G. Kruss & A. Kraak (eds), *A contested good? Understanding private higher education in South Africa.* New York: Palgrave.

Mabokela, R. O. & Mawila, K. F. N. (2004). The impact of race, gender, and culture in the South African education Roadmap. *International Journal of Educational Development*, 31, 86–94.

MacDonald, C. A. (1990). School-based learning experiences: A final report of the Threshold Project. Pretoria: HSRC Press.

Madue, S. M. (2008). How one university – and its faculties – respond to new national policies on the measurement of research output. *SAJHE*, 22 (1), 128–43.

Mafisa, I. & Malingo, B. (2014). Hundreds of public schools have closed in the past 20 years. *The New Age Online,* October 2014. http://thenewage.co.za/141367-1009-53-Hundreds_of_schools_shut. Retrieved October 2014.

Makgoba, M. (1997). From diversity to engaging difference: A novel approach to identity, knowledge production and curricula transformation. In N. Cloete, J. Muller, M. Makgoba & D. Ekong (eds), *Knowledge, identity and curriculum transformation in Africa.* Cape Town: Maskew Miller Longman.

Mahlomaholo, S. M. G. (2011). Gender differentials and sustainable learning environments. *South African Journal of Education*, 1, 312–21.

Mahlomaholo, S. M. G. & Francis D. (2011). Editorial: Learn together and work together for a more reasonable, unbiased, acceptable, and morally righteous nation. *South African Journal of Education*, 31, 295–97.

Mahomed, H. (2004). Challenges in curriculum transformation in South Africa. Fifth annual educationally speaking conference 15–18 May 2004, Birchwood Hotel, Boksburg. Gauteng.

Maile, S. (2004). School choice in South Africa. *Education and Urban Society*, 37 (1), 94–116.

Makoni, S. (2001). The merits of renting as opposed to owning English. In R. J. Balfour & D. Sarinjeive (eds), *English in transition: Research, debates, possibilities.* Pietermaritzburg: Brevitas, 55–72.

Malan, S. P. T. (2000). The 'new paradigm' of outcomes-based education in perspective. *Journal of Family Ecology and Consumer Sciences*, 28, 22–28.

Manik, S (2009). Understanding the exit of teachers from South Africa: Determinants of transnational teacher migration. *Perspectives in Education*, 27 (3), 267–77.

Mannah, S. (2005). The state of mobilisation of women teachers in the South African Democratic Teachers' Union. In Chisholm, L. & September, J. (eds), *Gender equity in South African education 1994-2004*, 46–151.

Maphosa, C., & Shumba, A. (2010). Educators' disciplinary capabilities after the banning of corporal punishment in South African schools. *South Africa Journal of Education.* http://www.scielo.org.za/scielo.php?pid=S0256100201000030004&script=sci_arttext&tlng=pt. Retrieved September 2015.

Marock, C. (2000). Quality assurance in higher education: The role and approach of professional bodies and SETAs to quality assurance. A report commissioned by the Higher Education Quality Committee.

Mason, M. (1999). Outcomes-based education in South African curricular reform: A response to Jonathan Jansen, *Cambridge Journal of Education*, 29 (1), 137–43. http://www.tandfonline.com/loi/ccje20. Retrieved June 2014.

Masondo, S. (2014). Study paints bleak picture of basic literacy levels. In *City Press*, 16 November 2014. http://www.news24.com/SouthAfrica/News/Study-paints-bleak-picture-of-basic-literacy-levels-20141116. Retrieved July 2015.

Mathebula, N. & Du Plessis, T. (2010). Language policy-making in the Free State: An analysis of language policy activities between 1994 and 2007, *The Language Learning Journal,* 38 (3), 307–26.

Matshedisho, K. R. (2007). The challenge of real rights for disabled students in South Africa. *SAJHE*, 21 (4), 706–16.

— (2010). Experiences of disabled students in South Africa: Extending the thinking behind disability support. *SAJHE* 24 (5), 730–44.

McDermott, L. (1998). The Future of English in South Africa. In J. Maartens & G. Extra, (eds), *Multilingualism in a multicultural context: Case studies on South Africa and Western Europe.* Tilburg: Tilburg University Press.

McKenna, S. (2004). The intersection between academic literacies and student identities. *SAJHE*, 18 (3), 269–80.

Mgqwashu, M. E. (2011). Academic literacy in the mother tongue: A prerequisite for epistemological access. *Alternation*, 18 (2), 159–78.

Mgqwashu, E. (2007). English studies and language teaching: Language acquisition and discursive critique. Unpublished PhD dissertation: University of KwaZulu-Natal.

Ministry of Education (2002). Language policy for higher education. Pretoria: Government Printing Press.

Mgijima, N. M. & Morobe, N. (2012). Training needs analysis for the improvement of the teaching of English, Life Orientation, Mathematics and Mathematics Literacy in FET Colleges. South African College Principals' Organisation (SACPO) and ETDP SETA, May 2012.

Mkhwanazi, V. & Baijnath, N. (2003). *Equity development programmes for academic staff at South African higher education institutions: Progress and promise. SAJHE,* 17 (3), 106–13.

Mncube, V. (2009). The perceptions of parents of their role in the democratic governance of schools in South Africa: Are they on board? *South African Journal of Education*, 29, 83–103.

Moletsane, R, Mitchell, C, de Lange, N, Stuart, J, Buthelezi, T, Taylor, M. (2009). What can a woman do with a camera? Turning the female gaze on poverty and HIV and AIDS in rural South Africa. *International Journal of Qualitative Studies in Education*, 22 (3), 315–31.

Moletsane, R. & Madiya, N. (2011). Postgraduate educational research on violence, gender, and HIV/AIDS in and around schools (1995–2004). *SAJHE*, 25 (2), 287–300.

Moll, I. & T. Welch. (2004). RPL in teacher education: Lessons being learned from the National Professional Diploma in Education. *Journal of Education*, 32, 159–81.

Molyneux, M. & Razavi S. (eds) (2002). *Gender justice, development, and rights.* Oxford: Oxford University Press.

Monteiro, A. R. (2010). The right of the child to education: What right to what education? *Procedia Social and Behavioural Sciences*, 9, 1988–1992. www.unhchr.ch/Huridocda/Huridoca.nsf/TestFrame/6a7.

Morley, L. (2013). The rules of the game: women and the leaderist turn in higher education. *Gender and Education*, Special Issue, Thinking Education Feminisms: Engagements with the work of Diana Leonard, 25 (1), 116–31.

Moreosele. N. (1988). Keeping mother tongue alive. *The Sowetan*, 31 March 1998.

Morrell, R. (2006). Corporal punishment in South African schools: A neglected explanation for its existence. *South African Journal of Education*, 21 (4), 292–99.

Morrell, R., Epstein, D., Unterhalter, E., Bhana, D. & Moletsane, R. (2012). Toward gender equality: South African schools during the HIV and AIDS epidemic. *Comparative Education Review*, 56 (1), 176–77. http://www.jstor.org/stable/10.1086/66442. Retrieved August 2014.

Motala, S. (2006). Education resourcing in post-apartheid South Africa: The impact of finance equity reforms in public schooling. *Perspectives in Education*, 24 (2), 79–93.

Motala, S. & Dieltiens, V. (2010). *Educational Access in South Africa, Country Research Summary*. Sussex, Consortium for Research on Educational Access, Transitions and Equity.

Mouton, N., Louw, G. P. & Strydom, G. L. (2012). A historical analysis of the post-apartheid dispensation education in South Africa (1994–2011), *International Business & Economics Research Journal*, 11 (11), 1211–22. http://www.cluteinstitute.com/. Retrieved April 2014.

MRC (2003). First National South African Youth Behaviour Survey. Medical Research Council.

Mtshali, N. (2014). School funding policy has been gazetted. 22 January 2014 at 12:16pm. In *IOL News*. http://www.iol.co.za/news/south-africa/school-funding-policy-has-been-gazetted-1.1635167#.VRy8a1L9los. Retrieved April 2014.

Mubangizi, J. C. (2004). Towards a human rights culture in South Africa's higher education policy and practice with specific reference to the right to equality. *Sabinet online*, 19 (1), 191–200. http://reference.sabinet.co.za/sa_epublication_article/sapr. Retrieved August 2014.

Mugaga, R. & Akumu, T. (2010). School drop-out rates for teenage girls worrying. *Education Observer*. http://www.observer.ug/inder.php?option=com_content@view +article&id=9434. Retrieved November 2010.

Mukora, J. (2008). Professions case study report: Artisans/Trades: Scarce and critical skills research project. A report commissioned by Department of Labour, South Africa.

Muller, J. (2005). The world is not enough: Knowledge in question. *SAJHE*, 19 (3), 497–511.

Muller, J. & Subotzky, G. (2001). What Knowledge is needed in the new millennium? *Organization*, 8 (2), 153–82.

Naicker, S. & Balfour, R. J. (2009). Policy and strategies for ESL pedagogy in multilingual classrooms: The classroom talk programme. *Language Learning Journal*, 37 (3), 339–58.

Naidoo, S. S. (2014). To what extent has the South African education system, post-1994, been democratised through the instrument of policy? Unpublished MEd. Cambridge: University of Cambridge Faculty of Education.

Naidoo, J. P. (2005). *Educational decentralisation and governance in South Africa: From policy to practice*. International institute of Educational planning, Paris: UNESCO.

Narismulu, P. & Dhunpath, R. (eds) (2011). Diversity, transformation and student experience in higher education teaching and learning. *Alternation* 18 (2), 1–14.

NEEDU (2012). National Education Evaluation & Development Unit national report, 2012.

National Qualifications Framework Act (2008). Higher Education Act 101 of 1997; no. 67 of 2008.

Ndebele, N., Badsha, N., Figaji, B., Gevers, W., Pityana, B., Scott, I. (eds) (2013). A proposal for undergraduate curriculum reform: The case for a flexible learning structure. Report of the Task Team on Undergraduate Curriculum Structure, August 2013.

Ndimande-Hlongwa, N., Balfour, R. J., Mkhize, N. & Engelbrecht, C. (2010). Progress and challenges for language policy implementation at the University of KwaZulu-Natal, *Language Learning Journal*, 38 (3), 347–57. http://dx.doi.org/10.1080/09571736.2010.5117 88. Retrieved September 2010.

Ndwheni, S. (2014). Concerns over management of NFSAS. In *Zoutnet*. Zoutnet.co.za/articles/news/27482/2014-10-23/concerns-over-management-of-NFSAS. Retrieved November 2014.

Ntshoe, I., Higgs, P., Wolhuter, C. C. & Higgs. L. G. (2010). Is quality assurance in higher education contextually relative? *SAJHE*, 24 (1), 111–31.

Ntuli, M. G. (2012). The effects of the educator post-provisioning model in the management of public schools in iLembe District. Unpublished MBA dissertation: University of KwaZulu-Natal.

Odhav, K. (2009). South African post-apartheid higher education policy and its marginalisation: 1994–2002. *Sa-Educ Journal*, 6 (1), 33–57.

Odlin, T. (1989. *Language Transfer*. Cambridge: Cambridge University Press.

Ono, Y. & Ferreira, J. (2010). A case study of continuing teacher professional development through lesson study in South Africa. *South African Journal of Education*, 30, 59–74.

Ozga, J. (2000). *Policy research in educational settings: Contested terrain*. Buckingham: Open University Press.

Pattman, R. (2011). Towards gender equality: South African Schools during the HIV and AIDS epidemic, *Gender and Education*, 23 (3), 360–61. DOI: 10.1080/09540253.2011.571813.

Petjé, M. (2002). Providing education in South Africa: The challenges. http://www.dpsa/documents/service_delivery_review/vol1no2/providing%20education%20in%20osa.pdf. Retrieved September 2004.

Pillay, G. & Balfour, R. J. (2011). Postgraduate supervision practices in South African universities in the era of democracy and educational change 1994–2004. *SAJHE* 25 (2), 358–71.

Pillay, V., Morrell, R., Epstein, D., Unterhalter, R., Bhana, D. & Moletsane, R. (2010). Towards gender equality: South African schools during the HIV and AIDS epidemic. *Perspectives in Education*, 28 (2), 87–89.

Pienemann, M. (1985). Learnability and syllabus construction. In M. Pienemann & K. Hyltenstam (eds), *Modelling and assessing second language acquisition*. Clevedon: Multilingual Matters.

Plüddemann P. (2002). Action and reflection: Dual-medium primary schooling as language policy realisation. *Perspectives in Education*, 20 (1), 47–64.

Planting, S. (2014). Seven critical facts about the education system (according to J. Jansen). *Moneyweb*. Moneyweb.co.za/ moneyweb – politica-economy. Retrieved November 2014.

Porteus, K., Vally, S. & Ruth, T. (2001). *Alternatives to corporal punishment: Growing discipline and respect in our classrooms*. Boston: Heinemann.

Pretorius, E. J. & Mampuru, D. M. (2007). Playing football without a ball: Language, reading and academic performance in a high poverty school. *Journal of Reading Research*, 30 (1), 38–58.

Prinsloo, D. (2007). The right to mother tongue education: A multidisciplinary, normative perspective. *Southern African Linguistics and Applied Language Studies*, 25 (1), 27–43.

Prunty, J. J. (1985). Signposts for a critical educational policy analysis. *Australian Journal of Education*, 29 (2), 133–40.

Puhrsch, D. (2007). Rainbow nation: Multilingualism and identity in South Africa (film). Johannesburg: Goethe Institut and University of Witwatersrand.

Raab, E., & Terway, A. (2010). *School Fees in South Africa: Increasing quality or decreasing equity. Educational Quality Improvement Program 2. Case Study of the School-level*

Implementation of the South African School Funding Norms: Perspectives of Principals. United States Agency of International Development (USAID).

Rassool, N., Edwards, V. & Bloch, C. (2006). Language and development in multilingual settings: A case study of knowledge exchange and teacher education in South Africa. *International Review of Education,* 52 (6), 533–52. http://www.jstor.org/stable/29737121. Retrieved August 2014.

Reddy, C. (2009). Integrated tales of policies, teaching and teacher education: Reflecting on an ongoing process. *SAJHE* 23 (6), 1161–73.

Reschovsky, A., (2006). Financing schools in the New South Africa. *Comparative Education Review,* 50 (1), 21–45. http://www.jstor.org/stable/10.1086/498327. Retrieved August 2014.

Roberts, J. (2014). Districts development: The new hope for educational reform. jet.org.za/publications/research/Roberts_District_Development.pdf. Retrieved August 2014.

Robinson, M. (2002). Teacher reforms In South Africa: Challenges, strategies and debates. Teachers for the twenty-first century. *Prospects,* 32 (3), 289–99.

Robus, D. & Macleod, C. (2006). 'White excellence and black failure': The reproduction of racialised higher education in everyday talk. *South African Journal of Psychology,* 36 (3), 463–80.

Rogan, J., & Macdonald, M. (1985). The in-service teacher education component of an innovation: A case study in an African setting. *Journal of Curriculum Studies,* 17 (1), 63–85.

Rothmann, J. (2014). (De)constructing the heterosexual/homosexual binary: The identity construction of gay male academics and students in South African tertiary education. Unpublished PhD dissertation, Potchefstroom Campus: North-West University.

Roux, C. D. (2012). *Safe Spaces: Human rights education in diverse contexts.* Rotterdam: Sense Publishers.

Roux, C. D. 2013. Faith-based schools: Is a critical engagement with social justice possible? REA annual meeting. http://www.religiouseducation.net/rea2013/files/2013/07/Roux.pd Retrieved August 2014.

Roux, C. D. (2012). *Safe spaces: Human rights education in diverse contexts.* Rotterdam: Sense.

— (2013). Faith-based schools: Is a critical engagement with social justice possible? REA annual meeting. http://www.religiouseducation.net/rea2013/files/2013/07/Roux.pdf. Retrieved August 2014.

Samuel, M. (1998). Changing lives in changing times: Pre-service teacher education in post-apartheid South Africa. *TESOL,* 576–84. onlinelibrary.wiley.com/doi/10.2307/3588128/abstract.

— (2009). Beyond the garden of Eden: Deep teacher professional development. *SAJHE,* 23 (4), 739–61.

Sayed, Y. (1999). Discourses of the policy of educational decentralisation in South Africa since 1994: An examination of the South African Schools Act (1) (2). *Journal of Comparative and International Education,* 29 (2), 141–52.

http://dx.doi.org/10.1080/0305792990290204. Retrieved August 2014.

— (2002). Democratising education in a decentralised system: South African policy and practice. *A Journal of Comparative and International Education,* 32 (1), 35–46.

Sayed, Y. & Soudien, C. (2005). Decentralisation and the construction of inclusion education policy in South Africa. *Compare: A Journal of Comparative and International Education,* 35 (2), 115–25.

Sayed, Y., Kanjee, A. & Nkomo, M. (2013). *The search for quality education in post-apartheid South Africa: Interventions to improve learning and teaching.* Cape Town: HSRC Press.

Schneider, M. & Buckley, J. (2002). What do parents want from schools? Evidence from the Internet. *Educational Evaluation and Policy Analysis,* 24 (2), 133–44.

Sehoole, M. T. C. (2014). The politics of mergers in higher education in South Africa. *Higher Education,* 50 (1), 159–79. http://www.jstor.org/stable/25068093. Retrieved March 2014.

Selves, S. (2008). The emergence of new identities in South African schools. *International Journal of Educational Development,* 28, 286–99.

Selinker, L. (1972). Interlanguage. *International Review of Applied Linguistics,* (10), 209–31.

Selves, S. (2008). The emergence of new identities in South African schools. *International Journal of Educational Development,* 28, 286–99.

Shackleton, l, Riordan, S. & Simonis, D. (2006). Including women: Gender in commonwealth higher education. Gender and the transformation agenda in South African higher education. *Women's Studies International Forum,* 29 (6), 572–80.

Sheik, A. (2011). 'My vuvuzela shall not be silenced': Towards linguistic equity in South Africa. *Alternation,* 18 (2), 179–94.

Shisana, O., Peltzer, K., Zungu-Dirwayi, N., & Louw, J. (eds) (2005). *The health of our educators: A focus on HIV/AIDS in South African public schools.* Cape Town: HSRC Press.

Shisana, O., Rehle, T., Simbayi, L. C., Zuma, K., Jooste, S., Zungu, N., Labadarios, D. &Onoya, D. (2014). *South African national HIV prevalence, incidence and behaviour survey, 2012.* Cape Town: HSRC Press.

Shulman, L. (1987). Knowledge and teaching: Foundations of the new reform. *Harvard Educational Review.* 57 (1), 1–22.

Simmonds, S. (2014). Curriculum-making in South Africa: Promoting gender equality and empowering women. *Gender and Education,* 26 (6), 636–52.

Singaram, V. S., Sommerville, T. E., Van der Vleuten, C. P. M. & Dolmans, D. H. J. M. (2011). 'Looking at the glass half full': Exploring collaborative mixed group learning as a transformative force for social inclusion in a South African higher education setting. *Alternation,* 18 (2), 96–114.

Smit, M. H. (2007). Public school language policy: Theory and practice. In R. Prinsloo, and E. Bray (eds), *Public School Governance in South Africa.* Pretoria: Centre for Inter-University Law and Education Policy (CELP), 59–70.

Smith, W. J. & Ngoma-Maema , W. Y. (2003). Education for all in South Africa: Developing a national system for quality assurance. *Comparative Education,* 39 (3), 345–65. http://www.jstor.org/stable/3593432. Retrieved August 2014.

Soudien, C. (2008). Report of the Ministerial Committee on transformation and social cohesion and the elimination of discrimination in public higher education institutions, November 2008.

— (2004). 'Constituting the class': An analysis of the process of integration in South African Schools. *Changing Class,* 89–114.

— (2007). Quality assurance in higher education and the management of South Africa's past: Some paradoxes. *Perspectives in Education,* 25 (3), 1–12.

— (2010a). Some issues in affirmative action in higher education in South Africa. *SAJHE,* 24 (2), 224–37.

— (2010b). Grasping the nettle? South African higher education and its transformative imper- atives. *SAJHE,* 24 (5), 881–96.

— (2011). The arhythmic pulse of transformation in South African higher education. *Alternation*, 18 (2), 15–34.

Soudien, C. & Sayed, Y. (2004). A new racial state? Exclusion and inclusion in education policy and practice in South Africa. *Perspectives in Education*, 22 (4), 102–15.

South African Qualifications Authority (2008). South African Qualifications Authority, 549 National Qualifications Framework (NQF) Act (67/2008): Publication of the General and Further Education and Training Qualifications Sub-framework and Higher Education Qualifications Sub-framework of the National Qualifications Framework.

Southall, R. (2003). *Democracy in Africa: Moving beyond a different legacy*. Cape Town: HSRC.

Spaull, N. (2013). South Africa's education crisis: The quality of education in South Africa 1994–2011. Commissioned report by Centre for Development Enterprise.

Spreen, C. A. & Vally, V. (2006). Education rights, education policies and inequality in South Africa. *International Journal of Educational Development*, 26, 352–62.

Spolsky, B. (1998). *Sociolinguistics*. Oxford: Oxford University Press.

Strevens, P. D. (1965). *Papers in language and language teaching*. London: Oxford University Press.

Steyn, A. G. W., & De Villiers, A. P. (2007). Public funding of higher education in South Africa by means of formulae. In *Review of higher education in South Africa: Selected themes*. Pretoria: Council on Higher Education, 11–51.

Strydom, A. H., & Fourie, M. (1999). Higher education research in South Africa: Achievements, conditions and new challenges. *Higher Education*, 38 (2), 155–67. In *Changes in higher education and its societal context as a challenge for future research* (ii). http://www.jstor. org/stable/3447931. Retrieved August 2014.

Strydom, J., Zulu, N. & Murray. L. (2004). Quality, culture and change. *Quality in Higher Education*, 10 (3), 207–17.

Subrahmanian, R. (2005). Gender, equity and education: Perspective from development. In Chisholm, L. & September, J. (eds), *Gender equity in South African education 1994–2004*, 27–38.

Taylor, N. (2008). Equity, efficiency and the development of South African schools. In Townsend, T. (ed.), *International handbook of school effectiveness and improvement*. Dordrecht: Springer.

Thaver, B. (2009). Transforming the Culture of Higher Education in South Africa. 95 (1),28–30. http://www.jstor.org/stable/40253294. Retrieved August 2014.

The Presidency (2104). Twenty-year review: South Africa, 1994–2014. www.thepresidency-dpme.gov.za/news/Pages/20-Year-Review.aspx. Retrieved August 2014.

Thomas, H. (2003). Association upward bias in the estimated returns to education: Evidence from South Africa. *The American Economic Review*, 93 (4), 1354–68. http://www.jstor.org/stable/3132292. Retrieved August 2014.

Tikly, L. (2011). *A roadblock to social justice? An analysis and critique of the South African*. College Park: University of Maryland.

Tikly, L. & Mabogoane, T. (1997). Marketization as a strategy for desegregation and redress: the case of historically white schools in South Africa. *International Review of Education*, 43 (2), 159–78.

Tooley, J. (2005). Private schools for the poor. *Education Next*, 5 (4), 22–32.

— (2007). Educating Amaretch: Private schools for the poor and the new frontier for inves-
tors. *Economic Affairs*, 27 (2), 37–43.

Tsung, L. & Clarke, M. (2010). Dilemmas of identity, language and culture in higher education in China. *Asia Pacific Journal of Education*, 30 (1), 57–69.

University of the Free State (UFS) (2003). Language policy of the University of the Free State.
www.uovs.ac.za/documents/ufs_facts/taal/E_Language%20Policy.pdf.

Unterhalter, E. (2003). The capabilities approach and gendered education: An examination of
South African complexities. *Theory and Research in Education*, 1 (1), 7–22.

Unterhalter, E. (2005). Gender equality and education in South Africa: Measurements, scores
and strategies. In Chisholm, L. & September, J. (eds), *Gender equity in South African education 1994-2004*, 77–85.

Unterhalter, E. (2007). *Gender schooling and global social justice*. London: Routledge.

Van Damme, D. (2001). Quality issues in the internationalisation of higher education. *Higher
Education*, 41 (4), 415–41. http://www.jstor.org/stable/3448132. Retrieved August 2014.

Vally, S. & Dalamba, Y. (1999). Racism, 'racial integration' and desegregation in South
African public secondary schools. A report on a study by the South African Human Rights
Commission.

Vally, S. & Motala, E. (eds) (2013). *Education, economy and society*. Pretoria: UNISA Press.

Van Damme, D. (2001). Quality issues in the internationalisation of higher education. *Higher
Education*, 41 (4), 415–41. http://www.jstor.org/stable/3448132. Retrieved August 2014.

Van der Berg, S. (2007). Apartheid's enduring legacy: Inequalities in education. *Journal of
African Economies*, 16 (5), 849–80.

Van der Berg S. (2001). The role of education in labour earnings, poverty and equality. Paper
to DPRU/FES Conference on Labour markets and poverty in South Africa, Johannesburg,
November 2001. http://www.commerce.uct.ac.za/DPRU/vanderberg.pdf. Retrieved June
2005.

Van der Walt, C. & C. Brink. (2005). Multilingual universities: A national and international
overview. *SAJHE*, 19 (4), 822–52.

Van Koller, J. F. (2010). The Higher Education Qualifications Framework: A review of its
implications for curricula. *SAJHE*, 24 (1), 157–74.

Van Louw, T. & Beets, P. A. D. (2008). The transformation of higher education: Context of the
establishment of the Centre for Leadership and Management in Education at Stellenbosch
University. *SAJHE*, 22 (3), 473–83.

Van Staden, S. & Howie, S. J. (2006). *South African teacher profiles and emerging teacher
factors: The picture painted by PIRLS*. University of Pretoria: Centre for Evaluation and
Assessment.

Vinjevold, P. (2007). FET College re-capitalisation. Powerpoint presentation to Southern
African Regional FET Conference, 15 November 2007.

Waghid, Y. (2007). Teacher mobility: A loss to South African schools? *Perspectives in
Education*, 25 (2), 101–108.

wakaMsimang, N. (1988). English Threatens African Languages and Culture. *The Mercury*,
22 February 1998, 6.

Wangenge-Ouma, G. & Cloete, N. (2008). Financing higher education in South Africa:
Public funding, non-government revenue and tuition fees. *SAJHE*, 22 (4), 906–19.

Wangenge-Ouma, G. (2012). Tuition fees and the challenge of making higher education in
South Africa. *SAJHE*, 20 (3), 38–50.

Webb, V. (1999). Multilingualism in democratic South Africa: The overestimation of language policy. *International Journal of Educational Development*, 19, 351–66. http:// www. elsevier.com/locate/ijedudev Retrieved May 2014.

Webb, V. (2012). Managing multilingualism in higher education in post-1994 South Africa. *Language Matters: Studies in the Languages of Africa*, 43 (2), 202–20.

Webb, V., Lafon, M. & Pare, p. (2010). Bantu languages in education in South Africa: An overview. Ongekho akekho! The absentee owner. *The Language Learning Journal*, 38 (3), 273–92.

Weber, E. (2011). Transforming higher education: Action research, learning and community politics. *Africa Education Review*, 8 (1), 1–16.

Weiher, G. H., & Tedin, K. L. (2002). Does choice lead to racially distinctive schools? Charter schools and household preference. *Journal of Policy Analysis and Management*. 21 (1), 79–92.

Weldon, G. (2009). History education in post-apartheid South Africa. http://www.minedu-cacion.gov.co/cvn/1665/article-240963.html, 1–7.

Widdowson, H.G. (2001). The monolingual teaching and bilingual learning of English. In R. Cooper, E. Shohamy & J. Walters (eds), *New perspectives and issues in educational language policy*. Philadelphia, PA: John Benjamins, 7–18.

Wilkinson, K. & Rademeyer, J. (2015). Can you really pass matric with a 30% average? The claim is misleading. *Africa Check*. https://africacheck.org/reports/can-you-really-pass-matric-with-30-the-claim-is-misleading/. Retrieved September 2015.

Williams, G. (2003). *Fragments of democracy: Nationalism, development and the state of Africa*. Cape Town: HSRC Press.

Williams, P. (1995). Metro broadcasting, Inc v FCC: Regrouping in singular times. In K. Crenshaw; N. Gotanda; G. Peller & K. Thomas (eds), *Critical race theory: The key writings that formed the movement*. New York: New Press, 82.

Wilson, F. (2007). *Gender-Based Violence in South African Schools*. UNESCO: working document.

Wilson-Strydom, M. (2011). University access for social justice: A capabilities perspective. *South African Journal of Education*, 31, 407–18.

Wolff, E.H. (2004). Marketing multilingual education in Africa: With special reference to bilingual approaches to basic education in Niger (Francophone Africa). In Joachim F. Pfaffe (ed.), *Making multilingual education a reality for all: Operationalizing good intentions*. Proceedings of the joint Third International Conference of the Association for the Development of African Languages in Education, Science and Technology (ADALEST) and the Fifth Malawian National Language Symposium held at Mangochi, Malawi, 30 August – 3 September 2004, 117–58.

Wolhuter, C. C. (2014). Research on higher education in South Africa: Stocktaking and assessment from international comparative perspectives, *SAJHE*, 28 (1), 275–91.

Wolhuter, C. C., Higgs, P., Higgs, L. G. & Ntshoe, I. Deacon, R., Osman, R. & Buchler, M. (2009). Education scholarship in Higher Education in South Africa, 1995–2006. *SAJHE*, 23 (6), 1072–85.

Wong-Fillmore, L. 1985. When does teacher-talk work as input? In S. Gass, and C. Madden (Eds). *Input in second language acquisition*. Rowley, MA: Newbury House, 17–50.

Wong-Fillmore, L. (1994). Second language learning in children: A model of language learning in a social context. In E. Bialystok (ed.), *Language processing in bilingual children*. Cambridge: Cambridge University Press, 40–60.

Woolman, S. & Fleisch, B. (2009). *The Constitution in the Classroom: law and education in South Africa 1994–2008.* Pretoria: Pretoria University Law Press.

World Economic Forum (2013). Global competitiveness report 2012–2013.

Wright, L. (1995). English in South Africa: Effective communication and the policy debate. In L. W. Lanham (et al.) (eds), *Getting the message in South Africa: Intelligibility, readability, comprehensibility.* Pietermaritzburg: Brevitas, 1–8.

Yamauchia, F. (2005). Race, equity, and public schools in post-apartheid South Africa: Equal opportunity for all kids. *Economics of Education Review,* 24 (2), 13–233.

Young, M. & Gamble, J. (eds) (2006). *Knowledge, curriculum and qualifications for South African further education,* Cape Town: HSRC Press.

Zobl, H. (1988). Configurationality and the subset principle: The Acquisition of 'V' by Japanese learners of English. In J. Pankhurst (et al.) (eds), *Learnability and second languages: a book of readings.* Dordrecht: Foris.

APPENDICES

The following appendices are available online at:

education.cambridge.org/balfourappendices

Appendix 1: Chronology of education legislation

Chronology of relevant policy developments in South African Education (1994 to present).

Appendix 2: Chronology of education crises

Chronology of selected media and other coverage relating to crises, issues and challenges in education (higher education and schools).

Appendix 3: Chronology of reports on violence in schools

Chronology of selected media coverage concerning violence in South African schools.

ACKNOWLEDGEMENTS

The time made available for this book is owed to the generosity of the Harry Oppenheimer Memorial Trust and the North-West University, both of which made funding and leave available. I am especially grateful for the Visiting Fellowship at the Institute of Education (UCL) in the United Kingdom, and the support provided by Professor Norbert Pachler, who hosted me at the Institute. The opportunity to engage with colleagues and for quiet reflection was priceless. I returned to my college (Clare Hall) in Cambridge to write the book in 2014, and was hosted at the Faculty of Education by Professors Maria Nicolajeva and Michael Evans, both of whom were encouraging and helpful to me. I am extremely grateful for the access to the library and resources of the faculty, as well as the college, and extend my thanks for the hospitality of Clare Hall to its president, Professor David Ibbetson.

The book could almost certainly not have been attempted without the support and dedication of my graduate assistant at North-West University, Mr. Dairai Dziwa, who undertook almost all of the data collection necessary for me to read and write the text (Dairai also helped to compile 'Appendix 1: Chronology of Education Legislation'). I have also been very fortunate to be assisted in the compilation of the two additional information appendices in the book: Ms. Cornia Pretorius assisted in the compilation of 'Appendix 2: Chronology of Education Crises', while Dr. Louise Postma assisted in the compilation of 'Appendix 3: Chronology of Selected Media Reports on Violence in South African Schools'. Professor Annette Combrinck (NWU) assisted with the editing of the text at a point at which I could no longer read my errors.

This book is a review and synopsis of writing and research undertaken by excellent and visionary education scholars. Naidoo, Heystek, De Villiers and Steyn, Moletsane and Karlsson, Chisholm and Hartshorne, Unterhalter, Jansen and Soudien, and the organisational reports from the Council on Higher Education, the Education, Training and Development Practices Skills Authority, and the Department of Basic Education and Higher Education and Training respectively for reports on funding, curriculum and gender violence. Insights offered in the book derive almost certainly from their work, and I make no claim to having conducted the original research from which many of my observations draw. Finally, thank you to Eugene le Roux, my beloved partner, for the support and encouragement in the time I was away from home to write the book, and the leadership of the Faculty of Education Sciences for allowing me the gap to pursue this work.

INDEX

access, xviii, xix, xxi, xxiii, 1, 4, 6, 8, 10–12, 18–20, 26, 28–9, 32, 35–6, 52, 57–9, 62, 67–8, 69, 71, 74, 81, 83–9, 90–1, 93–6, 98, 101, 108–10, 113–14, 122, 126, 130, 134, 138–9, 141, 154–5, 157, 159–60, 162–3, 167–80, 182–6, 193–5, 199, 210–13, 218–19, 222, 224, 227, 231–2, 234, 236, 238–9, 241–2

Adult Basic Education and Training (ABET), 64–5, 99, 122–4

Advanced Certificates in Education, 44

Afrikaans, xxi, 11, 36, 53, 107, 161, 164, 168–71, 177–8, 180–4, 186, 190

Afrikaner, xi, 202

Annual National Assessments, 22, 224–5,

Apartheid, x–xii, xv, xix–xxiii, 1–2, 10–12, 23–4, 28, 32, 35–6, 43, 47–8, 50–4, 62–3, 66–7, 90–1, 104–7, 110, 134, 151, 163, 168–9, 173–4, 178, 180, 191–2, 194, 196, 200, 202, 211, 214, 217, 221, 224, 229, 238, 242

apprenticeships (*see also learnerships*), xx, 97, 105, 109–10, 112, 115, 229–30, 238,

artisan, 89, 104–5, 112–13, 115–16, 126, 217, 238

arts and Culture, 27, 34, 116, 123

Bantustans, xi–ii, 10, 43, 202–3, 229

Basic Education xiii, 1, 3–4, 14, 21, 36, 51, 59, 64, 68, 122–3, 171, 174, 199–200, 225–6

Bill of Rights, 4–5, 108, 133, 161

Black Homelands Citizenship Act of 1970, xii

Boehm, U., 34–5

Chisholm, Linda, xv, xvii, 2, 4, 23, 32–3, 35, 42, 50, 52–3, 137, 139, 150

class, 2–3, 6–7, 11–13, 19, 40, 145, 156–7, 177, 187–9, 192, 195–6, 199, 201, 212–13, 217, 219
middle class, 7, 11–12, 27, 31, 33, 157, 180, 187–8, 195

Committee of College of Education Rectors of South Africa (CCERSA), 43

Committee on Teacher Education Policy (COTEP), 43

Congress of South African Trade Unions (COSATU), 134, 138

Constitution of South Africa, x, xv–xvi, xviii, 1, 4, 28, 33, 36, 133, 136, 139, 143, 147–8, 150–1, 153–4, 156–7, 160, 162–3, 165–8, 171–2, 175, 181, 188, 193, 197, 213, 228, 231

Convention on the Rights of Persons with Disabilities, 15

Council for Higher Education, (CHE) 43, 72–4, 81, 91, 94–5, 109, 192–3, 201–2, 208–10, 226–7, 229–30, 241

culture, influence of, 4–5, 15–16, 24, 27, 34, 43, 50, 59–60, 81–2, 97, 104, 116, 123, 133, 135–7, 143, 147, 155–7, 162, 172, 175, 178, 180, 231, 239

curriculum, xii, xvii, xxi, 3, 6, 8, 16, 21–4, 26–7, 32–7, 40–1, 43, 45–52, 54, 61, 64–5, 81, 90–2, 94, 97, 101, 109, 112, 115–16, 124, 126, 136, 141–4, 155–6, 165, 167, 175–6, 181, 184, 186, 189, 198, 201, 222–3, 225–7, 229, 233, 237–8, 241–2
change, xxi, 36, 50, 61, 175
Curriculum 2005, xii, 33, 35, 181
Curriculum 2021, xii
National Curriculum Statement (NCS), xii, 32, 142, 181, 237
reforms, 35, 47, 52, 91, 225
Revised National Curriculum Statement, (RNCS), xii, 6, 33, 36

Deacon, Roger, Osman, Ruksana and Buchler, Michelle, *survey by,* 56, 58, 60

democracy, xv, xx, 1, 3, 8, 26, 32, 40. 42, 61, 63–5, 72, 100, 130, 133, 150, 158, 168, 189, 197, 221, 234, 239–40

departments of education, centralisation of, xii, 42
Department of Basic Education (DBE), xiii, 1, 3, 14, 68, 199–200, 225–6
Department of Education and Training, 23–4, 42, 52, 106, 211
Department of Higher Education and Training

An environmentally friendly book printed and bound in England by www.printondemand-worldwide.com

PEFC Certified

This product is
from sustainably
managed forests
and controlled
sources

www.pefc.org

PEFC/16-33-415